Stoton, December 18, Woodland green.

# KARATE
## The Complete Kata

# KARATE
## The Complete Kata

## Hirokazu Kanazawa

**President of Shotokan Karate-do
International Federation**

TRANSLATED BY
**Richard Berger**

KODANSHA USA

For information concerning the Shotokan Karate-do International Federation, please refer to the below:

2–1–20 Minami-Kugahara
Ota-ku, Tokyo
146–0084 Japan
PHONE: 81–(0)3–3754–5481 FAX: 81–(0)3–3754–5483
E-MAIL: japan@skif.jp

Jacket photos and all step-by-step photos by Naoto Suzuki.

Techniques are demonstrated by the author, Manabu Murakami, Nobuaki Kanazawa, Ryusho Suzuki, Shinji Tanaka, Fumitoshi Kanazawa, and Daizo Kanazawa.

Originally published in Japanese as *Karate Kata Zenshu (two volumes)* by Ikeda Shoten in 1981 and 1982.

Edited in cooperation with Musashi Editorial Ltd., and Matt Cotterill.

Published by Kodansha USA, Inc.
451 Park Avenue South
New York, NY 10016

Distributed in the United Kingdom and continental Europe by Kodansha Europe Ltd.

Printed in South Korea through Dai Nippon Printing Co., Ltd.
ISBN: 978-1-56836-517-6

First edition published in Japan in 2009 by Kodansha International
First US edition 2013 by Kodansha USA

19 18          7 6 5 4 3

The Library of Congress has cataloged the earlier printing as follows:

Library of Congress Cataloging-in-Publication Data

Kanazawa, Hirokazu.
  Karate : the complete kata / Hirokazu Kanazawa, translated by Richard Berger.
    p. cm.
  ISBN 978-4-7700-3090-0
  1. Karate. I. Title.
  GV1114.3.K344 2009
  796.815'3--dc22

                    2009032405

*www.kodanshausa.com*

# CONTENTS

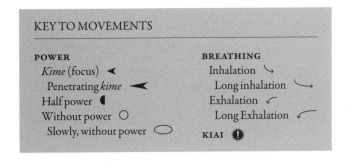

KEY TO MOVEMENTS

**POWER**
*Kime* (focus)  ◄
Penetrating *kime*  ◄
Half power  ◖
Without power  ○
Slowly, without power  ⬭

**BREATHING**
Inhalation  ↘
Long inhalation  ↘
Exhalation  ↙
Long Exhalation  ↙
**KIAI**  ✸

# FOREWORD

Karate represents a traditional culture of Japan that is now embraced worldwide. Accordingly, *kata* competitions have grown increasingly popular over the years. With this popularity, however, we are seeing more and more *kata* performances featuring acrobatic techniques like those seen in apparatus gymnastics, performances that are unlike those seen in the past. This development has provided me with many occasions for contemplation.

When viewed from a historical perspective, the path of karate encompasses a variety of styles, each with its own distinct teaching approach. One clear manifestation of these differences can be found in *kata*.

*Kata*, a technical system created by our ancestors, are the result of punishing training based on harsh emotional and technical experiences overcoming the divide between life and death, and were carried out as a part of martial arts practice to be passed on to future generations.

As for the practicing of *kata*, the initial step of the learning process today consists of students performing the *kata* together in the *dōjō* (training hall), moving in unison as the instructor calls out each movement. Traditionally, however, *kata* would be practiced over and over on an individual basis. (Joint training performed in the *dōjō* provides a decided advantage in that the collective *ki*, or life energy, of the group fills the *dōjō* with *ki*, which serves to further heighten each individual's *ki*.)

In the eighteenth of his twenty guiding principles of karate, Gichin Funakoshi states: "Perform *kata* exactly: Actual combat is another matter." As the master wisely points out, *kata* are made up of more than merely offensive and defensive techniques. They contain elements that offer opportunities for deep learning about physical education, art, history and, particularly, philosophy.

Performing *kata* in accordance with their fixed order of movements, executing each technique in earnest while visualizing an attacking opponent, poses a challenge to the self, as well as a battle with the self. Where there is no battle with one's self, there can be no training of the spirit. Therein, I believe, lies the value of martial arts.

In the same way that a calligrapher writes on a white piece of paper, the martial arts practitioner uses his body to express all he has to offer in the surrounding space, thus revealing his own philosophy and character.

While the performance of *kata* demands mental concentration from start to finish and the maintaining of *ki* throughout, it is also important to maintain an attitude of emotional openness, free of inhibition, moving as naturally as possible with aplomb. Breathing also plays a critical role. Movement, consciousness and power must be maintained through breathing. It is for this reason that, for every three times that one performs a *kata*, it should be practiced once in a relaxed manner, at a leisurely pace. A relaxed performance makes it possible to learn the correct way to make use of one's strength, and how to eliminate expending power where it is not needed.

One method of confirming the result of *kata* training is by viewing the performance not from the front, but rather from the rear—if it conveys an aesthetic beauty and a sense of overwhelming power, then I believe it is safe to consider that *kata* complete.

Recently, with the growing popularity of competitive karate, there is a strong tendency to focus practice only on one's favorite *kata*. When viewing karate as a martial art, however, I would encourage practitioners to also work to gain competence in *kata* that are not among one's favorites.

I hope that this book will prove a beneficial learning resource for the study of *kata*.

# KARATE
The Complete Kata

# Heian (Pinan)

Upon researching the Heian *kata*, perhaps the most peculiar thing that can be said about them is that, in contrast to other *kata*, although their origin and history are clearly understood, the vast majority of the people who learn these *kata* are unacquainted with their background.

Unlike ancient *kata* whose traditions remain obscure, or were kept secret and passed down through writing or word of mouth, the period in which the Heian *kata* were created, the name of their creator, and even the purpose behind their creation have been relatively well established.

Master Yasutsune Itosu (1830–1915), who had been bestowed the title "Sacred Fists," is recognized as the creator of the Heian *kata* and was said to have completed them in 1905. While middle school students in Okinawa at the time would practice the *kata* Naihanchi (Tekki) exclusively for two, or even three, years as part of their regular physical education curriculum, the Heian *kata* were conceived to provide an easier means for mastering basic karate techniques.

While some theories claim that the Heian *kata* derived from the *kata* Kūshankū (depending on the classification of Kūshankū *kata*), upon further investigation, it appears that they also incorporate assorted elements from the Bassai *kata* (which are covered in later chapters). Accordingly, it is believed that the Heian *kata* include highly advanced technical components.

Tradition, as an element of karate *kata*, represents a source of value and significance. As such, altering the original form of a *kata* created by our predecessors results in something of a different nature and sacrifices the very origins of that *kata*. For this reason, the creation of the Heian *kata* as basic, physical education-oriented *kata* from the traditional combat-oriented Kūshankū *kata* could be considered a drastic revision. Based on this development, the incorporation of karate as part of the curriculum employed in middle schools and normal schools, as previously mentioned, clearly indicates that karate was considered well suited as a self defense or physical education-oriented area of study rather than only a technique for killing. This, in turn, could be viewed as a product of the changing times.

As such, the generalization of secret fighting techniques, so to speak, as a more open, group-oriented activity necessitated extraordinary instructors, one of whom was Master Itosu. Because he created the Heian *kata* so that they would be suitable for physical education applications, they do not incorporate strikes targeting the eyes—such as one- and two-finger spear hand attacks—or return-wave or other types of kicks to the groin. From an educational standpoint, such techniques were deemed inappropriate.

Additionally, all of the Heian *kata* begin and end with blocking techniques. To begin with a block and end with a block serves to convey a humble attitude, which is why these *kata* were named Heian, meaning peace and tranquility. They are important *kata* and should not be forgotten.

# Heian Shodan (Heian No. 1)

Heian Shodan, comprising only five types of basic techniques—downward blocks, middle-level lunge punches, rising blocks, knife-hand blocks, and a hammer-fist strike—is the simplest of the five Heian *kata*.

Long ago, Heian No. 2 was the first *kata* introduced to students (which is still the case today in some other karate styles), but within the Shōtōkan school, Heian No. 1 represents the entry point for learning *kata*. It is believed that this change was made in accordance with the level of technical difficulty involved in performing these *kata*.

Why, however, was Heian No. 2 introduced before Heian No. 1? According to one theory, Master Itosu believed that repetitive practicing of the easier *kata*, No. 1, would prove beneficial after first learning the second, more difficult of the two, while another theory assumes it to be a renewed version of the *kata* Kūshankū.

Yōi · 1-A · 1 · 2-A · 2 · 3-A · 3 · 4-A · 4 · 5-A

### Yōi (Ready position)
*Soto hachiji-dachi* (open V stance) with both fists positioned in front of the hips

1-A) Turn the head to the left while drawing the left foot out and to the rear. At the same time, draw the left fist up to above the right shoulder and thrust the right fist out downward at an angle toward the left.

### 1) Zenkutsu-dachi/Hidari gedan-barai
Shift into a left front stance facing the left side while performing a left downward block.

2-A) Step forward with the right foot while maintaining the same upper body position.

### 2) Zenkutsu-dachi/Migi chūdan oi-zuki
Follow through with the step forward with the right foot into a right front stance while delivering a right middle-level lunge punch.

3-A) Turn the head to the right to face the opposite direction while pulling the right foot back and across to the

opposite side of the left foot, pivoting on the left foot to turn the body 180 degrees to the right. At the same time, pull the right fist up to above the left shoulder and thrust the left fist out across the front of the body.

### 3) Zenkutsu-dachi/Migi gedan-barai
Shift into a right front stance facing the opposite direction while performing a right downward block.

4-A) Twist the right wrist inward while pulling the right arm back sharply in front of the left hip and up to above the head in a large sweeping motion. At the same time, draw the right hip inward while pulling the right foot back one half-step for greater momentum.

### 4) Renoji-dachi/Migi tate-mawashi tettsui-uchi
Shifting into an L stance, draw the right fist down sharply to execute a vertical round hammer-fist strike.

5-A) Step forward with the left foot while maintaining the same upper body position.

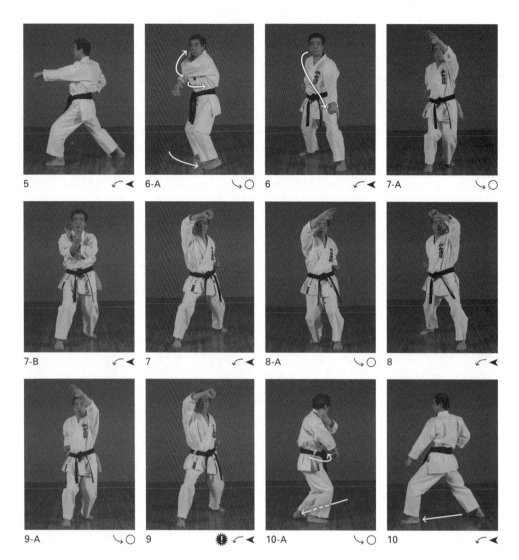

5 ↙◀ 6-A ↘○ 6 ↙◀ 7-A ↘○

7-B ↙◀ 7 ↙◀ 8-A ↘○ 8 ↙◀

9-A ↘○ 9 ✸↙◀ 10-A ↘○ 10 ↙◀

**5)** *Zenkutsu-dachi/Hidari chūdan oi-zuki*
Follow through with the step forward into a left front stance while delivering a left middle-level lunge punch.

**6-A)** Turn the head to the left while drawing the left foot across to the left, pivoting on the right foot to turn the body 90 degrees to the left. At the same time, pull the left fist back to above the right shoulder and thrust the right fist out across the front of the body.

**6)** *Zenkutsu-dachi/Hidari gedan-barai*
Shift into a left front stance while performing a left downward block.

**7-A)** Advancing the right foot forward, open the left hand and thrust it upward at an angle in front of the body, taking care to keep the hips facing forward.

**7-B)** Drive the right fist upward will pulling the left elbow downward, crossing the arms in front of the body.

**7)** *Zenkutsu-dachi/Migi jōdan age-uke*
Complete the step forward with the right foot into a right front stance while performing a right upper-level rising block, using the rotation of the hips to ensure a strong technique.

**8-A)** Stepping forward with the left foot, open the right hand and thrust it upward at an angle in front of the body.

**8)** *Zenkutsu-dachi/Hidari jōdan age-uke*
Complete the step forward into a left front stance while performing a left upper-level rising block.

**9-A)** Stepping forward with the right foot, open the left hand and thrust it upward in front of the body.

**9)** *Zenkutsu-dachi/Migi jōdan age-uke*
Complete the step forward into a right front stance while performing a right upper-level rising block with a *kiai* (a loud vocalization, such as "*eei*" or "*yaah*").

**10-A)** Draw the left foot across the rear to the right-hand side, pivoting on the right foot to turn the body 270 degrees to the left (facing the right side). At the same time, pull the left fist up to above the right shoulder and thrust the right fist out across the front of the body.

**10)** *Zenkutsu-dachi/Hidari gedan-barai*
Shift into a left front stance while performing a left downward block.

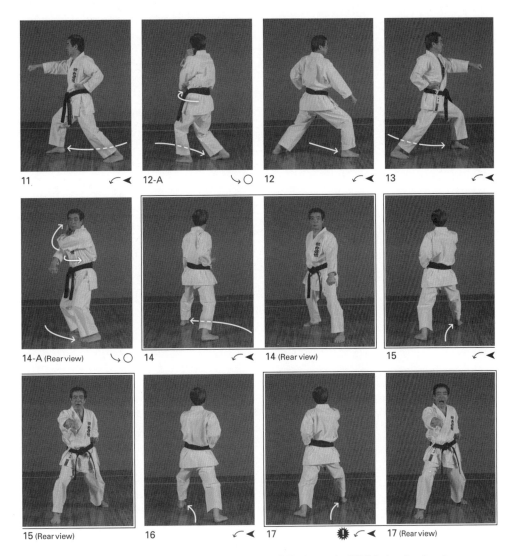

11    12-A    12    13

14-A (Rear view)    14    14 (Rear view)    15

15 (Rear view)    16    17    17 (Rear view)

**11)** *Zenkutsu-dachi/Migi chūdan oi-zuki*
Step forward with the right foot into a right front stance while delivering a right middle-level lunge punch.

**12-A)** Draw the right foot back and across to the opposite side of the left foot, turning 180 degrees to the right while simultaneously pulling the right fist to above the left shoulder and thrusting the left fist out across the front of the body.

**12)** *Zenkutsu-dachi/Migi gedan-barai*
Shift into a right front stance while performing a right downward block.

**13)** *Zenkutsu-dachi/Hidari chūdan oi-zuki*
Step forward with the left foot into a left front stance while delivering a left middle-level lunge punch.

**14-A)** Turn the head to the left while drawing the left foot across to the left, pivoting on the right foot to turn the body 90 degrees to the left. At the same time, pull the left fist back to above the right shoulder and thrust the right fist out across the front of the body.

**14)** *Zenkutsu-dachi/Hidari gedan-barai*
Assume a left front stance while executing a left downward block.

**15)** *Zenkutsu-dachi/Migi chūdan oi-zuki*
Returning down the center line of the *embusen* (performance line), step forward with the right foot into a right front stance while delivering a right middle-level lunge punch.

**16)** *Zenkutsu-dachi/Hidari chūdan oi-zuki*
Step forward with the left foot into a left front stance while delivering a left middle-level lunge punch.

**17)** *Zenkutsu-dachi/Migi chūdan oi-zuki*
Step forward with the right foot into a right front stance while delivering a right middle-level lunge punch with a *kiai*.

18-A     18     19-A     19     20-A

20     21-A     21     Yame-A     Yame

18-A) Draw the left foot across the rear to the right-hand side of the body, pivoting on the right foot to turn the body 270 degrees to the left. At the same time, pull the left hand, open and formed into a knife hand with the back of the hand facing outward, up to above the right shoulder and thrust the right hand, also formed into a knife hand with the palm facing the floor, out across the front of the chest.

**18) _Kōkutsu-dachi/Hidari chūdan shutō-uke_**
Assume a right back stance while performing a left middle-level knife-hand block.

**19-A)** Draw the right foot forward at a 45-degree angle to the right while pulling the right knife hand up to above the left shoulder and thrusting the left knife hand out in front of the solar plexus.

**19) _Kōkutsu-dachi/Migi chūdan shutō-uke_**
Complete the step forward into a left back stance while executing a right middle-level knife-hand block.

**20-A)** Draw the right foot back at a 135-degree angle to the right while pulling the right knife hand up to above the left shoulder and thrusting the left knife hand out across the front of the chest.

**20) _Kōkutsu-dachi/Migi chūdan shutō-uke_**
Shift into a left back stance while performing a right middle-level knife-hand block.

**21-A)** Draw the left foot forward at a 45-degree angle to the left while pulling the left knife hand up to above the right shoulder and thrusting the right knife hand out in front of the solar plexus.

**21) _Kōkutsu-dachi/Hidari chūdan shutō-uke_**
Complete the step forward into a right back stance while performing a left middle-level knife-hand block.

*Yame*-A) Draw the left foot back, placing it beside the right foot into an open V stance, while crossing the arms in front of the chest.

**_Yame_** (*Yame* is a command to cease performing an activity or action.)
Return to a natural-posture stance with the arms extended downward in front of the body so that the fists are positioned in front of the hips as in the original starting ready position. Maintain a state of physical and mental readiness (*zanshin*), prepared to respond to a potential attack, regardless of when or from where it may come.

## TECHNICAL ANALYSIS
### Movements 3–4 (1)

In response to an opponent grabbing the right wrist following a downward block (photo 1), pull the right arm back sharply in front of the hips to break the hold (photo 2) and, drawing the fist up to above the head (photo 3), follow through with a vertical round hammer-fist strike directed to the top of the opponent's head (photo 4).

1

2

3

4

## TECHNICAL ANALYSIS
### Movements 3–4 (2)

In response to an opponent's front snap kick, block with a downward block (photo 1). As the opponent then delivers a middle-level reverse punch, draw the blocking arm back to perform a back-arm block (photo 2). Follow through with the motion of the arm, bringing the fist up to above the head (photo 3) and downward to counter with a vertical round hammer-fist strike (photo 4).

1

2

3

4

## TECHNICAL ANALYSIS
## Movements 9–10

Upon blocking an opponent's punch with a rising block (photo 1), grab his wrist with both hands while turning the hips to the left (photo 2), following through with the motion to execute a shoulder throw (photos 3-5).

1

2

3

4

5

# Heian Nidan (Heian No. 2)

Heian Nidan adds numerous basic techniques to those already introduced in Heian Shodan: upper-level inside-to-outside back-arm blocks, close punches, a combined side snap kick and back-fist strike, a four-finger spear-hand strike, and front snap kicks. The *kata* also features an increased number of knife-hand blocks and back stances, making it more *kata*-like in appearance.

Yōi     1-A     1     2-A     2-B

2     3-A     3     4-A     4

### *Yōi* (Ready position)

*Soto hachiji-dachi* (open V stance) with both fists positioned in front of the hips.

1-A) Turn the head to the left and, leaving the fists in place, draw the left foot out to the left side.

### 1) *Kōkutsu-dachi/Hidari jōdan uchi haiwan-uke/Migi ude soete*

Shift into a right back stance facing the left-hand side while pulling both arms up in a sharp, whipping motion to perform a left upper-level inside-to-outside back-arm block. The right arm accompanies the technique, moving in synchronization with the left arm to provide additional momentum, making possible a more powerful block. In the completed position, the arms should describe a large horizontally oriented rectangle.

### 2-A) *Kōkutsu-dachi/Hidari ude-uke/Migi jōdan tettsui-uchi* (*Migi ura-zuki*)

In response to an opponent's punch to the face, draw the left fist back toward the right shoulder to deflect the attack with a forearm block, rotating the wrist so that the back of the fist faces outward upon completing the motion. At the same time, launch the right fist along a narrow arcing course downward to the front to deliver a right upper-level hammer-fist strike. (Depending on the application, the right arm could also deliver a right close punch.) Turn the hips to the left when performing the technique while maintaining a strong back stance, being

careful not to allow the right knee to collapse inward.

2-B) Turning the hips to the right, draw the right elbow back toward the body while driving the left elbow out toward the direction of the left foot.

### 2) *Kōkutsu-dachi/Hidari chūdan zuki*

Extend the left arm out sharply to the left to deliver a left middle-level punch while pulling the right fist back to above the right hip.

3-A) Turn the head to the right to face the opposite direction while driving the right fist across the body to the left-hand side and lowering the left fist.

### 3) *Kōkutsu-dachi/Migi jōdan uchi haiwan-uke/Hidari ude soete*

Transfer the center of gravity toward the left leg to assume a left back stance while swinging both arms up to perform a right upper-level inside-to-outside back-arm block. The left arm accompanies the technique, providing momentum for a more powerful block.

### 4-A) *Kōkutsu-dachi/Migi ude-uke/Hidari jōdan tettsui-uchi* (*Hidari ura-zuki*)

Draw the right fist back toward the left shoulder to perform a forearm block while executing a left upper-level hammer-fist strike (or left close punch).

### 4) *Migi chūdan zuki*

Deliver a right middle-level punch to the right while pulling the left fist back to above the left hip.

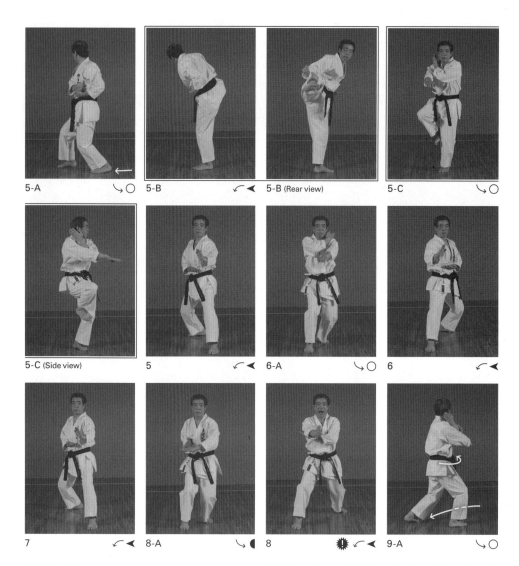

5-A  ↘○   5-B  ↗◄   5-B (Rear view)   5-C  ↘○

5-C (Side view)   5  ↗◄   6-A  ↘○   6  ↗◄

7  ↗◄   8-A  ↘◑   8  ☀↗◄   9-A  ↘○

**5-A)** *Koshi-gamae*

Turn the head to the right while drawing the left foot one half-step toward the right foot. At the same time, pull the right fist back to the left side of the body, positioning it on top of the left fist with the thumb-side of the fist facing upward.

**5-B)** *Migi yoko ke-age/Migi yoko-mawashi uraken-uchi*

Deliver a right side snap kick to the right side while simultaneously executing a right side round back-fist strike in the same direction.

**5-C)** Turn the head to the left to face the opposite direction (the same orientation as the original ready position) while pulling back the kicking leg. At the same time, pull the left hand, formed into a knife hand, up to above the right shoulder with the back of the hand facing outward while thrusting the right hand, also formed into a knife hand, out across the chest to the left-hand side with the palm facing the floor.

**5)** *Kōkutsu-dachi/Hidari chūdan shutō-uke*

Plant the right foot back in the direction of the side snap kick, shifting into a right back stance facing the front while performing a left middle-level knife-hand block.

**6-A)** Step forward with the right foot while pulling the right knife hand up to above the left shoulder and thrusting the left knife hand out in front of the chest.

**6)** *Kōkutsu-dachi/Migi chūdan shutō-uke*

Complete the step forward with the right foot into a left back stance while performing a right middle-level knife-hand block.

**7)** *Kōkutsu-dachi/Hidari chūdan shutō-uke*

Step forward with the left foot into a right back stance while executing a left middle-level knife-hand block.

**8-A)** *Hidari osae-uke*

Drawing the right foot forward, drop the left hand along a circular course centered on the elbow to perform a left pressing block while extending the right hand, formed into a spear hand, in a course straight in front of the body just above the left hand.

**8)** *Zenkutsu-dachi/Migi chūdan shihon-nukite*

Complete the step forward with the right foot into a right front stance while delivering a right middle-level spear hand with a *kiai*. The left hand is positioned beneath the right arm for added support.

9 ↙◄ 10-A ↘○ 10 ↙◄ 11-A ↘○

11 ↙◄ 12-A ↘○ 12 ↙◄ 12 (Rear view)

13-A ↘○ 13-A (Rear view) 13-B ↙○ 13-B (Rear view)

9-A) Pull the left foot across the rear to the right-hand side, pivoting on the right foot to turn the body 270 degrees to the left (facing the right side). At the same time, pull the left hand, formed into a knife hand, up to above the right shoulder and thrust the right hand, also formed into a knife hand, out across the chest and below the left underarm.

### 9) *Kōkutsu-dachi/Hidari chūdan shutō-uke*
Shift into a right back stance while performing a left middle-level knife-hand block.

10-A) Draw the right foot forward at a 45-degree angle to the right while pulling the right knife hand up to above the left shoulder and thrusting the left knife hand out in front of the body.

### 10) *Kōkutsu-dachi/Migi chūdan shutō-uke*
Shift into a left back stance while delivering a right middle-level knife-hand block.

11-A) Draw the right foot across to the right to turn the body 135 degrees in the same direction while pulling the right knife hand up to above the left shoulder and thrusting the left knife hand out across the front of the chest.

### 11) *Kōkutsu-dachi/Migi chūdan shutō-uke*
Shift into a left back stance while performing a right middle-level knife-hand block.

12-A) Draw the left foot forward at a 45-degree angle to the left while pulling the left knife hand up to above the right shoulder and thrusting the right knife hand out in front of the body.

### 12) *Kōkutsu-dachi/Hidari chūdan shutō-uke*
Shift into a right back stance while executing a left middle-level knife-hand block.

13-A) Turn the head to the left and draw the left foot across to the left, turning the body 45 degrees in the same direction (so as to look down the center line of the *embusen* (performance line) from the end opposite to the original starting position). At the same time, draw the right arm back at an angle to the right in a large sweeping motion. The left arm remains in the same knife-hand-block position relative to the upper body.

13-B) Transfer the center of gravity toward the left leg while swinging the right arm across the front of the body and downward to below the right underarm.

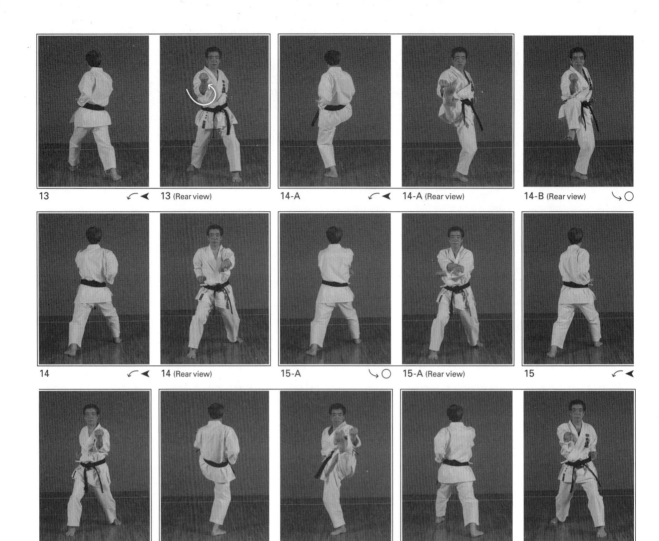

13      13 (Rear view)      14-A      14-A (Rear view)      14-B (Rear view)

14      14 (Rear view)      15-A      15-A (Rear view)      15

15 (Rear view)      16-A      16-A (Rear view)      16      16 (Rear view)

### 13) Zenkutsu-dachi/Migi chūdan gyaku uchi-uke/Gyaku-hanmi

Assume a slightly shortened left front stance while performing a right middle-level reverse inside-to-outside block, turning the hips to *gyaku-hanmi* (45-degree angle to the front, with the hip on the side opposite to the front leg pushed forward).

### 14-A) Migi mae-geri

Keeping the arms in place, deliver a right front snap kick.

14-B) Retract the right leg following the kick.

### 14) Zenkutsu-dachi/Hidari chūdan gyaku-zuki

Plant the right foot forward into a right front stance while executing a left middle-level reverse punch.

15-A) Extend the right arm straight out in front of the body while drawing the left fist back to below the right underarm with the back of the fist facing upward.

### 15) Zenkutsu-dachi/Hidari chūdan gyaku uchi-uke/Gyaku-hanmi

Perform a left middle-level reverse inside-to-outside block while turning the hips to *gyaku-hanmi*. As the hips rotate, the front foot moves back slightly but the front knee remains bent at the same angle.

### 16-A) Hidari mae-geri

Keeping the arms in place, deliver a left front snap kick.

### 16) Zenkutsu-dachi/Migi chūdan gyaku-zuki

Plant the left foot forward into a left front stance while executing a right middle-level reverse punch.

17-A) Step forward with the right foot while extending the left arm out at an angle to the left, leaving the elbow bent slightly. At the same time, pull the right fist back to the left arm so that the inside of the right wrist is positioned just above the left elbow.

### 17) Zenkutsu-dachi/Migi chūdan morote-uke

Complete the step forward with the right foot into a right front stance while performing an inside-to-outside block with the right arm, augmented by the left fist, which presses against the inside of the right elbow. The left fist provides support when blocking to enable a stronger technique.

18-A) Draw the left foot across the rear to the right, pivoting on the right foot to turn the body 270 degrees to the left (to face toward the right side). At the same time, pull the left fist up to above the right shoulder and thrust the right fist out across the front of the body.

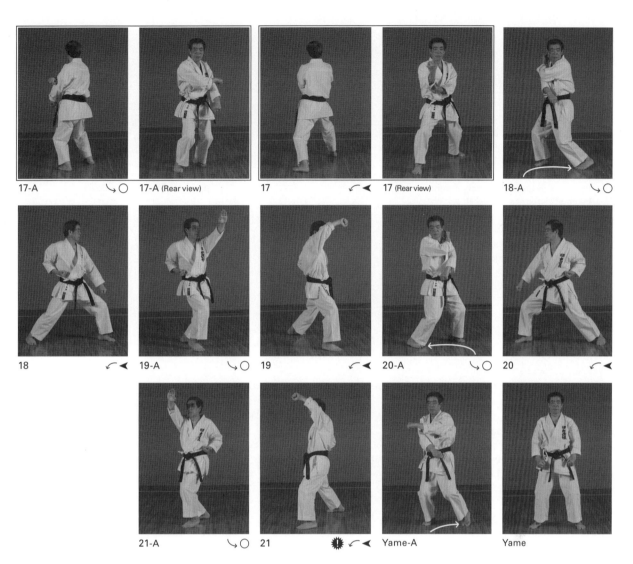

17-A    ↘○    17-A (Rear view)    17    ↙◀    17 (Rear view)    18-A    ↘○

18    ↙◀    19-A    ↘○    19    ↙◀    20-A    ↘○    20    ↙◀

21-A    ↘○    21    ✴①↙◀    Yame-A    Yame

**18) *Zenkutsu-dachi/Hidari gedan-barai***
Shift into a left front stance while performing a left downward block.

19-A) Open the left hand and thrust it upward in front of the body at an angle to the right while drawing the right foot forward in the same direction.

**19) *Zenkutsu-dachi/Migi jōdan age-uke***
Complete the step forward with the right foot at a 45-degree angle to the right into a right front stance while performing a right upper-level rising block.

20-A) Draw the right foot back, pivoting on the left foot to turn the body 135 degrees to the right, simultaneously pulling the right fist up to above the left shoulder and thrusting the left fist out across the front of the body.

**20) *Zenkutsu-dachi/Migi gedan-barai***
Shift into a right front stance while performing a right downward block.

21-A) Open the right hand and thrust it upward in front of the body at an angle to the left while drawing the left foot forward in the same direction.

**21) *Zenkutsu-dachi/Hidari jōdan age-uke***
Complete the step forward with the left foot at a 45-degree angle to the left into a left front stance while performing a left upper-level rising block with a *kiai*.

*Yame*-A) Draw the left foot back, placing it beside the right foot into an open V stance. At the same time, cross the arms in front of the body with the left arm above the right.

***Yame***
Extend the arms downward in front of the body so that the fists are positioned in front of the hips as in the original starting ready position and maintain a state of physical and mental readiness (*zanshin*)

### TECHNICAL ANALYSIS
### Movements 1–2

In response to an opponent's upper-level punch from the left-hand side, execute a left upper-level inside-to-outside back-arm block (photo 1). As the opponent follows with an upper-level reverse punch, sweep the fist past the right side of the head with a left forearm block while simultaneously delivering a counterattack to the elbow using a right hammer-fist strike (photo 2). As the opponent then responds with a right middle-level punch, use the left elbow to deflect the strike (photo 3), following through with the motion of the left arm to deliver a punch to the midsection (photo 4).

1

2

3

4

### TECHNICAL ANALYSIS
### Movements 4–5-C

As an opponent delivers a punching attack from the rear (photo 1), sidestep the assault by sliding the rear foot one half-step forward and counter with a simultaneous side snap kick and back-fist strike (photo 2). Immediately turn the head to the left in preparation for an attack from the opposite direction.

1

2

3

### TECHNICAL ANALYSIS
### Movements 13-B–13

In response to an opponent's front snap kick, block with a reverse inside-to-outside block (photo 1), following through with the motion of the arm to deflect a subsequent middle-level lunge punch attack to the midsection (photo 2).

1

2

# Heian Sandan (Heian No. 3)

Heian Sandan incorporates a range of varied techniques, beginning with an inside-to-outside block, followed immediately by a simultaneous inside-to-outside block/downward block combination. The *kata* includes a response to a situation in which the wrist has been grabbed upon delivering a spear-hand strike, which involves the twisting and rotating of the body followed by an attack. The final sequence of Heian Sandan assumes that an opponent has seized from behind, calling for a back elbow strike performed simultaneously with an over-the-shoulder vertical punch to the opponent's face.

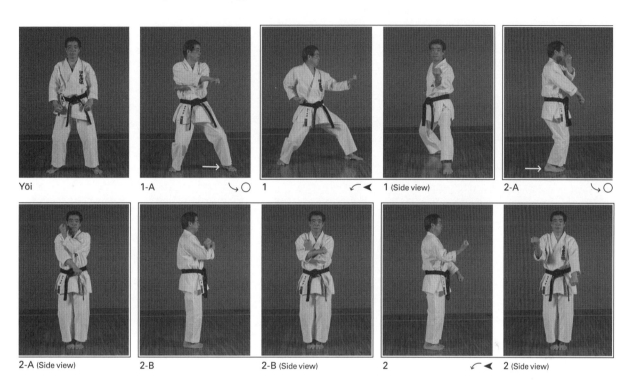

Yōi   1-A ↘○   1 ↙◀   1 (Side view)   2-A ↘○

2-A (Side view)   2-B   2-B (Side view)   2 ↙◀   2 (Side view)

### *Yōi* (Ready position)
*Soto hachiji-dachi* (open V stance) with both fists positioned in front of the hips.

1-A) Turn the head to the left and, drawing the left foot out to the left, pull the left fist back to the right side of the body and below the right underarm while extending the right arm across the front of the chest to the left.

### 1) *Kōkutsu-dachi/Hidari chūdan uchi-uke*
Shift into a right back stance facing the left side while executing a left middle-level inside-to-outside block.

2-A) Drawing the right foot forward to alongside the left foot into a closed parallel stance, pull the left fist up to above the right shoulder with the back of the fist facing outward while thrusting the right fist downward at an angle in front of the body.

2-B) The left fist travels down in front of the body to perform a downward block while the right fist, pivoting at the elbow, simultaneously arcs upward to deliver an inside-to-outside block.

### 2) *Heisoku-dachi/Kōsa-uke*
The arms complete a cross block (the right arm executing an inside-to-outside block and the left arm a downward block) while maintaining a closed parallel stance. When performing cross blocks, the arm delivering the downward block always travels closest to the body, between the chest and the arm executing the inside-to-outside block.

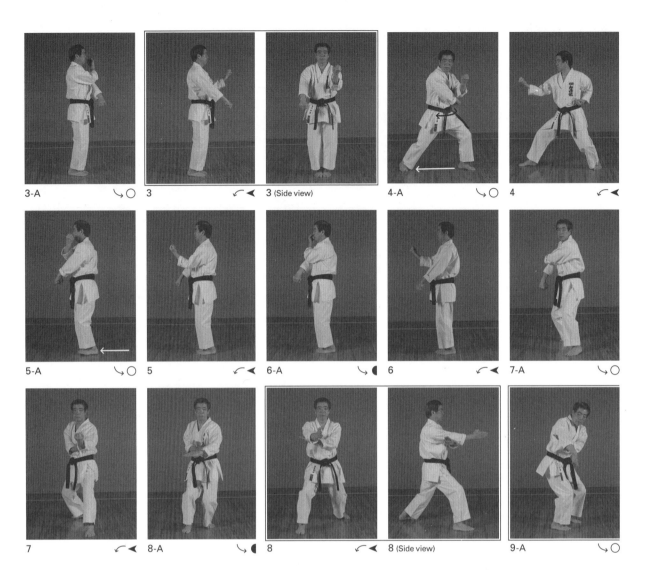

3-A) Pull the right fist up to the left shoulder with the back of the fist facing outward while drawing the left fist across toward the right side of the body.

### 3) *Heisoku-dachi/Kōsa-uke*
Execute another cross block, driving the right fist down to deliver a downward block while arcing the left fist upward into an inside-to-outside block.

4-A) Draw the right foot straight back while pulling the right fist across the front of the body to below the left underarm as the left hand extends in the opposite direction above the right arm. At the same time, look over the right shoulder to the rear while turning the upper body in the same direction.

### 4) *Kōkutsu-dachi/Migi chūdan uchi-uke*
Turning the hips 180 degrees to the right, shift into a left back stance facing the opposite direction from the previous orientation while executing a right middle-level inside-to-outside block.

5-A) Drawing the left foot forward to alongside the right foot into a closed parallel stance, pull the right fist up to above the left shoulder with the back of the fist facing outward while thrusting the left fist down at an angle in front of the body to the right-hand side.

### 5) *Heisoku-dachi/Kōsa-uke*
Standing in a closed parallel stance, launch the right fist down to deliver a downward block while drawing the left fist across toward the left side of the body.

6-A) Pull the left fist up to above the right shoulder while drawing the right fist across toward the left side of the body.

### 6) *Heisoku-dachi/Kōsa-uke*
Maintaining a closed parallel stance, perform another cross block, with the right arm executing an inside-to-outside block while the left arm delivers a downward block.

9-A (Side view)

9-B

9-C

9

9 (Side view)

10-A

10-A (Side view)

10

10 (Side view)

11-A

11

7-A) Turning the head to the left (the same orientation as the original ready position), extend the left leg straight out to the left side. At the same time, thrust the right fist downward at an angle to the right while simultaneously drawing the left arm across the front of the body, positioning the thumb-side of the left fist just above the right elbow.

### 7) *Kōkutsu-dachi/Hidari chūdan morote-uke*
Shift into a right back stance while sharply drawing the left arm around the body to the front to deliver a left middle-level augmented inside-to-outside block. The right fist is positioned at the base of the left elbow upon completion of the block to ensure a powerful technique.

### 8-A) *Hidari osae-uke*
Drawing the right foot forward, drop the left hand along a circular course centered on the elbow to perform a left pressing block while extending the right hand, formed into a spear hand, in a course straight in front of the body just above the left hand.

### 8) *Zenkutsu-dachi/Migi chūdan shihon-nukite*
Complete the step forward with the right foot into a right front stance while executing a right middle-level spear hand attack. The left hand, open with the back of the hand pressing against the right arm just above the elbow, provides support for the right arm.

9-A) In response to an opponent grasping the right wrist, extend the right arm forward while twisting the wrist counter-clockwise. Keeping the left hand positioned behind the right elbow, draw the left foot forward while rotating the hips to the left.

12-A

12-A (Rear view)

9-B) Continue drawing the left foot forward and behind the right foot, further rotating the hips while pulling the right hand up to the small of the back with the palm facing outward.

9-C) Draw the right arm around to the front of the body above the left arm.

### 9) *Kiba-dachi/Hidari chūdan tettsui-uchi*
Plant the left foot forward into a straddle-leg stance, taking advantage of the rotation of the hips to launch a left middle-level hammer-fist strike while pulling the right fist back sharply to above the right hip.

10-A) Keeping the left fist positioned out in front of the body, step forward with the right foot,.

### 10) *Zenkutsu-dachi/Migi chūdan oi-zuki*
Complete the step forward with the right foot into a right front stance while delivering a right middle-level lunge punch with a *kiai*

11-A) Pull the left foot forward toward the right foot, pivoting on the right foot to turn the body to the left. At the same time, pull the right fist back toward the right hip while drawing the left elbow out from the body, keeping the left fist in contact with the left hip.

### 11) *Heisoku-dachi/Ryōken koshi-gamae*
Draw the left foot alongside the right foot, completing a 180-degree turn to the left into a closed parallel stance while gradually straightening the legs. Upon completion of the turn, the fists are positioned above the hips with the first knuckles of the index and middle fingers pressing into the sides of the body and the elbows extending out to the sides.

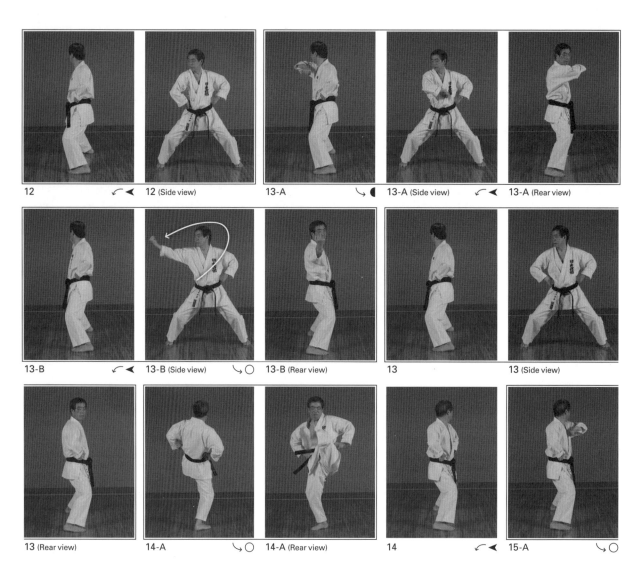

12    ↙◀    12 (Side view)     13-A    ↘◖  13-A (Side view)   ↙◀    13-A (Rear view)

13-B    ↙◀    13-B (Side view)   ↘○  13-B (Rear view)      13         13 (Side view)

13 (Rear view)      14-A   ↘○  14-A (Rear view)     14    ↙◀    15-A   ↘○

12-A) Swing the right leg up sharply in front of the body.

**12) *Kiba-dachi/Fumikomi/Migi empi-uke***
Deliver a stamping kick with the right leg, assuming a straddle-leg stance while driving the right elbow inward to execute a right elbow block.

**13-A) *Kiba-dachi/Migi jōdan uraken-uchi***
Maintaining a strong straddle-leg stance, draw the right fist back and upward along the side of the head in a sharp arcing motion along a path perpendicular to the floor to deliver a right upper-level back-fist strike.

13-B) Complete the back-fist strike utilizing the snapping motion of the elbow and wrist.

13) Withdraw the right fist, pulling it back to above the right hip.

14-A) Swing the left leg up sharply across the front of the body.

**14) *Kiba-dachi/Fumikomi/Hidari empi-uke***
Deliver a stamping kick with the left leg, assuming a straddle-leg stance while simultaneously performing a left elbow block.

**15-A) *Kiba-dachi/Hidari jōdan uraken-uchi***
Maintaining a strong straddle-leg stance, launch the left fist back and upward along an arcing path perpendicular to the floor to deliver a left upper-level back-fist strike.

15-B) Follow through with the motion of the arm to complete the strike.

15) Immediately return the left fist to above the left hip.

16-A) Swing the right leg up sharply across the front of the body.

**16) *Kiba-dachi/Fumikomi/Migi empi-uke***
Deliver a stamping with the right leg, assuming a straddle-leg stance while delivering a right elbow block.

**17-A) *Kiba-dachi/Migi jōdan uraken-uchi***
Maintaining a strong straddle-leg stance, deliver a right upper-level back-fist strike.

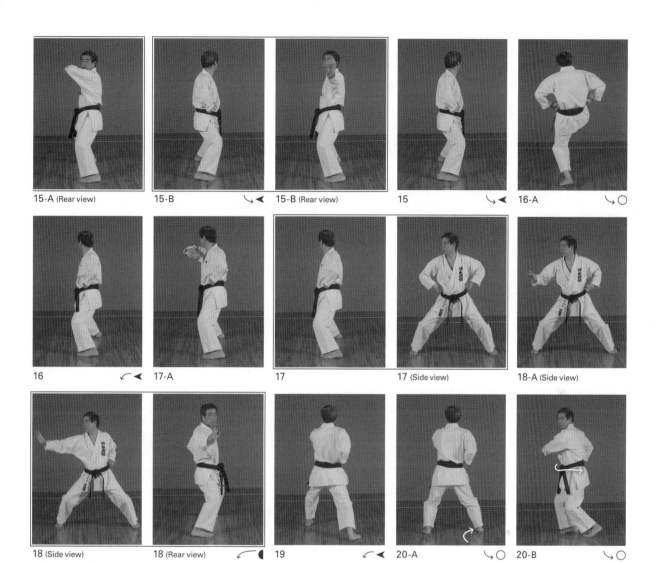

15-A (Rear view)  15-B  ↘◄  15-B (Rear view)  15  ↘◄  16-A  ↘○

16  ↙◄  17-A  17  17 (Side view)  18-A (Side view)

18 (Side view)  18 (Rear view)  ↙●  19  ↙◄  20-A  ↘○  20-B  ↘○

20  ↙◄

17) Upon completing the technique, pull the right fist back to above the right hip.

18-A) Draw the right hand, formed into a knife-hand, out to the right side of the body while drawing the left elbow back, keeping the left fist positioned above the left hip.

**18) *Kiba-dachi/Migi chūdan tate shutō-gamae***
Maintaining a strong straddle-leg stance, fully extend the right hand to the right side of the body as if to execute a right middle-level vertical knife-hand block. The left elbow is pulled tightly toward the left side of the body.

**19) *Zenkutsu-dachi/Hidari chūdan oi-zuki***
Step forward, in the direction of the right hand, with the left foot into a left front stance while delivering a left middle-level lunge punch

20-A) Without moving the upper body, draw the right foot forward in line with the left foot. The right foot travels along a curved path, first inward toward the left foot, and then out to the right.

20-B) Pivoting on the right foot, draw the left foot across the back of the right leg to the opposite side, sharply rotating the hips 180 degrees to the left.

**20) *Kiba-dachi/Migi tate-zuki/Hidari ushiro empi-uchi***
Assuming a straddle-leg stance, swing the right fist across the front of the body to deliver a right vertical-fist punch over the left shoulder to the rear. At the same time, drive the left elbow back sharply to execute a left elbow strike to the rear

21

✳ Yame-A

Yame

**21) *Kiba-dachi/Hidari tate-zuki/Migi ushiro empi-uchi***
Thrusting off the left foot to shift the body to the right, launch the left fist across the front of the body to execute a left vertical-fist punch over the right shoulder to the rear while driving the right elbow back sharply to deliver a right elbow strike to the rear with a *kiai*.

*Yame*-A) Draw the right foot inward, placing it beside the left foot into an open V stance. At the same time pull the right arm across the front of the chest while lowering the left fist.

***Yame***
Return to a natural-posture stance with the arms extended downward in front of the body, maintaining a state of physical and mental readiness (*zanshin*).

**TECHNICAL ANALYSIS**
## Movements 8–9

In response to an opponent grabbing the right wrist following a spear hand attack (photo 1), extend the right arm forward (photo 2), twisting the wrist while pivoting on the right foot to turn the hips to the left (photo 3). Follow through with the motion of the hips (photo 4), countering with a left hammer fist strike to the side of the body (photo 5).

1

2

3

4

5

## TECHNICAL ANALYSIS
### Movements 11–12

As an opponent launches a middle-level lunge punch, deflect the attack with a right crescent kick (photo 2) and, utilizing the rotation of the hips, deliver a front-elbow-strike counterattack (photo 3).

1

2

3

## TECHNICAL ANALYSIS
### Movement 20

In response to an opponent grabbing from behind (photo 1), break the hold by raising both elbows sharply while lowering the hips to (photo 2). Counter by driving the left elbow back to deliver an elbow strike while launching the right fist over the left shoulder to execute a vertical-fist punch to the rear (photo 3).

1

2

3

# Heian Yondan (Heian No. 4)

The opening movement of Heian Yondan is similar to that of Heian Nidan except that the hands are open. Heian No. 4, however, includes a greater number of kicking techniques, knife-hand blocks and back stances. This *kata* also introduces several advanced techniques, such as upper-level front snap kicks, reverse wedge blocks in response to simultaneous double-punch attacks, and a knee strike to the face performed while grasping an imagined opponent's head.

Yōi     1-A     1     2-A

2     3-A     3     4-A

### *Yōi* (Ready position)
*Soto hachiji-dachi* (open V stance) with both fists positioned in front of the hips.

1-A) Turn the head to the left while simultaneously opening both hands and drawing the left foot out to the left side into a right back stance. The hands remain in the same position as the initial ready position so that they appear to have been pulled back once the left foot has been planted.

### 1) *Kōkutsu-dachi/Kaishu haiwan-uke*
Maintaining a strong back stance, raise both arms upward in a flowing arcing motion to deliver a left open-hand back-arm block. During the technique, the right arm, moving in synchronization with the left, serves to provide additional momentum for a more effective block. In the completed position, the arms should describe a large horizontally oriented rectangle.

2-A) Transfer the center of gravity toward the left leg while dropping the arms straight downward. Shift into a left back stance as the hands drop level to the waist, maintaining the same basic orientation as the block technique performed in the previous step.

### 2) *Kōkutsu-dachi/Kaishu haiwan-uke*
Maintaining a strong back stance, raise both arms in a smooth arcing motion to perform a right open-hand back-arm block.

3-A) Turning the head to the left, draw the left foot toward the right foot and then out to the left-hand side while pulling the left hand toward the right hand, tucking the left elbow in against the body. At the same time, draw the right elbow back behind the head.

### 3) *Zenkutsu-dachi/Gedan jūji-uke*
Plant the left foot forward into a left front stance while driving both arms down sharply in front of the body to execute a downward X-block. The left hand, closing into a fist, travels along a curved path to deliver a downward block while the right hand moves in a direct path down from the shoulder to deliver a downward vertical fist punch.

4-A) Step forward with the right foot while drawing the left fist out to the left side of the body with the right wrist positioned above the left elbow.

### 4) *Kōkutsu-dachi/Migi chūdan morote-uke*
Complete the step forward with the right foot into a left back stance while performing an inside-to-outside block with the right arm, augmented by the left fist, which presses against the inside of the right elbow.

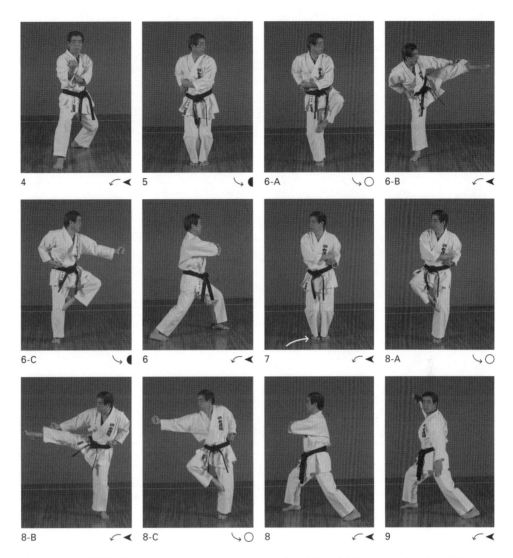

4    5    6-A    6-B

6-C    6    7    8-A

8-B    8-C    8    9

### 5) *Heisoku-dachi/Koshi-gamae*

Turning the head to the left, draw the left foot forward to alongside the right foot into a closed parallel stance while pulling both fists to above the right hip with the left fist resting on top of the right fist. The back of the left hand faces away from the body.

6-A) Raise the left foot to above the right knee in preparation to deliver a left side snap kick.

### 6-B) *Hidari yoko ke-age/Hidari yoko-mawashi ura-ken-uchi*

Deliver a left side snap kick while simultaneously executing a left side round back-fist strike.

6-C) Snap the left foot back to above the right knee following the kick.

### 6) *Zenkutsu-dachi/Migi mae empi-uchi*

Plant the left foot in the direction of the kick into a left front stance while simultaneously delivering a right front elbow strike against the palm of the left hand.

### 7) *Heisoku-dachi/Koshi-gamae*

Turning the head to the right, draw the right foot inward

to alongside the left foot into a closed parallel stance while pulling both fists to above the left hip with the right fist resting above the left fist.

8-A) Raise the right foot to above the left knee in preparation for a right side snap kick.

### 8-B) *Migi yoko ke-age/Migi yoko-mawashi uraken-uchi*

Deliver a right side snap kick while simultaneously performing a right side round back-fist strike.

8-C) Snap the right foot back to above the left knee after the kick.

### 8) *Zenkutsu-dachi/Hidari mae empi-uchi*

Plant the right foot in the direction of the kick into a right front stance while executing a left front elbow strike against the palm of the right hand.

### 9) *Zenkutsu-dachi/Hidari shutō gedan-barai*

Turning the head to the left, drop the left hand, formed into a knife hand, down to the left side of the body to deliver a downward knife-hand block while simultaneously drawing the right elbow back sharply behind the head.

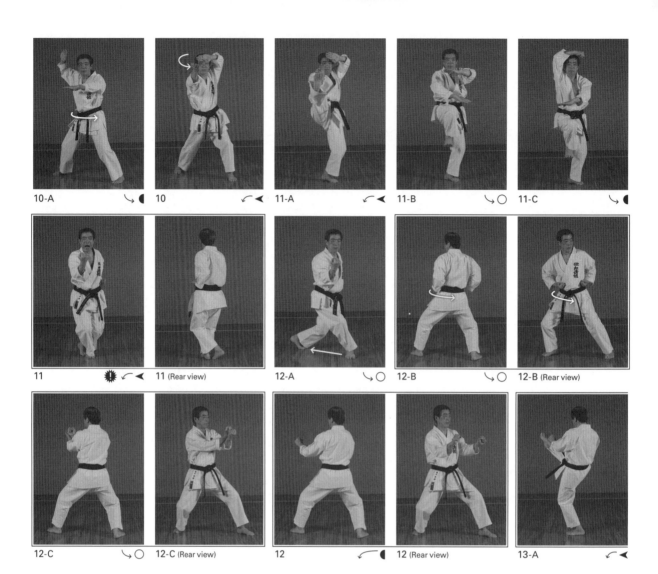

10-A) ↘ ◖    10   ◞◄    11-A ◞◄    11-B ↘○    11-C ↘◖

11 ✹◞◄    11 (Rear view)    12-A ↘○    12-B ↘○    12-B (Rear view)

12-C ↘○    12-C (Rear view)    12 ◞◖    12 (Rear view)    13-A ◞◄

**10-A)** Rotating the hips sharply to the left, draw the left hand directly upward while launching the right knife hand along a circular path around the right side of the head.

**10) *Zenkutsu-dachi/Migi jōdan shutō-uchi/Gyaku-hanmi***

Complete the rotation of the hips into a left front stance with the hips at *gyaku-hanmi* (45-degree angle to the front, with the hip on the side opposite to the front leg pushed forward) while executing a right upper-level knife-hand strike. The left knife hand is positioned above the forehead with the palm facing outward and the left elbow pulled back at an angle.

**11-A) *Migi jōdan mae-geri***

Maintaining the same upper body position, deliver a right upper-level front snap kick.

11-B) Upon retracting the kicking leg, pull the right hand back toward the chest while drawing the left hand out in front of the body.

**11-C) *Hidari chūdan osae-uke***

Thrusting off the left foot, drive the hips forward while dropping the left hand out in front of the body to perform a left middle-level pressing block. Moving in synchronization with the left hand, draw the right hand, closed into a fist, up to above the head.

**11) *Kōsa-dachi/Migi chūdan uraken-uchi***

Plant the right foot on the floor and immediately draw the left leg behind it into a cross-legged stance while delivering a right middle-level back-fist strike with a *kiai*.

12-A) Without moving the arms, extend the left leg back and to the right at a 45-degree angle.

12-B) Turning the hips to the left while keeping the right knee bent at the same angle, shift into a right back stance while drawing the right fist back to the right hip.

12-C) Draw both fists upward and out in front of the chest, crossing the arms at the wrists with the left arm on the far side of the right arm and the backs of the fists facing outward.

13-A (Rear view)

13-B (Rear view)

13-C

13-C (Rear view)

13

13 (Rear view)

14-A

14-A (Rear view)

14-B (Rear view)

14

14 (Rear view)

15-A

15-A (Rear view)

15-B

15-B (Rear view)

**12)** *Kōkutsu-dachi/Chūdan kakiwake-uke*
Pull the elbows back toward the body, drawing the fists away from each other while rotating the fists outward to perform a separating block, paying special attention to keep the elbows tucked in near the body.

**13-A)** *Migi jōdan mae-geri*
Keeping the arms in place, deliver a right upper-level front snap kick.

13-B) Retract the kicking leg following the kick.

**13-C)** *Zenkutsu-dachi/Migi chūdan oi-zuki*
Plant the right foot forward into a right front stance while delivering a right middle-level lunge punch.

**13)** *Zenkutsu-dachi/Hidari chūdan gyaku-zuki*
From the same front stance position, deliver a left middle-level reverse punch.

14-A) Turning the head 90 degrees to the right, draw the right foot back toward the left foot and out at a 45-degree angle to the right while pulling the left fist back toward the left hip.

14-B) Shift into a left back stance while drawing both fists upward and out in front of the chest, crossing the arms at the wrists with the right arm on the far side of the left arm and the backs of the fists facing outward.

**14)** *Kōkutsu-dachi/Chūdan kakiwake-uke*
Pull the elbows back toward the body while drawing the fists apart to perform a separating block.

**15-A)** *Hidari jōdan mae-geri*
Keeping the arms in place, deliver a left upper-level front snap kick.

**15-B)** *Zenkutsu-dachi/Hidari chūdan oi-zuki*
Step forward following the kick with the left foot into a left front stance while delivering a left middle-level lunge punch.

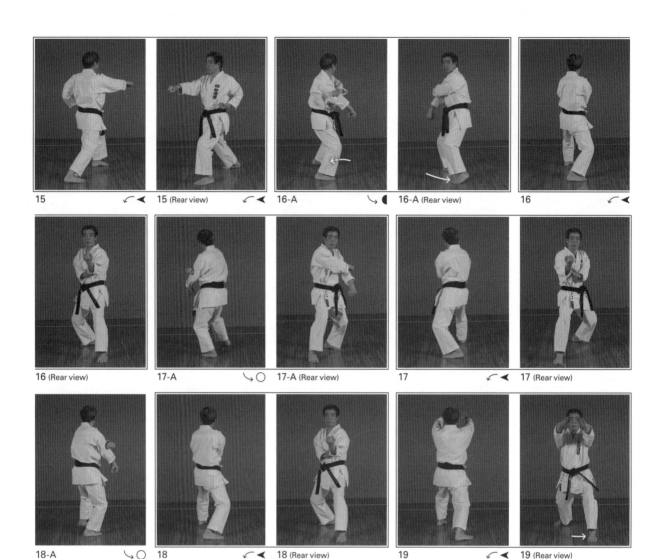

15    15 (Rear view)    16-A    16-A (Rear view)    16

16 (Rear view)    17-A    17-A (Rear view)    17    17 (Rear view)

18-A    18    18 (Rear view)    19    19 (Rear view)

### 15) *Zenkutsu-dachi/Migi chūdan gyaku-zuki*
From the same front stance position, deliver a right middle-level reverse punch.

16-A) Turning the head 45 degrees to the left, shift the center of gravity toward the right leg and slide the left foot to the left side. At the same time, extend the right arm downward at an angle to the right while simultaneously drawing the left arm across the front of the body, positioning the thumb-side of the left fist just above the right elbow.

### 16) *Kōkutsu-dachi/Hidari chūdan morote-uke*
Assuming a right back stance, sharply sweep the left arm around the body to deliver a left middle-level augmented inside-to-outside block.

17-A) Step forward with the right foot, drawing the left fist out to the left side of the body with the right wrist positioned above the left elbow.

### 17) *Kōkutsu-dachi/Migi chūdan morote-uke*
Complete the step forward with the right foot into a left back stance while executing an augmented inside-to-outside block with the right arm.

18-A) Step forward with the left foot, extending the right arm out to the right side of the body with the left wrist positioned above the right elbow.

### 18) *Kōkutsu-dachi/Hidari chūdan morote-uke*
Complete the step forward with the left foot into a right back stance, delivering an augmented inside-to-outside block with the left arm.

### 19) *Zenkutsu-dachi/Morote kubi-osae*
Slide the left foot to the left while simultaneously transferring the center of gravity forward and shifting into a left front stance. At the same time, extend both arms out in front of the body and upward, holding the hands open at approximately eye level to perform a two-handed head hold.

### 20-A) *Migi hiza-uchi*
Sharply drive the right knee up to deliver a knee strike with a *kiai*, pulling both hands down to either side of the knee. Both hands close into fists as they travel downward and the toes of the right foot point toward the floor during the knee strike.

20-A

20-A (Rear view)

20-B

20

21

Yame-A

Yame

20-B) Turning the head to the left to face the opposite direction, pull the left hand, opened into a knife hand, back to above the right shoulder and thrust the right hand, also formed into a knife hand, across the front of the body toward the rear.

### 20) *Kōkutsu-dachi/Hidari chūdan shutō-uke*
Turning the body to the left, plant the right foot to the rear into a right back stance facing the opposite direction while delivering a left middle-level knife-hand block.

### 21) *Kōkutsu-dachi/Migi chūdan shutō-uke*
Step forward with the right foot into a left front stance while performing a right middle-level knife-hand block.

*Yame*-A) Draw the right foot back, positioning it in line with the left foot into an open V stance. At the same time extend the left arm downward to the right side and the right arm downward to the left side so that the arms cross in front of the body.

### *Yame*
Return to a natural-posture stance with the arms extended downward in front of the body, maintaining a state of physical and mental readiness (*zanshin*).

**TECHNICAL ANALYSIS**
## Movements 9–10

In response to a front snap kick from the left-hand side, execute a downward knife-hand block while pulling the right elbow back behind the head (photo 2). As the opponent steps forward with an upper-level lunge punch, deflect the attack with a left knife-hand block (photo 3) while simultaneously countering with a right knife-hand strike to the side of the head (photo 4).

1

2

3

4

## TECHNICAL ANALYSIS
### Movements 18–20-A

Upon blocking an opponent's middle-level lunge punch with an augmented inside-to-outside block (photo 1), shift the hips forward to assume a front stance while grasping his head with both hands (photo 2), and then pull downward while executing a knee strike (photo 3).

1

2

3

# Heian Godan (Heian No. 5)

Heian Godan features an assortment of advanced techniques befitting the final *kata* of the Heian series. It begins with an inside-to-outside block/reverse punch combination delivered from a back stance, followed by a transition to the water-flow posture in a closed parallel stance. Other techniques include downward and upper-level X-blocks, a crescent kick, a front elbow strike, an augmented uppercut punch to the rear, downward spear-hand strikes, simultaneous upper- and lower-level blocks, and a leap to evade a stick attack to the lower legs followed by a counterattack to an opponent's shin upon landing.

Yōi  1-A  ↘○ 1  ⤹◄ 2  ⤹◄ 3-A  ↘○

3     4-A     4     5     6-A

6     7-A     7     8-A     8-A (Side view)

8

8 (Side view)

### *Yōi* (Ready position)
*Soto hachiji-dachi* (open V stance) with both fists positioned in front of the hips.

1-A) Turn the head to the left and, drawing the left foot out to the left, pull the left fist back to the right side of the body and below the right underarm while extending the right arm across the front of the chest to the opposite side.

### 1) *Kōkutsu-dachi/Hidari chūdan uchi-uke*
Shift into a right back stance facing the left side while executing a left middle-level inside-to-outside block.

### 2) *Kōkutsu-dachi/Migi chūdan gyaku-zuki*
Turning the hips to the right, deliver a right middle-level reverse punch, paying special attention not to allow the right knee to collapse inward.

3-A) Pull the right foot in toward the left foot while turning the head to the right. At the same time, draw the right fist across the front of the chest and down toward the right hip while bringing the left fist out and around the body.

### 3) *Heisoku-dachi/Hidari kagi-gamae*
Draw the right foot alongside the left foot into a closed parallel stance as the head turns to face the right side. At the same time, pull the right fist back to above the right hip while drawing the left arm around the front of the chest into the position of a completed hook punch. This position is also known as *mizu-nagare no kamae* (water-flow posture).

4-A) Draw the right foot out to the right side while pulling the right fist across the front of the body to below the left underarm as the left arm extends in the opposite direction.

### 4) *Kōkutsu-dachi/Migi chūdan uchi-uke*
Shifting into a left back stance facing the right side, deliver a right middle-level inside-to-outside block.

### 5) *Kōkutsu-dachi/Hidari chūdan gyaku-zuki*
Maintaining a strong back stance, turn the hips to the right while executing a left middle-level reverse punch.

6-A) Draw the left foot toward the right foot, turning the head 90 degrees to the left while pulling the left fist back toward the left hip and the right fist out in front of the chest.

### 6) *Heisoku-dachi/Migi kagi-gamae*
Bringing the left foot alongside the right foot into a closed parallel stance, pull the left fist back to above the left hip while drawing the right arm around the body into the position of a completed hook punch.

7-A) Step forward with the right foot, drawing the left fist out at an angle to the left with the right wrist positioned just above the left elbow.

### 7) *Kōkutsu-dachi/Migi chūdan morote-uke*
Complete the step forward with the right foot into a left back stance while performing a right inside-to-outside block, augmented by the left fist.

8-A) Step forward with the left foot, bringing both fists back to above the right hip with the right fist positioned above the left.

### 8) *Zenkutsu-dachi/Gedan jūji-uke*
Complete the step forward with the left foot into a left front stance while driving both fists down sharply in front of the body to execute a downward X-block.

9-A) Keeping the arms crossed at the wrists, pull both elbows back sharply toward the body, drawing the fists toward the chest.

9-A

9     10-A     10-B     10-C

10     11-A     11-B     11

12-A     12-B     12     13-A

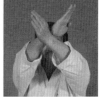

Detail: Movements
9–10-B

### 9) *Zenkutsu-dachi/Jōdan haishu jūji-uke*
Thrust both hands upward at an angle while opening them to deliver an upper-level back-hand X-block.

10-A) Keeping the wrists crossed, drop the right hand down toward the left-hand side while rotating the left hand so that the palm faces upward, then swing the right hand back toward the right while drawing the left hand downward along the same path.

### 10-B) *Zenkutsu-dachi/Chūdan osae-uke*
Continue the rotation of both hands while dropping them level with the chest to perform a middle-level pressing block.

10-C) Stepping forward with the right foot, thrust the left hand, formed into a vertical knife hand, out in front of the body while pulling the right fist back to above the right hip.

### 10) *Zenkutsu-dachi/Migi chūdan oi-zuki*
Complete the step forward into a right front stance while delivering a right middle-level lunch punch with a *kiai*.

11-A) Pivoting on the left foot, swing the right foot up and around the left side of the body, rotating the hips in the same direction while drawing the right fist up to above the head.

11-B) Completing a 180-degree turn of the body, drive the right leg and right arm downward.

### 11) *Kiba-dachi/Fumikomi/Migi sokumen gedan-barai*
Deliver a stamping kick with the right leg, assuming a straddle-leg stance while simultaneously executing a side downward block with the right arm.

12-A) Turning the head to the left, draw the left arm across the front of the body to the right while extending the right arm in the opposite direction.

12-B) Draw the left arm out to the left-hand side while pulling the right elbow in the opposite direction.

### 12) *Kiba-dachi/Hidari chūdan haishu-uke*
Complete the motion of the arms to deliver a middle-level back-hand block with the left arm.

### 13-A) *Mikazuki-geri*
Swing the right leg up across the body to deliver a crescent kick, striking the palm of the left hand. The

13-B ↶○

13 ↖◀

14-A ↘○

14 ↶◀

15 ↶◀

16-A ↘○

16-B ✸ ↶◀

16-C ↶◀

16-D ↘○

16 ↶◀

16 (Rear view)

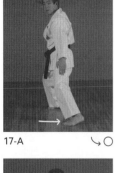

17-A ↘○

17 ↶◀

right fist remains in place above the right hip.

13-B) Keeping the left hand in place, draw the right foot down in the same direction as the kick.

### 13) *Kiba-dachi/Migi mae empi-uchi*
Plant the right foot into a straddle-leg stance while delivering a right front elbow strike against the palm of the left hand.

14-A) Turning the head to the right, shift the weight of the body to the right leg while drawing the left foot in toward the right leg and behind the right foot. At the same time, begin turning the hips to the right, drawing the right arm around the body toward the right-hand side.

### 14) *Kōsa-dachi/Migi chūdan morote-uke*
Complete the rotation of the hips, shifting into a cross-legged stance while sharply drawing the right arm around the body to deliver a right middle-level augmented inside-to-outside block.

### 15) *Renoji-dachi/Kōhō tsuki-age*
Turning the head to the left to face the opposite direction, draw the left foot out into an L-stance while driving the right fist upward behind the head to deliver an upper-cut punch to the rear. The left fist, positioned at the base of the right elbow, provides added support to the technique while the left elbow remains tucked against the chest.

16-A) Pivoting on the left foot, rapidly rotate the body 180 degrees to the right while sharply raising the right knee and dropping the fists to the hips.

16-B) Pulling both elbows back and up sharply, leap upward as if yanking the body into the air with the hands and draw the legs up and under the body. This technique is executed with a *kiai*.

16-C) Land on the floor into a cross-legged stance while delivering a downward X-block with the right fist above the left fist. Upon landing, the legs are bent at the knees with the right foot in front of the left foot.

16-D) Turning the head to the right, thrust off the left leg and move the right foot out to the right side of the body while drawing the right fist back to above the elbow of the left arm.

### 16) *Zenkutsu-dachi/Migi chūdan morote-uke*
Shift into a right front stance while delivering an augmented inside-to-outside block with the right arm.

### 17-A) *Hidari shutō gedan-barai*
Turn the head to the left to face the rear while shifting the left foot across the back to the opposite side. At the same time, draw the left hand, formed into a knife hand, around to the left-hand side of the body to deliver a downward knife-hand block while pulling the right elbow out sharply in the opposite direction. The right fist opens into a knife hand upon pulling back the right elbow.

### 17) *Zenkutsu-dachi/Hidari nagashi-uke/Migi gedan nukite*
Turning the hips to the left to assume a left front stance, drive the right hand down at an angle in front of the body to deliver a downward spear-hand attack while pulling the left hand back to above the right shoulder to simultaneously perform a sweeping block. The left elbow should remain low, positioned relatively close to the chest.

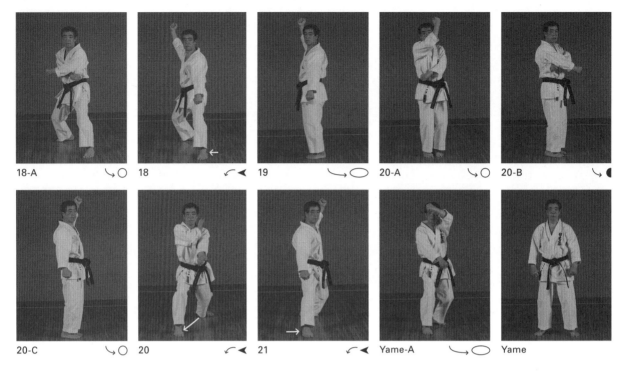

18-A)   ↘○  18   ↙◄  19   ↘◯  20-A   ↘○  20-B   ↘●

20-C   ↘○  20   ↙◄  21   ↙◄  Yame-A   ↘◯  Yame

18-A) Transferring the center of gravity to the rear while shifting the left foot to the right, sharply draw the right elbow back while launching the left arm downward in front of the body.

### 18) *Kōkutsu-dachi/Manji-uke*
Shifting into a right back stance, complete the motion of the arms to execute a hi-low block. The right arm performs an upper-level inside-to-outside block to the rear while the left arm performs a downward block to the front.

### 19) *Heisoku-dachi/Manji-gamae*
Draw the left foot back to alongside the right foot into a closed parallel stance while maintaining the hi-low block position with the upper body.

20-A) Rotate the hips to the left, turning in place while simultaneously drawing the left fist upward in front of the body and lowering the right elbow.

20-B) Continue to rotate the body to the left while drawing the left fist below the right arm toward the rear and sweeping the right arm down across the front of the body to the right-hand side.

### 20-C) *Heisoku-dachi/Manji-gamae*
Upon completing the rotation of the body, the legs are again in a closed parallel stance while the upper body is in a hi-low block position. The left arm is pulled behind the head in an upper-level block to the rear while the right arm extends downward to the right side of the body in a downward block.

### 20) *Zenkutsu-dachi/Migi nagashi-uke/Hidari gedan nukite*
Stepping out with the right foot into a right front stance, drive the left hand down at an angle in front of the body to deliver a downward spear-hand attack while pulling the right hand back to above the right shoulder to perform a sweeping block.

### 21) *Kōkutsu-dachi/Manji-uke*
Sliding the right foot to the left while transferring the center of gravity to the rear, shift into a left back stance while sharply pulling the left hand back and driving the right arm downward to perform a hi-low block.

Yame-A) Slide the right foot back and out to the right into an open V stance while shifting the right fist across to the left-hand side and drawing the left arm forward and downward, initially passing the forearm in front of the face.

### *Yame*
Return to a natural-posture stance with the arms extended downward in front of the body, maintaining a state of physical and mental readiness (*zanshin*).

## TECHNICAL ANALYSIS
### Movements 8–10

Block an opponent's front snap kick with a downward X-block (photo 1) and, as he follows with an upper-level lunge punch, drive the hands upward to execute a back-hand X-block (photo 2). Immediately pull the opponent's arm downward (photo 3) while twisting it to prevent a subsequent strike (photo 4), and then drive forward, deflecting the attacker's arm (photo 5) and countering with a lunge punch to the mid-section (photo 6).

1

2

3

4

5

6

## TECHNICAL ANALYSIS
### Movements 14–15

In response to a lunge-punch attack from the right-hand side, shift into a cross-legged stance while executing an inside-to-outside augmented block (photo 1), followed by an upper-cut punch (photo 2).

1

2

## TECHNICAL ANALYSIS
### Movements 16–18

In response to a front-snap kick attack from the rear, turn around and deliver a downward knife-hand block (photo 2). As the attacker follows through with an upper-level lunge punch, sweep the strike past the side of the head with the left hand while simultaneously countering with a right palm-heel strike to the midsection (photo 3). Finally, topple the opponent with a leg sweep while sharply pulling his punching arm downward to the side (photo 4).

1

2

3

4

The author practices a reverse punch using a *makiwara* (punching board).

# Tekki Shodan

This *kata*, also known as Naihanchi, was given the name Tekki by Master Funakoshi. Just as Heian represent important Itosu-school basic *kata*, and Sanchin represents an important basic *kata* within the Naha-te style of Master Higaonna, Tekki Shodan represents an important basic *kata* within the Shuri-te style.

According to legend, this was the only *kata* known by Master Chōki Motobu, who was called "Motobu the Monkey" for his outstanding agility, and "Teijikun" (Real Fighter) for his combat skills. In other words, it was believed that, due to some mysterious quality, through the practice of this *kata* alone, one could realize the true essence of karate. And it is this quality that also makes Tekki Shodan a unique and difficult *kata* to master.

One of the distinctive characteristics of this *kata*, which applies to all three of the Tekki *kata* (Tekki Shodan, Tekki Nidan and Tekki Sandan) is its *embusen* (performance line), which is a straight line extending to the left and right. The type of stance used exclusively throughout these *kata*—including *uchi hachiji-dachi*, *naihanchi-dachi* and *kiba-dachi*—differs slightly depending on the style of karate being practiced, with *kiba-dachi* (straddle-leg stance) being the stance used in the Shōtōkan style. Each of these stances, however, while consistent throughout this series of *kata*, has changed gradually over time, the result of ongoing research.

It was said that karate instructors could determine the abilities of their students simply by watching them perform this *kata*, which is why the diligent practice of Tekki Shodan every morning and evening is considered a means to earning one's credentials in karate. According to past masters, this *kata* should only be demonstrated after having practiced it at least ten thousand times.

## Tekki Shodan

Shizentai

Yōi-A

Yōi

1

### Shizentai (Natural posture)
*Soto hachiji-dachi* (open V stance) with both fists positioned in front of the hips.

*Yōi*-A) Slide the right foot inward toward the left foot, drawing the hands together in front of the body while opening them into knife hands as they approach each other.

### Yōi (Ready position)
Shift into *heisoku-dachi* (closed parallel stance) while

overlapping the hands. The left hand is positioned on top of the right and both arms extend downward at an angle in front of the body with the elbows bent slightly.

### 1) Kōsa-dachi
Turn the head to the right and sharply lower the hips, transferring the body's weight to the right leg. Cross the left foot in front of the right leg, placing it on the far side of the right foot to assume a cross-legged stance. The arms and hands remain in place.

2-A | 2 | 3 | 4 | 5

6 | 7 | 8-A | 8 | 9-A

2-A) Transfer the body's weight fully to the left leg and swing the right leg up in front of the body while crossing the arms in a large motion in front of the chest with the left arm above the right arm.

### 2) *Kiba-dachi/Fumikomi/Migi chūdan haishu-uke*
Deliver a stamping kick with the right leg, assuming a straddle-leg stance while performing a middle-level back-hand block with the right arm, employing a snapping motion of the elbow to ensure an effective technique.

### 3) *Kiba-dachi/Hidari sokumen empi-uchi*
Execute a left elbow strike to the right side. Turn only the upper body to perform the technique, striking the elbow against the palm of the right hand while taking care not to allow the left knee to collapse inward.

### 4) *Kiba-dachi/Koshi-gamae*
Turn the head to the left while drawing the right fist down to above the right hip, simultaneously dropping the left fist on top of the right fist so that the back of the left hand faces outward.

### 5) *Kiba-dachi/Hidari sokumen gedan-barai*
Drive the left fist down to the left-hand side to execute a left downward block.

### 6) *Kiba-dachi/Migi chūdan kagi-zuki*
Deliver a right middle-level hook punch to the left side. The fist travels along a course parallel to the floor and level with the solar plexus. The right elbow is bent so that the forearm is parallel to the hips upon completion.

### 7) *Kōsa-dachi*
Without moving the upper body or raising the hips, draw the right foot in front of the left leg, placing it on the far side of the left foot to assume a cross-legged stance.

8-A) Turning the head to face the front, swing the left leg up in front of the body toward the right while driving the right fist back over the left shoulder. During this movement the left foot and the right fist move in opposite directions, twisting the upper body to generate momentum for the following technique.

### 8) *Kiba-dachi/Fumikomi/Migi chūdan uchi ude-uke*
Deliver a stamping kick with the left leg, assuming a straddle-leg stance while performing a right middle-level inside-to-outside block to the front.

9-A) Keeping both elbows bent, draw the left fist out and upward while pulling the right elbow back and downward, crossing the arms in front of the chest with the left arm traveling on the far side of the right arm.

### 9-B) *Kiba-dachi/Hidari jōdan nagashi-uke/Migi uke-zuki*
Pull the left elbow back behind the shoulder, drawing the left fist back to beside the left ear with the back of the hand facing inward to perform an upper-level sweeping block. At the same time, thrust the right arm down in front of the body to execute a blocking punch.

### 9) *Kiba-dachi/Hidari jōdan uraken-uchi*
Pull the right fist back toward the body at the height of the solar plexus while delivering a left upper-level back-fist strike. The right fist supports the left elbow at the moment of impact for a more powerful strike.

10-A) Turn the head to the left.

### 10-B) *Hidari nami-gaeshi*
Keeping the arms in place, snap the left foot up toward the lower abdomen to perform a left return-wave kick. Neither the hips nor center of gravity should move during the technique.

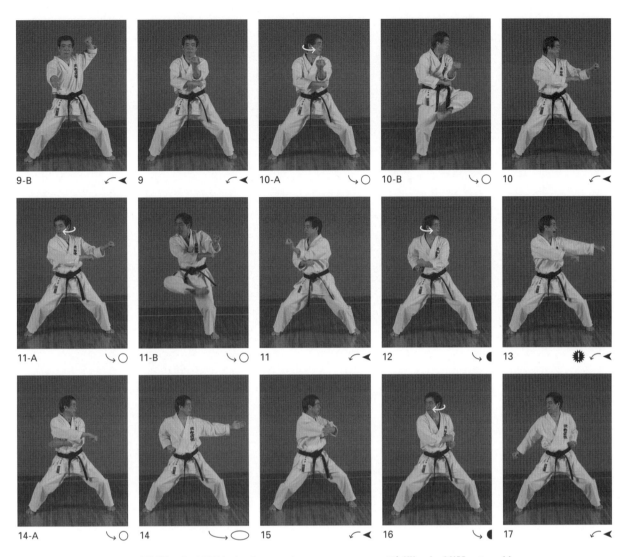

9-B ↙◄    9 ↙◄    10-A ↘○    10-B ↘○    10 ↙◄

11-A ↘○    11-B ↘○    11 ↙◄    12 ↘◗    13 ☀ ↙◄

14-A ↘○    14 ↷○    15 ↙◄    16 ↘◗    17 ↙◄

**10) *Kiba-dachi/Hidari sokumen-uke***
Plant the left foot into a straddle-leg stance while delivering a side block to the left with the left arm, keeping the back of the right fist in contact with the bottom of the left elbow. Turn only the upper body to perform the technique while maintaining a strong straddle-leg stance.

11-A) Turn the head to the right.

**11-B) *Migi nami-gaeshi***
Maintaining the same arm position, execute a return-wave kick with the right leg.

**11) *Kiba-dachi/Hidari sokumen-uke***
Plant the right foot into a straddle-leg stance and execute a side block to the right with the left arm, turning only the upper body to perform the technique. The lower body remains in a strong straddle-leg stance and the right fist stays positioned below the left elbow.

**12) *Kiba-dachi/Koshi-gamae***
Turn the head to the left while drawing both fists down to above the right hip.

**13) *Kiba-dachi/Morote-zuki***
Deliver a double-fist punch to the left side with a *kiai*. The left fist is level with the shoulder and the right fist is level with the solar plexus.

14-A) Open the left hand and draw it back across the chest and below the right underarm.

**14) *Kiba-dachi/Hidari chūdan haishu-uke***
Slowly draw the left hand out to the left side to perform a middle-level back-hand block while pulling the right fist back to above the right hip.

**15) *Kiba-dachi/Migi sokumen empi-uchi***
Deliver a right elbow strike to the left side, striking the elbow against the palm of the left hand.

**16) *Kiba-dachi/Koshi-gamae***
Turn the head to the right while dropping both fists down to above the left hip.

**17) *Kiba-dachi/Migi sokumen gedan-barai***
Execute a right downward block to the right-hand side.

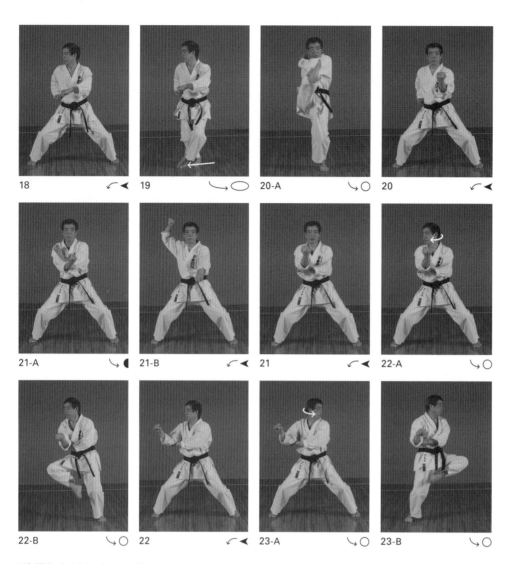

18    19    20-A    20

21-A    21-B    21    22-A

22-B    22    23-A    23-B

### 18) *Hidari chūdan kagi-zuki*

Deliver a left middle-level hook punch in the same direction.

### 19) *Kōsa-dachi*

Without moving the upper body or raising the hips, draw the left foot in front of the right leg, placing it on the far side of the right foot to assume a cross-legged stance.

20-A) Swing the right leg up in front of the body toward the left while thrusting the left fist back over the right shoulder and turning the head to face the front.

### 20) *Kiba-dachi/Fumikomi/Hidari chūdan uchi ude-uke*

Deliver a stamping kick with the right leg, assuming a straddle-leg stance while performing a left middle-level inside-to-outside block to the front.

21-A) Keeping both elbows bent, draw the right fist out and upward while pulling the left elbow back and downward, crossing the arms in front of the chest with the right arm traveling on the far side of the left arm.

### 21-B) *Kiba-dachi/Migi jōdan nagashi-uke/Hidari uke-zuki*

Draw the right arm back to the right side of the body to perform an upper-level sweeping block while thrusting the left arm down toward the front to execute a blocking punch.

### 21) *Kiba-dachi/Migi jōdan uraken-uchi*

Pull the left fist back toward the body while delivering a right upper-level back-fist strike. The left fist provides support underneath the right elbow at the moment of impact.

22-A) Turn the head to the right.

### 22-B) *Migi nami-gaeshi*

Keeping the arms in place, execute a return-wave kick with the right leg.

### 22) *Kiba-dachi/Migi sokumen-uke*

Plant the right foot into a straddle-leg stance and, turning only the upper body, execute a side block to the right with the right arm, keeping the left fist positioned underneath the right elbow.

23-A) Turn the head to the left.

### 23-B) *Hidari nami-gaeshi*

Maintaining the same upper-body position, perform a return-wave kick with the left leg.

23      24      25      Yame-A      Yame-B

Yame

### 23) *Kiba-dachi/Migi sokumen-uke*
Plant the left foot into a straddle-leg stance while executing a side block to the left with the right arm, turning only the upper body to perform the technique while keeping the left fist in contact with the right elbow.

### 24) *Kiba-dachi/Koshi-gamae*
Turn the head to the right while drawing both fists down to above the left hip.

### 25) *Kiba-dachi/Morote-zuki*
Deliver a double-fist punch to the right side with a *kiai*.

*Yame*-A) Draw the right foot inward toward the left foot and open the hands while bringing them together in front of the body. At the same time, begin turning the head to face the front.

*Yame*-B) Bring the right foot alongside the left into a closed parallel stance while drawing the left hand over the right hand, the same ready position in which the *kata* began.

### *Yame*
Draw the right foot out to the right side into an open V stance with both fists positioned in front of the hips, the same natural-posture stance assumed prior to starting the *kata*.

**TECHNICAL ANALYSIS**
## Movements 20–21

Block an opponent's middle-level lunge punch with an inside-to-outside block (photo 1). As the opponent responds with an upper-level reverse punch, deflect the attack with an upper-level sweeping block while countering with a punch to the midsection (photo 2), followed by a back-fist strike to the face (photo 3).

1

2

3

**TECHNICAL ANALYSIS**
## Movements 22-A–22

Evade an opponent's leg-sweep attempt from the side with a return-wave kick (photo 2). As the opponent follows with a reverse punch, deflect the attack with an augmented side block (photo 3).

1

2

3

The *dōjō-kun*, or code of ethics for the training hall, are as follows:
1  Seek perfection of character
2  Be faithful
3  Endeavor
4  Respect others
5  Refrain from violent behavior

# Tekki Nidan, Tekki Sandan

As already mentioned in the previous chapter, around the time that Master Gichin Funakoshi changed the Chinese characters used to write the word "karate," he assigned the name Tekki to the *kata* that had, till then, been known as Naihanchi. As a basic Itosu-style *kata*, it, along with the Heian *kata*, is representative of the Shuri-te style. One of its most distinguishing characteristics is its performance line: a straight line.

Although we know Tekki Shodan to be an extremely old *kata* that was passed down to the Shuri region, its creator and origins remain shrouded in obscurity, which creates something of an air of mystery.

There are several legends that provide reasons as to why the movements in Tekki Shodan describe a straight performance line: one explains that it was due to the limited space on the decks of the ships that brought martial artists from China; another describes the *kata* as a lethal encounter at the edge of a cliff with no room to back up; and yet another claims that the techniques were meant to be practiced while sitting astride a horse. As for Tekki Nidan and Sandan, however, the reason for straight performance lines is well known: the two *kata* were created by Shuri-te master Yasutsune Itosu based on Tekki Shodan.

While the Tekki *kata* may appear easy because the feet only move along a straight line and the offensive and defensive techniques employed are of a basic nature, they are rightly considered to be quite challenging *kata*, especially Tekki Nidan and Sandan. In fact, the third of the three Tekki *kata* is said to incorporate a collection of the techniques featured in the first two.

It is commonly acknowledged that Master Itosu created Tekki Nidan and Sandan as training

*kata* for physical education applications. Accordingly, it should be noted that neither *kata* contain kicking techniques or strikes targeting such vulnerable points as the groin or the eyes.

In his book *Ryūkyū Kempō Karate*, Master Funakoshi introduces Naihanchi Shodan, Nidan and Sandan, providing photographs to illustrate the techniques used in each *kata*. The explanation for Naihanchi Shodan specifies the use of *naihanchi-dachi* (naihanchi stance), including a note that, when in the stance, tension is placed on both legs, the buttocks protrude to the rear, the chest is drawn out, and power in both legs is focused from the outside inward. By contrast, Funakoshi indicates that in Naihanchi Nidan and Sandan, *hachiji-dachi* (open V stance) is used. It should be noted that in modern Shōtōkan, the straddle-leg stance (*kiba-dachi*) is used for all three *kata*.

At the very least, it is easy to deduce that the thinking behind the techniques employed in the second and third Tekki *kata* differ from those in the first. As such, there are still many aspects about these *kata* that are deserving of further research.

# Tekki Nidan

Yōi | 1-A | ↘○ 1 | ↘◗ 2-A | ↘○ 2 | ↙◀

3 | ↙◀ 4 | ↙◀ 5-A | ↘○ 5 | ↘◗ 6-A | ↘○

### Yōi (Ready position)
*Soto hachiji-dachi* (open V stance) with both fists positioned in front of the hips.

1-A) Turn the head to the right and draw the left foot in toward the right foot, lowering the hips while raising both fists vertically in front of the body, extending the elbows out to the sides as the hands rise.

### 1) Kōsa-dachi/Ryō-hiji harai-age
Move the left foot in front of the right leg, placing it on the far side of the right foot to assume a cross-legged stance while raising the fists level with the chest to perform a double rising elbow sweep.

2-A) Transferring the body's weight fully to the left leg, swing the right leg up in front of the body while sharply raising the fists and drawing the elbows together in front of the chest.

### 2) Kiba-dachi/Fumikomi/Sokumen-uke
Deliver a stamping kick with the right leg to the right-hand side, assuming a straddle-leg stance while executing a side block in the same direction with the right arm, augmented by the accompanying motion of the left arm.

### 3) Kōsa-dachi/Gedan soto ude uke
Draw the left foot in front of the right leg, placing it on the far side of the right foot into a cross-legged stance while driving the right arm down to the front of the body to deliver a lower-level outside to inside block. The left hand opens to meet the right arm as it approaches with the thumb of the left hand against the underside of the right arm and the remaining fingers positioned above the crook of the elbow.

### 4) Kiba-dachi/Sokumen soete gedan uchi ude-uke
Thrusting off the left foot, drive the right foot out to the right into a straddle-leg stance while simultaneously swinging the right arm out in the same direction to deliver a lower-level inside-to-outside block, accompanied by the left hand, which remains against the right elbow.

5-A) Turning the head to the left, draw the left foot in toward the right foot while bringing the hands to the front of the hips. The left hand closes into a fist as it moves away from the right arm.

### 5) Heisoku-dachi/Ryō-hiji harai-age
Draw the feet together into a closed parallel stance, raising the hips while lifting the fists up vertically in front of the body to perform a double rising elbow sweep.

6-A) Swing the left leg up in front of the body while sharply raising the fists and drawing the elbows together in front of the chest.

6-B) Deliver a stamping kick to the left with the left leg.

### 6) Kiba-dachi/Fumikomi/Sokumen-uke
Assuming a straddle-leg stance, execute a side block to the left with the left arm, augmented by the accompanying motion of the right arm.

### 7) Kōsa-dachi/Gedan soto ude uke
Draw the right foot in front of the left leg, placing it on the far side of the left foot into a cross-legged stance while driving the left arm down to the front of the body to deliver a lower-level outside to inside block.

### 8) Kiba-dachi/Sokumen soete gedan uchi ude-uke
Step out with the left foot into a straddle-leg stance while swinging the left arm out to the left-hand side to deliver a lower-level inside-to-outside block.

6-B      6      7      8

9      10      11-A      11

12-A      12      13      14

### 9) *Kiba-dachi/Soete koshi-gamae*
Turn the head to the right while pulling both hands back to above the left hip, simultaneously opening the left hand and closing the right hand into a fist. The front of the right fist presses into the palm of the left hand and the inside of the left wrist rests against the side of the body.

### 10) *Kiba-dachi/Soete sokumen-uke*
Drive the right arm around the front of the body to deliver a side block to the right, augmented by the left hand, which provides support by pressing against the inside of the right forearm below the wrist.

11-A) Turning the head to face the front, swing the right leg up in front of the body while driving the right elbow straight back. The left hand accompanies the motion of the right arm, pressing against the front of the right fist.

### 11) *Kiba-dachi/Fumikomi/Soete mae empi-uchi*
Plant the right foot, executing a stamping kick into a straddle-leg stance while driving the right elbow for-ward to deliver a front elbow strike, keeping the front of the right fist pressed against the palm of the left hand. When executing the strike, pull the back of the left hand back sharply to the solar plexus and keep the left elbow tucked tightly against the left side of the body.

12-A) Draw the right hand out and around the body at chest level, opening the hand into a knife hand during the movement. The head turns to the right in synchro-nization with the motion of the right arm.

### 12) *Kiba-dachi/Sokumen tate shutō-uke*
Complete the motion of the right arm, bending the wrist upward along the way to deliver a vertical knife-hand block to the right side.

### 13) *Kiba-dachi/Hidari kagi-zuki*
Deliver a middle-level hook punch with the left arm.

### 14) *Kōsa-dachi*
Without moving the upper body or raising the hips, draw the left foot in front of the right leg, placing it on the far side of the right foot to assume a cross-legged stance.

15-A     15     16-A     16-B     16

17     18     19-A     19     20-A

15-A) Turning the head to face the front, swing the right leg up in front of the body while driving the left fist back over the right shoulder.

### 15) *Kiba-dachi/Fumikomi/Hidari chūdan uchi-uke*

Deliver a stamping kick with the right leg, assuming a straddle-leg stance while performing a left middle-level inside-to-outside block to the front.

16-A) Keeping both elbows bent, draw the right fist forward and upward while pulling the left elbow back and downward, crossing the arms in front of the chest with the right arm traveling on the far side of the left arm.

### 16-B) *Kiba-dachi/Migi jōdan nagashi-uke/Hidari uke-zuki*

Pull the right elbow back behind the shoulder, drawing the right fist back to beside the right ear to perform an upper-level sweeping block. At the same time, thrust the left arm down in front of the body to execute a blocking punch.

### 16) *Kiba-dachi/Migi jōdan ura-uchi zuki*

Pull the left fist back toward the body at the height of the solar plexus while delivering a right upper-level close punch with a *kiai*.

### 17) *Kiba-dachi/Soete koshi-gamae*

Turn the head to the left while drawing the right elbow straight back sharply, pulling both hands to above the right hip. Open the right hand when pulling the right elbow back and press the front of the left fist against the palm of the right hand.

### 18) *Kiba-dachi/Soete sokumen-uke*

Drive the left arm around the front of the body to deliver a side block to the left augmented by the right hand, which presses against the inside of the left forearm.

19-A) Turning the head to face the front, swing the left leg up sharply in front of the body while driving the left elbow straight back. The right hand presses against the front of the left fist during the motion.

### 19) *Kiba-dachi/Fumikomi/Soete mae empi-uchi*

Execute a stamping kick with the left leg, assuming a straddle-leg stance while driving the left elbow forward to deliver a front elbow strike, keeping the front of the left fist pressed against the palm of the right hand.

20-A) Draw the left hand out and around the body while opening the hand into a knife hand, turning the head to the left in synchronization with the left arm.

### 20) *Kiba-dachi/Sokumen tate shutō-uke*

Complete the motion of the left arm to deliver a vertical knife-hand block to the left-hand side.

### 21) *Kiba-dachi/Migi kagi-zuki*

Deliver a middle-level hook punch with the right arm.

### 22) *Kōsa-dachi*

Without raising the hips, draw the right foot in front of the left leg, placing it on the far side of the left foot into a cross-legged stance.

23-A) Turning the head to face the front, swing the left leg up in front of the body while driving the right fist back over the left shoulder.

### 23) *Kiba-dachi/Fumikomi/Migi chūdan uchi-uke*

Deliver a stamping kick with the left leg, assuming a straddle-leg stance while executing a right middle-level inside-to-outside block to the front.

24-A) Draw the left fist forward and upward while pulling the right elbow back and downward, crossing the arms in front of the chest with the left arm traveling on the far side of the right arm.

20    ↘○◖  21    ↶◀  22    ↘◯  23-A    ↘◖  23    ↶◀

24-A    ↘○  24-B    ↙◀  24    ✴ ↙◀  Yame-A  Yame

### 24-B) *Kiba-dachi/Hidari jōdan nagashi-uke/Migi uke-zuki*

Pull the left elbow back behind the shoulder, drawing the left fist back to beside the right ear to perform an upper-level sweeping block while thrusting the right arm downward to execute a blocking punch.

### 24) *Kiba-dachi/Hidari jōdan ura-uchi zuki*

Pull the right fist back toward the body at the height of the solar plexus while delivering a left upper-level close punch with a *kiai*.

*Yame*-A) Draw the right foot inward into an open V stance while pulling the left fist back toward the right shoulder and then downward.

### *Yame*

Return to a natural-posture stance with the arms extended downward in front of the body, maintaining a state of physical and mental readiness (*zanshin*).

---

**TECHNICAL ANALYSIS**
## Movements 10–11

After blocking an opponent's punch with an augmented side block (photo 1), grab the attacker's wrist (photo 2) and deliver a kick to the back of the leg (photo 3) followed by an elbow strike (photo 4).

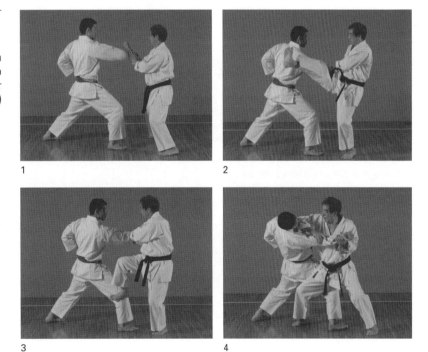

1

2

3

4

# Tekki Sandan

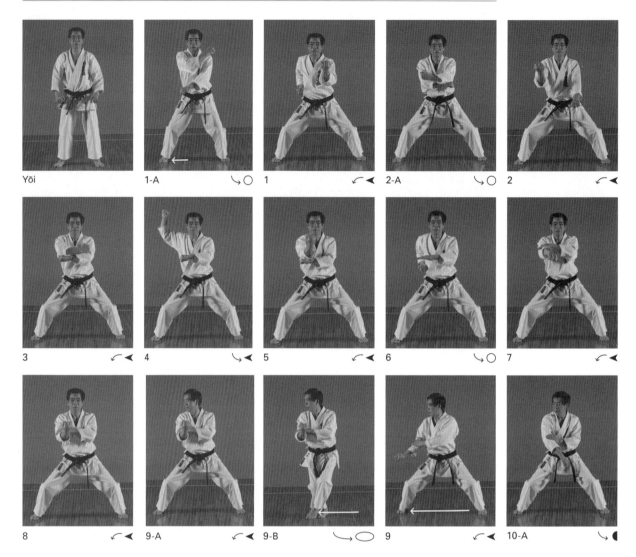

Yōi     1-A     1     2-A     2

3     4     5     6     7

8     9-A     9-B     9     10-A

## Yōi (Ready position)
Soto hachiji-dachi (open V stance) with both fists positioned in front of the hips.

1-A) Drawing the right foot out to the right-hand side, thrust the right fist up to above the left shoulder while driving the left fist across the front of the body in the opposite direction.

### 1) Kiba-dachi/Hidari chūdan uchi-uke
Assuming a straddle-leg stance, complete a middle-level inside-to-outside block to with the left arm while sharply pulling back the right elbow.

2-A) Draw the right fist across the front of the body and then upward to deliver an inside-to-outside block while driving the left forearm downward with the right arm traveling on the far side of the left arm.

### 2) Kiba-dachi/Kōsa-uke
The arms complete a cross block with the right arm performing an inside-to-outside block and the left arm a downward block.

### 3) Kiba-dachi/Yoko ude-hasami
Keeping the elbows in place, drive the right fist down to the left elbow while simultaneously bringing the left fist up to the right elbow to execute a side forearm scissors block. The back of the right fist faces outward while the back of the left fist faces upward.

### 4) Kiba-dachi/Migi jōdan nagashi-uke/Hidari kagi-gamae
Pull the right elbow back behind the shoulder to perform an upper-level sweeping block, leaving the left arm in place.

### 5) Kiba-dachi/Migi jōdan ura-uchi zuki
Keeping the left arm in place, deliver a right upper-level close punch.

### 6) Kiba-dachi/Ryūsui no kamae
Pull the right elbow back sharply, drawing the right fist to above the right hip while opening the left hand. This position is known as ryūsui no kamae (flowing-water posture).

10-B     ↘○    10     ↙◀    11     ↘○    12     ↙◀    13     ↙◀

14     ↙◀    15-A     ↘◀    15     ✹↙◀    16-A     ↘○    16     ↘○

### 7) Kiba-dachi/Soeshō migi chūdan-zuki

Deliver a right middle-level straight punch beneath the open left hand. Upon completion of the technique, the left palm rests on the right arm just above the elbow.

### 8) Kiba-dachi/Soeshō kaeshi-ude

Pull the right elbow back slightly and turn the right fist clockwise so the back of the right fist faces downward. Keep the left hand positioned on the right arm during the technique.

9-A) Turn the head to the right.

### 9-B) Kōsa-dachi

Without moving the upper body or raising the hips, draw the left foot in front of the right leg, placing it on the far side of the right foot to assume a cross-legged stance.

### 9) Kiba-dachi/Migi sokumen gedan uchi ude-uke

Thrusting off the left foot, drive the right foot out to the right into a straddle-leg stance while simultaneously swinging the right arm out in the same direction to deliver a lower-level inside-to-outside block, accompanied by the left hand, which remains positioned above the right elbow.

### 10-A) Kiba-dachi/Hazushi-te

Keeping the left hand positioned against the right arm, pull the right fist back sharply to the left side of the body as if to release the arm from an opponent's grasp, turning the wrist inward to lead with the thumb-side of the fist during the motion.

10-B) Keeping the left hand in place, follow through with the motion, driving the right fist upward and over the head.

### 10) Kiba-dachi/Migi sokumen tettsui otoshi-uchi

Drop the right fist down sharply to the right side to deliver a downward hammer-fist strike, keeping the left hand positioned against the right arm above the elbow.

### 11) Kiba-dachi/Soeshō hiki-te

Turn the head to face the front while pulling the right elbow back, drawing the right fist to above the right hip.

### 12) Kiba-dachi/Soeshō migi chūdan-zuki

Deliver a right middle-level straight punch beneath the open left hand.

### 13) Kiba-dachi/Kōsa-uke

Draw the right fist upward while driving the left fist downward to execute a cross block, with the right arm performing an inside-to-outside block as the left arm delivers a downward block.

### 14) Kiba-dachi/Kōsa-uke

Deliver another cross block, with the left arm performing an inside-to-outside block and the right arm a downward block.

### 15-A) Kiba-dachi/Hidari jōdan nagashi-uke

Draw the left elbow back to perform an upper-level sweeping block.

### 15) Kiba-dachi/Hidari jōdan ura-uchi zuki

Pull the right fist back toward the body at the height of the solar plexus while delivering a left upper-level close punch with a kiai.

16-A) Turn the head to the left.

### 16) Kōsa-dachi

Without raising the hips, draw the right foot in front of the left leg, placing it on the far side of the left foot into a cross-legged stance.

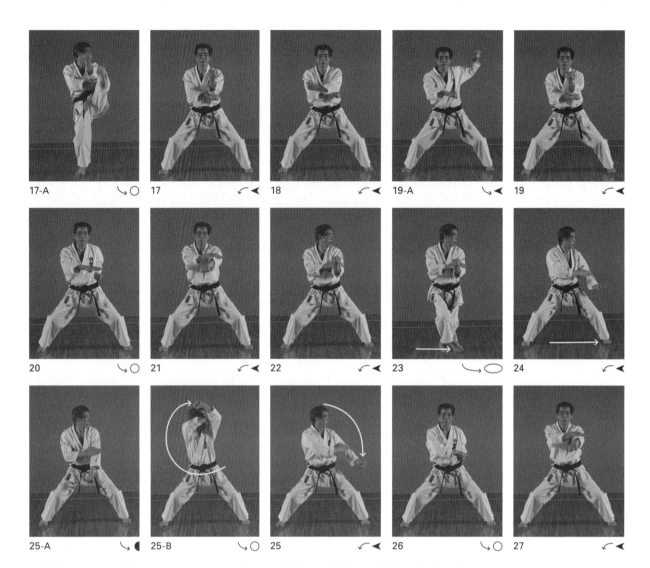

17-A    17    18    19-A    19

20    21    22    23    24

25-A    25-B    25    26    27

17-A) Transfer the body's weight fully to the right leg and swing the left leg up in front of the body.

**17) *Kiba-dachi/Fumikomi/Soete uraken-gamae***
Maintaining the same upper body position, turn the head to face the front while delivering a stamping kick to the left with the left leg, assuming a straddle-leg stance.

**18) *Kiba-dachi/Yoko ude-hasami***
Drive the left fist down to the right elbow to deliver a side forearm scissors block.

**19-A) *Kiba-dachi/Hidari jōdan nagashi-uke/Migi kagi-gamae***
Pull the left elbow back to perform an upper-level sweeping block.

**19) *Kiba-dachi/Hidari jōdan ura-uchi zuki***
Keeping the right arm in place, deliver a left upper-level close punch.

**20) *Kiba-dachi/Ryūsui no kamae***
Drive the left elbow back, pulling the left fist back to above the left hip while opening the right hand.

**21) *Kiba-dachi/Soeshō hidari chūdan-zuki***
Deliver a left middle-level straight punch beneath the open right hand.

**22) *Kiba-dachi/Soeshō kaeshi-ude***
Pull the left elbow back slightly, turning the left fist counter-clockwise, then turn the head to the left.

**23) *Kōsa-dachi***
Draw the right foot in front of the left leg, placing it on the far side of the left foot into a cross-legged stance.

**24) *Kiba-dachi/Hidari sokumen gedan uchi ude-uke***
Drive the left foot out to the left into a straddle-leg stance while swinging the left arm in the same direction to deliver a lower-level inside-to-outside block accompanied by the right hand.

**25-A) *Kiba-dachi/Hazushi-te***
Pull the left fist back sharply to the right-hand side of the body, turning the wrist inward to lead with the thumb-side of the fist.

25-B) Follow through with the motion of the left arm, driving the left fist upward and over the head.

28    ↘○    29    ↙◀    30    ↘○    31-A    ↘○    31    ↙◀

32    ↙◀    33-A    ↙◀    33    ✺ ↙◀    Yame-A    Yame

### 25) *Kiba-dachi/Hidari sokumen tettsui otoshi-uchi*

Drop the left fist down sharply to the left-hand side of the body to deliver a downward hammer-fist strike, keeping the right hand against the left arm.

### 26) *Kiba-dachi/Soeshō hiki-te*

Turn the head to face the front while pulling the left fist back to above the left hip.

### 27) *Kiba-dachi/Soeshō hidari chūdan-zuki*

Deliver a left middle-level straight punch beneath the open right hand.

### 28) *Kiba-dachi/Migi sokumen tate shutō-uke*

Turning the head to the right, draw the right arm around the body to execute a vertical knife-hand block to the right-hand side while pulling the left fist back to above the left hip.

### 29) *Kiba-dachi/Hidari kagi-zuki*

Deliver a middle-level hook punch with the left arm.

### 30) *Kōsa-dachi*

Without raising the hips, draw the left foot in front of the right leg, placing it on the far side of the right foot into a cross-legged stance.

31-A) Turning the head to face the front, swing the right leg up in front of the body while driving the left fist back over the right shoulder.

### 31) *Kiba-dachi/Fumikomi/Hidari chūdan uchi-uke*

Deliver a stamping kick with the right leg into a straddle-leg stance while delivering a left middle-level inside-to-outside block to the front.

### 32) *Kiba-dachi/Kōsa-uke*

Draw the right fist out and upward while driving the left fist downward to execute a cross block, with the right arm performing an inside-to-outside block as the left arm delivers a downward block.

### 33-A) *Kiba-dachi/Migi jōdan nagashi-uke*

Draw the right elbow back to perform an upper-level sweeping block.

### 33) *Kiba-dachi/Migi jōdan ura-uchi zuki*

Pull the left fist back toward the body while delivering a right upper-level close punch with a *kiai*.

Yame-A) Draw the right foot inward into an open V stance while pulling the right fist back toward the left shoulder and then downward.

### *Yame*

Return to a natural-posture stance with the arms extended downward in front of the body, maintaining a state of physical and mental readiness (*zanshin*).

## TECHNICAL ANALYSIS
### Movements 9–10

Block an opponent's front snap kick from the side using a lower-level inside-to-outside block (photo 2), swinging the blocking arm back across the front of the body to deflect a subsequent lunge-punch attack (photo 3), and following through with the motion of the arm to counter with a hammer-fist strike to the neck (photo 4).

1

2

3

4

The author demonstrates an inside-to-outside block against a lunge-punch attack during a training session in Durban, South Africa.

# Bassai Dai

Bassai is a powerful *kata* that conveys the feeling of storming a fortress, a characteristic evident in its various incarnations in other karate styles, including those passed down from Itosu, Matsumura, Tomari, Oyadomari and Ishimine.

Within the Itosu style (today's Shōtōkan style), there are two variations of the Bassai *kata*: Bassai Dai and Bassai Shō. Although Master Itosu is credited with having created Bassai Shō, it differs considerably from Bassai Dai in many respects.

Even though both *kata* share the same name, their contents vary. While it is not clear as to which style the original form of this *kata* belongs, according to current consensus, it was introduced by Master Kōkan Oyadomari. Does this mean, then, that the influence of Bassai Dai leans more toward the Tomari-te style of Master Oyadomari? If not, perhaps toward the Shuri-te style linked to Master Itosu, the creator of Bassai Shō? While it goes without saying that more research is required, we can state with a considerable degree of confidence that this *kata* is not related to the Naha-te style.

Bassai Dai is distinctive for its powerful, dynamic techniques, as well as the diverse variety of techniques it contains, including consecutive blocking sequences, upper-, middle- and lower-level attacks, and wide U-punches.

Bassai Dai, along with Kankū Dai, are the two most representative *kata* within the Shōtōkan karate style and must be learned after the basic *kata* have been mastered. As such, it would be impossible to attain the rank of black belt without first being able to properly perform these two important *kata*.

## Bassai Dai

Shizentai

Yōi

1-A

1

### *Shizentai* (Natural posture)
*Soto hachiji-dachi* (open V stance) with both fists positioned in front of the hips.

### *Yōi* (Ready position)
Slide the right foot in toward the left foot to assume a closed parallel stance (*heisoku-dachi*) while drawing the hands together in front of the body. The left hand opens and wraps around the right fist and both arms extend downward at an angle in front of the body with the elbows bent slightly.

1-A) Thrust off the left leg, leaping forward with great force while drawing the hands around to the left side of the body. The left hand remains wrapped around the right fist.

### 1) *Kōsa-dachi/Migi uchi ude-uke/Hidari soete*
Plant the right foot strongly on the floor and immediately draw the left foot behind it into a cross-legged stance while delivering an inside-to-outside block with the right arm. The left hand presses against the inside of the right forearm just below the wrist for added support.

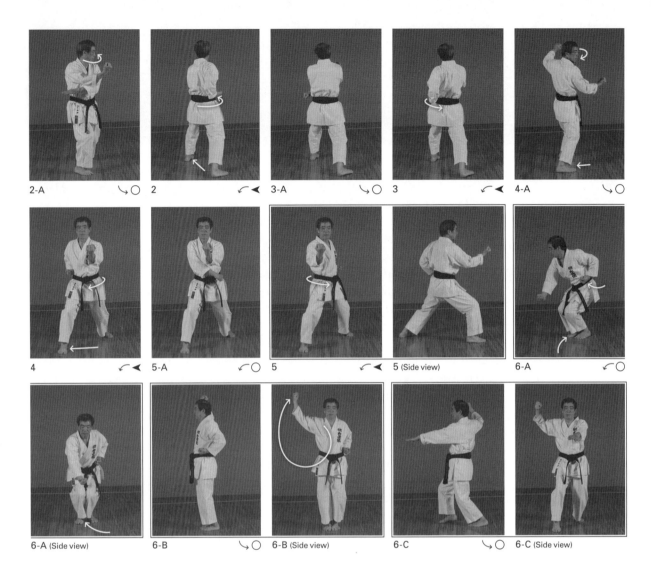

2-A   ↘○    2   ↙◀    3-A   ↘○    3   ↙◀    4-A   ↘○

4   ↙◀    5-A   ↙○    5   ↙◀    5 (Side view)    6-A   ↙○

6-A (Side view)    6-B   ↘○    6-B (Side view)    6-C   ↘○    6-C (Side view)

2-A) Turn the head to the left and extend the left leg to the rear while pulling the left hand across the front of the body beneath the right arm.

**2) *Zenkutsu-dachi/Hidari chūdan uchi-uke***
Turning the hips to the left, shift into a left front stance facing the opposite direction while delivering a left middle-level inside-to-outside block.

3-A) Drive the right fist across the front of the body and underneath the left arm, which remains in the blocking position.

**3) *Zenkutsu-dachi/Migi chūdan uchi-uke/Gyaku-hanmi***
Draw the right fist out to the right to perform a middle-level inside-to-outside block, turning the hips to *gyaku-hanmi* (45-degree angle to the front, with the hip on the side opposite to the front leg pushed forward).

4-A) Turning the head to the right, draw the right foot across the rear to the opposite side while raising the left arm up and back behind the left shoulder. The right arm remains in the blocking position in front of the chest.

**4) *Zenkutsu-dachi/Hidari chūdan soto-uke/Gyaku-hanmi***
Turning the hips to the right, assume a right front stance

facing the opposite direction while executing a left middle-level outside-to-inside block with the hips turned to *gyaku-hanmi.*

5-A) Drive the right fist across the front of the body and underneath the left arm.

**5) *Zenkutsu-dachi/Migi chūdan uchi-uke***
Turning the hips to the left, draw the right fist out to deliver a middle-level inside-to-outside block.

**6-A) *Gedan sukui-uke***
Draw the right foot back to alongside the left foot while turning 90 degrees to the right, bending the knees and crouching slightly to perform a downward scooping block.

6-B) Draw the right fist up to the right side of the head with the back of the fist facing outward while straightening the back but keeping the knees bent slightly. The left fist remains firmly in place above the left hip.

6-C) Step forward with the right foot while extending the left arm out in front of the body and pulling the right elbow back in preparation for the subsequent block.

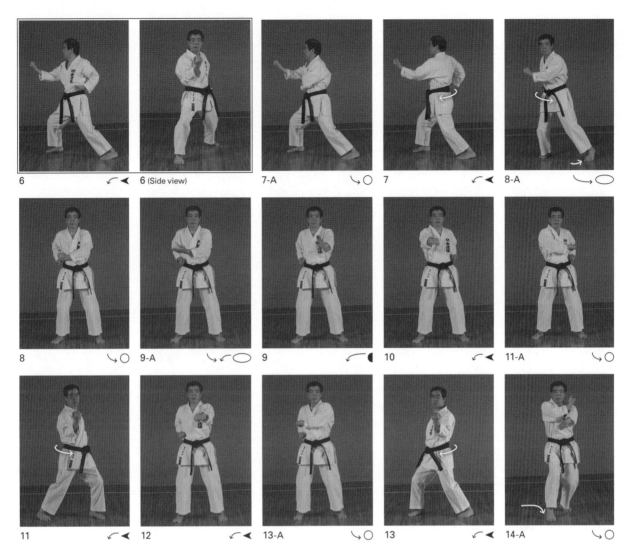

6     6 (Side view)     7-A     7     8-A

8     9-A     9     10     11-A

11     12     13-A     13     14-A

### 6) *Zenkutsu-dachi/Migi chūdan soto-uke*
Complete the step forward into a right front stance while delivering a right middle-level outside-to-inside block.

7-A) Drive the left fist across the front of the body and underneath the right arm.

### 7) *Zenkutsu-dachi/Hidari chūdan uchi-uke/Gyaku-hanmi*
Draw the left fist out to perform a middle-level inside-to-outside block while turning the hips to *gyaku-hanmi*.

8-A) Draw the left foot back and in toward the right foot while lowering the left fist in the direction of the right hip.

### 8) *Shizentai/Koshi-gamae*
Shift into a natural posture (open V stance), placing the left fist on top of the right fist.

9-A) Draw the left hand out in front of the body, opening it into a knife hand as it leaves the hip.

### 9) *Shizentai/Hidari chūdan tate shutō-uke*
Fully extend the left arm in front of the chest to perform a middle-level vertical knife-hand block.

### 10) *Shizentai/Migi chūdan zuki*
Deliver a middle-level straight punch with the right arm.

11-A) Pull the right fist back and across the front of the body to the left side.

### 11) *Migi chūdan uchi-uke*
Turning the hips sharply to the left, perform a right middle-level inside-to-outside block to the front. As the hips rotate, turn the right foot inward, extending the right leg sharply while bending the left knee.

### 12) *Shizentai/Hidari chūdan zuki*
Straighten the left leg to return to a natural posture while delivering a left middle-level straight punch.

13-A) Pull the left fist back and across the body to the right side.

### 13) *Hidari chūdan uchi-uke*
Turning the hips sharply to the right, deliver a left middle-level inside-to-outside block to the front.

14-A) Draw the right foot in toward the left foot and out in front of the body while pulling the right hand, opened into a knife hand, back to above the left shoulder and extending the left arm out in front of the chest.

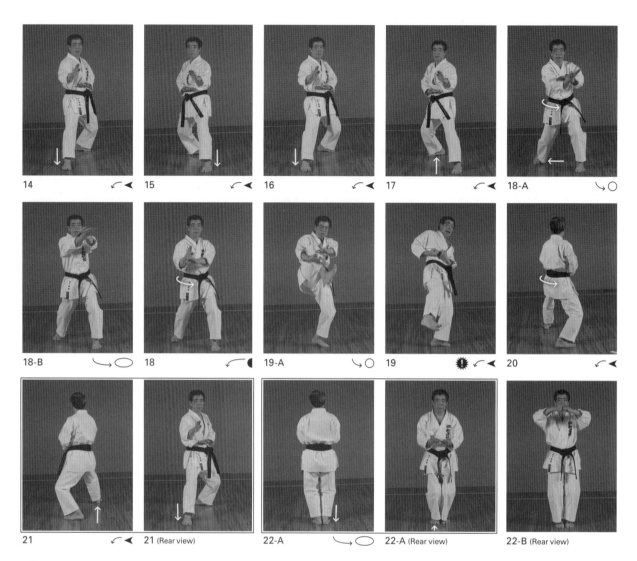

14     15     16     17     18-A

18-B     18     19-A     19     20

21     21 (Rear view)     22-A     22-A (Rear view)     22-B (Rear view)

### 14) *Kōkutsu-dachi/Migi chūdan shutō-uke*
Complete the step forward with the right foot into a left back stance while executing a right middle-level knife-hand block.

### 15) *Kōkutsu-dachi/Hidari chūdan shutō-uke*
Step forward with the left foot into a right back stance while performing a left middle-level knife-hand block.

### 16) *Kōkutsu-dachi/Migi chūdan shutō-uke*
Step forward again with the right foot into a left back stance while delivering a right middle-level knife-hand block.

### 17) *Kōkutsu-dachi/Hidari chūdan shutō-uke*
Step back with the right foot into a right back stance while executing a left middle-level knife-hand block.

18-A) Draw the right foot out to the right side to shift into a slightly shortened left front stance (*moto-dachi*) while extending the right arm out and upward in front of the chest along a course directly below the left hand, which remains in the same blocking position. The palm of the right hand remains facing upward as the right arm extends forward.

18-B) Draw the right hand up and over to the right in an arcing motion while rotating the right hand counterclockwise. The left hand rests on top of the right wrist.

### 18) *Moto-dachi/Kaeshi-dori/Gyaku-hanmi*
Turning the hips to *gyaku-hanmi*, draw the right elbow back toward the body to perform a reverse grasp with the right hand. The left elbow is also held close to the body while the tips of the fingers of the left hand rest at the base of the thumb of the right hand.

19-A) Draw the right knee up sharply into the triangle formed by the forearms and chest.

### 19) *Gedan ke-sage*
Drive the right leg downward to deliver a strong thrust kick with a *kiai*, closing both hands into fists while pulling them back sharply to above the right hip with the backs of the hands facing the direction of the kick.

### 20) *Kōkutsu-dachi/Hidari chūdan shutō-uke*
Retract the kicking leg and then plant the right foot back in the direction of the kick, assuming a right back stance facing the opposite direction while delivering a left middle-level knife-hand block.

22

22 (Rear view)

23-A

23-A (Rear view)

23

23 (Rear view)

24

24 (Rear view)

25-A

25

26

### 21) *Kōkutsu-dachi/Migi chūdan shutō-uke*

Step forward with the right foot into a left back stance while delivering a right middle-level knife-hand block.

### 22-A) *Heisoku-dachi*

Draw the right foot back to alongside the left foot into a closed parallel stance while pulling the right elbow back toward the body. The knees remain bent slightly and the elbows rest above the hips with both forearms extending upward at a slight angle in front of the body. The hands remain formed into knife hands with the palms facing upward and the little fingers almost touching.

22-B) Raise the arms while straightening the knees, drawing the elbows outward and rotating the forearms in a "rolling" motion. Close the hands into fists as they travel upward, keeping them almost touching during the motion.

### 22) *Heisoku-dachi/Morote age-uke*

Complete the upward motion of the arms to perform a two-handed rising block, bringing the fists to just above the forehead.

23-A) Thrust both forearms outward at angles to the sides while sharply lifting the right knee.

### 23) *Zenkutsu-dachi/Chūdan tettsui hasami-uchi*

Planting the right foot forward into a right front stance, draw the fists around along circular paths and downward to the front to perform a middle-level hammer-fist scissors strike.

### 24) *Zenkutsu-dachi/Migi chūdan oi-zuki*

Maintaining a front stance, thrust off the left foot to shift the body forward roughly one half-step while delivering a right middle-level lunge punch.

25-A) Turning the head to the left to face the rear, shift the left foot across the back to the opposite side while delivering a downward knife-hand block to the rear with the left hand.

### 25) *Zenkutsu-dachi/Hidari nagashi-uke/Migi gedan nukite*

Completing a 180-degree turn to the left, shift into a left front stance while delivering a right downward spear-hand attack with a left upper-level sweeping block.

### 26) *Heisoku-dachi/Manji-gamae*

Draw the left foot back alongside the right into a closed parallel stance, turning the hips 90 degrees to the right while pulling the right arm back and extending the left arm downward into a hi-low block position.

27-A) Keeping the left arm extended downward in place, sharply lift the right knee up toward the left side of the body and, pivoting on the left foot, turn the body 180 degrees to the left.

### 27) *Kiba-dachi/Migi sokumen gedan-barai*

Plant the right foot into a straddle-leg stance while driving the right arm downward in the same direction to execute a downward block.

27-A

27

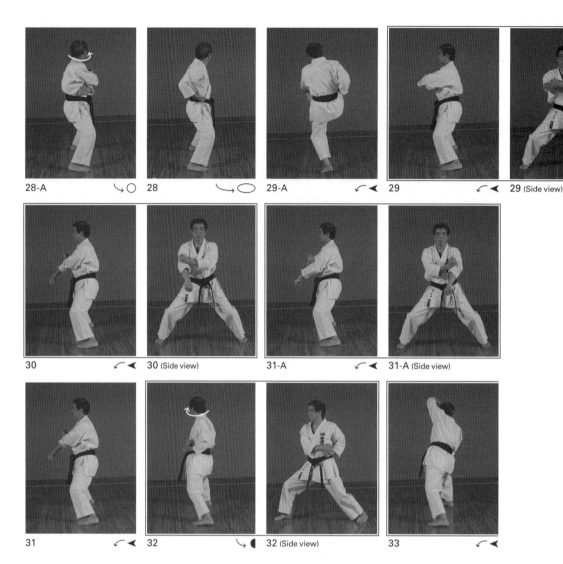

28-A    28    29-A    29    29 (Side view)

30    30 (Side view)    31-A    31-A (Side view)

31    32    32 (Side view)    33

28-A) Turn the head to the left and pull the left hand, opened into a knife hand, across to the right side of the body and beneath the right arm while extending the right arm in the opposite direction.

### 28) *Kiba-dachi/Hidari chūdan haishu-uke*
Draw the left arm out to the left side to deliver a middle-level back-hand block while pulling the right fist back to above the right hip.

### 29-A) *Migi mikazuki-geri*
Swing the right leg up and across the front of the body to deliver a crescent kick, striking the open palm of the left hand with the sole of the right foot. The right fist remains in place above the right hip.

### 29) *Kiba-dachi/Migi empi-uchi*
Plant the right foot in the direction of the kick into a straddle-leg stance while delivering a right front elbow strike against the palm of the left hand.

### 30) *Kiba-dachi/Migi gedan-barai/Hidari soete*
Drive the right fist down to deliver a downward block. The left hand immediately closes into a fist and rests just above the right elbow during the technique.

### 31-A) *Kiba-dachi/Hidari gedan-barai/Migi soete*
Drive the left fist down to perform a downward block while simultaneously drawing the right fist up to above the left elbow.

### 31) *Kiba-dachi/Migi gedan-barai/Hidari soete*
Deliver another downward block with the right arm while drawing the left fist up to above the right elbow.

### 32) *Zenkutsu-dachi/Koshi-gamae*
Turning the head to the right, slide the right foot back slightly, shifting into a narrow right front stance facing the right while drawing both fists back to above the left hip with the right fist resting on top of the left fist.

### 33) *Zenkutsu-dachi/Yama-zuki*
Deliver a wide-U punch to the front, with the left fist targeting an imagined opponent's face, and the right fist delivering a close punch to the midsection. In the completed position, the fists should be aligned vertically.

### 34) *Heisoku-dachi/Koshi-gamae*
Draw the right foot back to alongside the left foot into a closed parallel stance while pulling both fists back to above the right hip.

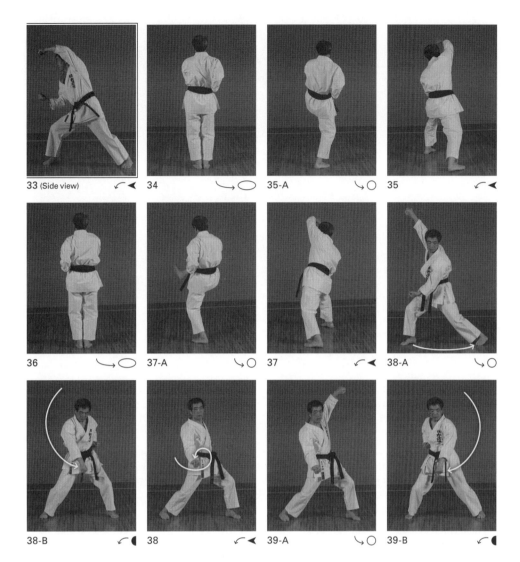

33 (Side view)    34    35-A    35

36    37-A    37    38-A

38-B    38    39-A    39-B

### 35-A) *Harai-fumikomi*
Deliver a sweeping stamping kick to the front with the left leg.

### 35) *Zenkutsu-dachi/Yama-zuki*
Plant the left foot forward, completing the stamping kick into a narrow left front stance while executing a wide-U punch with the right fist above the left.

### 36) *Heisoku-dachi/Koshi-gamae*
Draw the left foot back into a closed parallel stance while pulling both fists back to above the left hip.

### 37-A) *Harai-fumikomi*
Deliver a sweeping stamping kick to the front with the right leg.

### 37) *Zenkutsu-dachi/Yama-zuki*
Plant the right foot forward to complete the stamping kick into a narrow right front stance while executing a wide-U punch with the left fist above the right.

38-A) Draw the left foot back sharply across the rear to the right-hand side of the body in line with the right foot, pivoting on the right foot to turn the body 90 degrees to

the left. At the same time, drop the left shoulder toward the chest and draw the right arm back and upward behind the body.

38-B) Swing the right arm downward strongly along an arcing path around the right side of the body. At the same time, extend the right leg, shifting the weight toward the left leg while pulling the left fist back sharply to above the left hip.

### 38) *Migi gedan sukui-uke*
Complete the sweeping motion of the right arm to execute a downward scooping block to the front, following through with a smaller circular motion of the forearm to deliver a downward back-fist strike. The back remains straight and perpendicular to the floor.

39-A) Keeping the right arm and lower body in the same position, draw the left arm back and upward behind the body.

39-B) Drive the left arm downward strongly around the left side of the body, pulling the right fist back to above the right hip while shifting the weight toward the right leg.

39       40-A       40       41

42-A       42       Yame-A       Yame

### 39) *Hidari gedan sukui-uke*

Complete the sweeping motion of the left arm to deliver a downward scooping block to the front followed by a downward back-fist strike.

40-A) Turning the head 45 degrees to the right, pull the left foot alongside the right foot. At the same time, extend the left arm out in front of the chest at a 45-degree angle to the right while pulling the right hand, opened into a knife hand, back to above the left shoulder.

### 40) *Kōkutsu-dachi/Migi chūdan shutō-uke*

Step out with the right foot at a 45-degree angle to the right into a left back stance while delivering a right middle-level knife-hand block.

41) Pivoting on the left foot, draw the right foot around to the right to turn the body 90 degrees in the same direction while turning the head to the left. The lower body remains in a left back stance while the upper body maintains a right knife-hand block position.

42-A) Keeping the left leg bent at the knee, pull the right foot alongside the left foot, extending the right arm across the chest to the left while pulling the left hand back to above the right shoulder.

### 42) *Kōkutsu-dachi/Hidari chūdan shutō-uke*

Step out with the left foot into a right back stance while delivering a left middle-level knife-hand block with a *kiai*.

Yame-A) Draw the left foot back toward the right foot, aligning the feet into a closed parallel stance. At the same time, extend the arms downward in front of the body, wrapping the left hand around the right fist to assume the same ready position in which the *kata* began.

### Yame

Draw the right foot out to the right side into an open V stance with both fists positioned in front of the hips, the same natural-posture stance assumed prior to starting the *kata*.

**TECHNICAL ANALYSIS**
## Movements 17–19

After blocking an opponent's middle-level lunge punch with a knife-hand block (photo 1), draw the opposite hand around to the far side of the opponent's wrist (photo 2), grab the wrist (photo 3) and pull it inward while delivering a downward thrust kick to the knee (photos 4 and 5).

1            2

3

4

5

## TECHNICAL ANALYSIS
### Movements 21–24

In response to an opponent's lunge-punch attack, block with a knife-hand block (photo 1). As the attacker lunges forward with both arms, step back and execute a two-armed rising block (photos 2 and 3), then counter by driving forward with a hammer-fist scissors strike to the midsection (photo 4) followed by a lunge punch (photo 5).

1

2

3

4

5

# Bassai Shō

As mentioned in the previous chapter, various versions of the Bassai *kata* exist today, including those passed down from Itosu, Matsumura, Tomari, Oyadomari, and Ishimine. It is now generally accepted, however, that the model on which this *kata* is based came from Master Kōkan Oyadomari. The Dai and Shō variations, however, are only found within the Itosu school.

Major characteristics of Bassai Shō, which was created by Shuri-te karate's Master Yasutsune Itosu, include sequences appearing in the first half of the *kata* in response to stick attacks. These begin with a two-handed block, after which the attacker is disarmed and thrown off balance while turning to face the next approaching assailant. Featuring numerous grappling techniques, Bassai Shō is an advanced *kata* that stresses the positioning of the hips when employing back stances and cat stances to ensure a proper center of gravity.

Although not many people perform Bassai Shō today, because it places importance on balance and requires the effective use of the hips, it is very much a *kata* worthy of practice.

## Bassai Shō

Shizentai

Yōi

Yōi (Side view)

1-A ↘○

1-A (Side view)

1-B ↘○

1-B (Side view)

1 ↙◀

1 (Side view)

2 ↙◀

### *Shizentai* (Natural posture)
*Soto hachiji-dachi* (open V stance) with both fists positioned in front of the hips.

### *Yōi* (Ready position)
Slide the right foot in toward the left foot to assume a closed parallel stance (*heisoku-dachi*) while opening and drawing the hands together in front of the body with both arms extending downward at an angle in front of the body. The hands, formed into knife hands, are crossed to form a narrow X with the left hand resting on top of the right hand and the thumb-side of the hands facing upwards.

2 (Side view)

3

3 (Side view)

4-A

4-B

4-C

4-D

4

5

6

7-A

1-A) Leaning forward with the upper body, drive both hands back toward the left-hand side of the body as if to block an attack from the rear. As the hands move, the left hand "folds over" so that the palm presses against the back of the right hand.

1-B) As the hands reach the rear, thrust off the left foot, leaping forward with great force.

### 1) *Kōsa-dachi/Jōdan haishu awase-uke*

Plant the right foot strongly on the floor and immediately draw the left foot behind it into a cross-legged stance while delivering an upper-level two-handed back-hand block. The hands cross at a right angle with the back of the right hand pressing against the fingers of the left hand.

### 2) *Kōkutsu-dachi/Morote jō-uke*

Turn the head to the left and extend the left leg to the rear into a right back stance facing the opposite direction while delivering a two-handed block against a *jō* (stick, or staff) attack. Drop the left elbow to the left hip and extend the left hand forward at approximately waist level with the palm of the hand facing upward while driving the right hand forward over the head with the palm of the hand facing upward.

### 3) *Kōkutsu-dachi/Suihei jō-dori*

Pull the right elbow back and rotate the right hand clockwise while extending and raising the left arm out in front of the body to perform a horizontal *jō* grasp. When completed, the right hand is positioned level with the right ear while the left arm extends forward at approximately the height of the shoulder.

4-A) Pivoting on the left foot, turn the hips to the right while drawing the right foot in toward the left foot. At the same time, raise the right hand, drawing the right

elbow across to the far side of the head while closing the left hand and pulling it back to the left hip.

### 4-B) *Heisoku-dachi/Migi haitō sukui-nage*

Completing a 180-degree turn of the hips, bring the right foot alongside the left foot into a closed parallel stance while lowering the hips and sweeping the right arm downward and across the front of the knees to deliver a ridge-hand scooping throw.

4-C) Straighten the legs and raise the hips to stand upright while following through with the sweeping motion of the right arm, drawing the right elbow out to the right side of the body.

4-D) Continue the motion of the right arm, bringing the right hand up and over the head.

### 4) *Heisoku-dachi/Migi gedan tettsui-uchi*

Draw the right arm around the left-hand side of the body and downward to the front while closing the right hand into a fist to deliver a downward hammer-fist strike.

### 5) *Kōkutsu-dachi/Morote jō-uke*

Drawing the left foot forward into a right back stance, open the left hand with the palm facing upward in front of the left hip while opening and pulling the right hand back to execute a two-handed block against a *jō* attack.

### 6) *Kōkutsu-dachi/Suihei jō-dori*

Draw the right elbow back and rotate the right hand clockwise while extending and raising the left arm out in front of the body to perform a horizontal *jō* grasp.

7-A) Keeping the head facing the same direction, pull the left foot back toward the right foot while turning the hips to the left and drawing the hands back to the left hip.

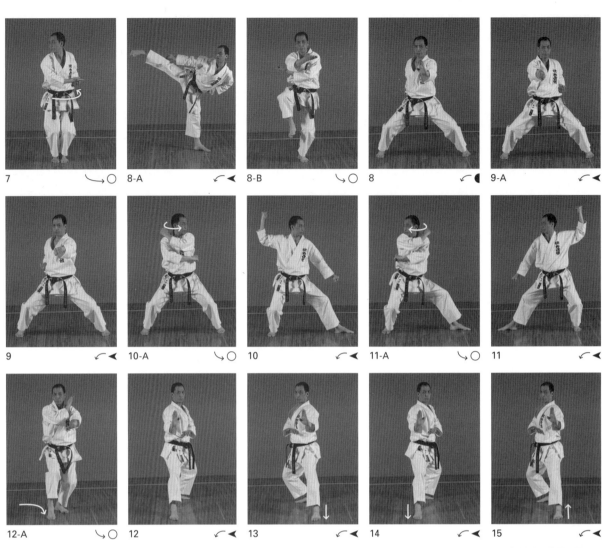

7      8-A      8-B      8      9-A

9      10-A      10      11-A      11

12-A      12      13      14      15

### 7) *Heisoku-dachi/Haitō koshi-gamae*

Align the left foot alongside the right foot into a closed parallel stance while pulling both hands back to above the left hip. As the hands travel toward the hip, the left hand closes into a fist while the right hand remains open, forming a ridge hand with the palm facing upward.

### 8-A) *Migi yoko keage/Migi haitō-uchi*

Deliver a right side snap kick while simultaneously executing a right ridge-hand strike in the same direction.

8-B) Turn the head to the left to face the front while pulling back the kicking leg. At the same time, thrust the left hand, formed into a knife hand, across the front of the body toward the right-hand side while drawing the right hand across the chest in the opposite direction.

### 8) *Kiba-dachi/Hidari tate shutō-uke*

Plant the right foot out to the right-hand side into a straddle-leg stance while delivering a left vertical knife-hand block to the front.

### 9-A) *Kiba-dachi/Migi chūdan-zuki*

Deliver a right middle-level straight punch.

### 9) *Kiba-dachi/Hidari chūdan-zuki*

Deliver a left middle-level straight punch.

10-A) Turning the head to the left, pull the left fist up to above the right shoulder and thrust the right fist across the front of the body.

### 10) *Kōkutsu-dachi/Manji-uke*

Shift the center of gravity back toward the right leg to assume a right back stance while drawing the right arm back strongly and driving the left arm downward to execute a hi-low block. The right arm performs an upper-level inside-to-outside block to the rear while the left arm delivers a downward block to the front.

11-A) Turn the head to the right while pulling the right fist back to above the left shoulder and driving the left fist across the front of the body to the right side.

### 11) *Kōkutsu-dachi/Manji-uke*

Transferring the center of gravity toward the left leg, shift into a left back stance while drawing the left arm back strongly and driving the right arm downward to execute a hi-low block.

16-A

16

17-A

17

18-A

18-A (Rear view)

18

18 (Rear view)

19-A

19-A (Rear view)

19

19 (Rear view)

20-A

20-A (Rear view)

12-A) Draw the right foot back toward the left foot and out in front of the body while pulling the right hand, formed into a knife hand, back to above the left shoulder and extending the left arm out in front of the chest.

### 12) *Kōkutsu-dachi/Migi chūdan shutō-uke*

Complete the step forward with the right foot into a left back stance while executing a right middle-level knife-hand block.

### 13) *Kōkutsu-dachi/Hidari chūdan shutō-uke*

Step forward with the left foot into a right back stance while performing a middle-level knife-hand block with the left arm.

### 14) *Kōkutsu-dachi/Migi chūdan shutō-uke*

Step forward again with the right foot into a left back stance while delivering a middle-level knife-hand block with the right arm.

### 15) *Kōkutsu-dachi/Hidari chūdan shutō-uke*

Draw the right foot straight back into a right back stance while delivering a left middle-level knife-hand block.

16-A) Draw the right foot out to the right side to shift into a slightly shortened left front stance (*moto-dachi*) while extending the right arm out and upward in front of the chest along a course directly below the left hand, which remains in the same blocking position. The back of the right hand remains facing the floor as the right arm extends forward.

### 16) *Moto-dachi/Kaeshi-dori/Gyaku-hanmi*

Turning the hips to *gyaku-hanmi*, draw the right hand up and over to the right in an arcing motion, rotating the right hand counter-clockwise while pulling the right elbow back toward the body to perform a reverse grasp.

17-A) Draw the right knee up sharply into the triangle formed by the forearms and chest.

### 17) *Gedan ke-sage*

Drive the right leg downward to deliver a strong thrust kick with a *kiai*, closing both hands into fists while pulling them back sharply to above the right hip with the backs of the hands facing the direction of the kick.

18-A) Retract the kicking leg while turning the hips to the left to face the opposite direction. At the same time, cross the arms in front of the chest with the right arm on the far side of the left arm.

### 18) *Kōkutsu-dachi/Ryōwan uchi-uke*

Plant the right foot back in the direction of the kick, assuming a right back stance while executing a double inside-to-outside block.

### 19-A) *Kōkutsu-dachi/Jōdan heikō ura-zuki*

Thrusting off the right foot, drive the left foot forward with a gliding step (*suri-ashi*), immediately followed by the right foot, while executing an upper-level parallel close punch.

### 19) Draw the elbows downward immediately following the two-handed close punch to return the arms to the position they were in prior to punching.

### 20-A) *Ashi-barai/Migi chūdan soto-uke*

Drawing the right foot forward and turning the hips to the left, execute a leg sweep to the front with the right foot while simultaneously performing a middle-level outside-to-inside block with the right arm.

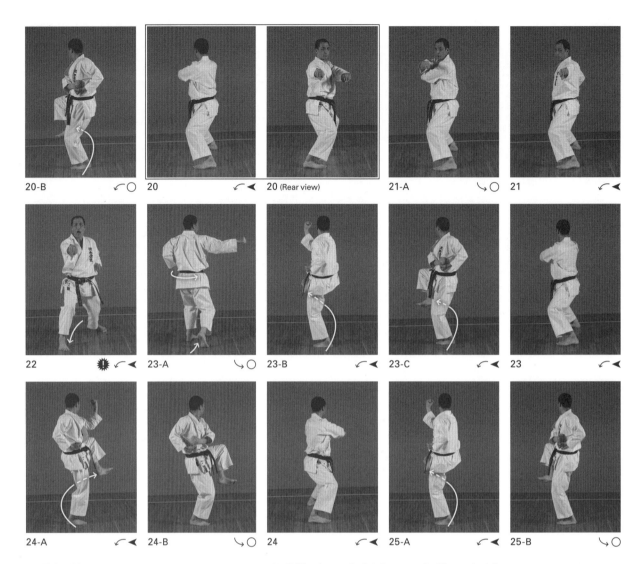

20-B     20     20 (Rear view)     21-A     21

22     23-A     23-B     23-C     23

24-A     24-B     24     25-A     25-B

### 20-B) *Koshi-gamae*
Upon completing the leg sweep, pull the right fist back to the left side of the body, positioning it on top of the left fist.

### 20) *Kiba-dachi/Sokumen morote-zuki*
Plant the right foot in the direction of the block, assuming a straddle-leg stance while delivering a side double-fist punch to the right-hand side.

21-A) Turning the head to the left to face the opposite side, draw the right arm across the front of the chest above the left arm while pushing the left fist out to the opposite side of the body.

### 21) *Kiba-dachi/Hidari chūdan tettsui-uchi*
Drive the left fist out to the left side of the body to deliver a middle-level hammer-fist strike.

### 22) *Zenkutsu-dachi/Migi chūdan oi-zuki*
Pivoting on the left foot, draw the right foot across the front of the left leg to the opposite side, turning the hips 90 degrees to the left to assume a right front stance while delivering a right middle-level lunge punch with a *kiai*.

23-A) Pivoting on the left foot, turn the hips to the left to face the opposite direction while drawing the right leg and right arm around the body.

### 23-B) *Ashi-barai/Migi chūdan soto-uke*
Perform a leg sweep with the right foot while simultaneously executing a middle-level outside-to-inside block with the right arm.

### 23-C) *Koshi-gamae*
Upon completing the leg sweep, draw the right fist back to the left side of the body, positioning it above the left fist.

### 23) *Kiba-dachi/Sokumen morote-zuki*
Plant the right foot into a straddle-leg stance while executing a side double-fist punch to the right.

### 24-A) *Ashi-barai/Hidari chūdan soto-uke*
Pivoting on the right foot, draw the left foot in front of and around the far side of the right leg, turning the hips 180 degrees to the right while executing a simultaneous leg sweep and left middle-level outside-to-inside block.

25

26-A

26-B

26-C

26-D

26

27

28-A

28-B

28-C

28

### 24-B) *Koshi-gamae*

Following the leg sweep, bring the left fist back to above the right hip, positioning it above the right fist.

### 24) *Kiba-dachi/Sokumen morote-zuki*

Plant the left foot into a straddle-leg stance while delivering a side double-fist punch to the left-hand side.

### 25-A) *Ashi-barai/Migi chūdan soto-uke*

Pivoting on the left foot, draw the right foot in front of and around the far side of the left leg, turning the hips 180 degrees to the left to deliver a leg sweep while simultaneously performing a middle-level outside-to-inside block with the right arm.

### 25-B) *Koshi-gamae*

Upon completing the leg sweep, draw the right fist back to above the left fist.

### 25) *Kiba-dachi/Sokumen morote-zuki*

Plant the right foot into a straddle-leg stance while performing a side double-fist punch to the right.

26-A) Turn the head to the left and draw the right hand out in front of the body and around toward the left shoulder, opening the hand as it travels in front of the chest.

26-B) As the right hand approaches the left shoulder, open and draw out the left hand in a large sweeping motion upward toward the left side of the body while extending the left leg back at an angle to the left, leading with the heel of the foot without turning the hips.

### 26-C) *Ura ashi-gake/Hidari jōdan shutō-uke*

Keeping the hips in place, completely extend the left leg to perform a back leg hook while extending the left arm in the same direction to execute an upper-level knife-hand block.

26-D) Turning the hips to the left, draw the heel of the left foot back toward the right foot while pulling both hands down in front of the body.

### 26) *Neko-ashi-dachi/Morote hiki-otoshi*

Complete the turning of the hips to assume a cat stance while lowering the hands to perform a two-handed pull-down.

### 27) *Yoko sashi-ashi*

Without changing the position of the arms or the orientation of the upper body, turn the head to the right and step across the front of the right leg with the left foot.

28-A) Draw the left hand up to the right shoulder while extending the right leg out at an angle to the right.

### 28-B) *Ura ashi-gake/Migi jōdan shutō-uke*

Leading with the heel of the right foot, completely extend the right leg to perform a back leg hook while drawing the right arm around and upward in a large sweeping motion in the same direction to execute an upper-level knife-hand block.

28-C) Turning the hips to the right, pull the heel of the right foot back toward the supporting leg while drawing the hands downward in front of the body.

### 28) *Neko-ashi-dachi/Morote hiki-otoshi*

Complete the turning of the hips to assume a cat stance while performing a two-handed pull-down.

Yame-A

Yame

*Yame*-A) Draw the right foot back to alongside the left foot and straighten the legs to assume a closed parallel stance. At the same time, lower the right hand to below the left hand in front of the body with the arms extended downward and the hands crossed, the same ready position in which the *kata* began.

### Yame

Draw the right foot out to the right side into an open V stance while closing the hands into fists and positioning them in front of the hips, the same natural-posture stance assumed prior to starting the *kata*.

**TECHNICAL ANALYSIS**
## Movements 1–3

Block a punching attack from the rear with a two-handed open-hand block (photos 1 and 2), immediately lunging forward to suppress a punching attack from the front with a two-handed backhand block (photo 3). Turning to face the rear, thrust the hands forward to block a stick attack (photo 4) and then raise the front arm to disarm the opponent while throwing him off-balance (photo 5).

1

2

3

4

5

## TECHNICAL ANALYSIS
### Movements 24-A–24

In response to an opponent's lunge-punch attack, block with an outside-to-inside block while sweeping his front leg (photos 1 and 2) and immediately counter with a double-fist punch (photo 3).

1

2

3

## TECHNICAL ANALYSIS
### Movements 26-A–26

As an opponent punches from the rear, deflect the attack with a left knife-hand block while extending the left leg behind the attacker's ankle (photo 1). Draw the leg back, executing a leg hook and sweep while pulling the opponent's punching arm forward (photo 2), dropping him to the floor to finish with a downward kick (photo 3).

1

2

3

# Kankū Dai

A special envoy from China during the Ming Dynasty named Kōsōkun, who was an accomplished practitioner of Chinese martial arts, is credited with having created Kankū Dai, a *kata* which is also known by the name Kūshankū.

With 65 movements, Kankū Dai is the longest of all the Shōtōkan *kata*, requiring approximately one and a half minutes to perform. The *kata* includes blocks and counterattacks in response to attacks from eight supposed opponents.

According to rumor, Master Funakoshi assigned this *kata* the Japanese name of Kankū (written using the characters 観空, literally "viewing the sky") based on the opening movement in which the practitioner casts his gaze skyward through the hands. As a favorite *kata* of Master Funakoshi's, it was one he often enjoyed practicing.

Kankū Dai is characterized by sequences of richly diverse techniques that include a leap in the air and a drop to the floor, along with a twisting technique accompanying the rotation of the body. While there are two variations of this *kata* within the Shōtōkan style—Dai and Shō—other known variations include Shihō Kūshankū and, within the Shuri-te style, Chihana Kūshankū, as well as the Kūshankū of Kitayara and of Kuniyoshi.

As mentioned in an earlier chapter, Master Itosu broke up the Kūshankū *kata* (Dai and Shō) to create the five *Heian* kata for practice by middle school students. As such, for those who have fully mastered the Heian *kata* Nos. 1 through 5, Kūshankū (Kankū) should prove fairly easy to learn.

This *kata*, along with Bassai, are important *kata* representative of the Shōtōkan style and are compulsory *kata* for the Japan Karatedo Federation. It is definitely a *kata* that all students of karate should make every effort to master.

## Kanku Dai

Shizentai

Yōi

Yōi (Detail)

1-A

### Shizentai
*Soto hachiji-dachi* (open V stance) with both fists positioned in front of the hips.

### Yōi (Ready position)
Open both hands, extending the thumbs out at right angles, and bring them together in front of the body. The tips of the index and middle fingers of the right hand rest above the tips of the corresponding fingers of the left hand while the tip of the right thumb rests above the left thumbnail.

1-A) Keeping both arms extended, raise the hands smoothly in front of the body.

1

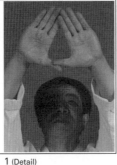
1 (Detail)

2-A

2-B

2-C

2

3-A

3

4-A

4-B

4

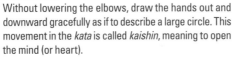
5-A

5

1) Continue raising the hands until the arms extend at a roughly 45-degree angle above the head. Once the hands reach eye level, follow the path of the hands with the eyes, lifting the head to peer through the opening between the hands as they rise.

2-A) Break the arms apart in a single sharp motion while dropping the chin to look straight ahead. The elbows are level with the shoulders while the forearms are perpendicular to the floor.

**2-B) *Kaishin***

Without lowering the elbows, draw the hands out and downward gracefully as if to describe a large circle. This movement in the *kata* is called *kaishin*, meaning to open the mind (or heart).

2-C) Once the hands are level with the elbows, continue the circular motion of the hands, bringing the arms downward in front of the body.

2) Once the distance separating the hands is roughly equivalent to the width of the hips, snap the hands together, bisecting the palm of the left hand with the outer edge of the right hand.

3-A) Turning the head to the left, draw the left foot out to the left side while pulling the hands back slightly to the right side.

**3) *Kōkutsu-dachi/Kaishu haiwan-uke***

Assume a right back stance facing the left, performing an open-hand back-arm block with the left arm while pulling the right hand to the solar plexus. Initiate the block with the feeling of "launching" the left hand on its course with a pushing motion of the right hand.

4-A) Turning the head to the right, shift the hips toward the left leg while bringing the left arm back toward the body and drawing the right arm out to the right-hand side.

4-B) Transfer the center of gravity to the left leg while sweeping the right arm around the body.

**4) *Kōkutsu-dachi/Kaishu haiwan-uke***

Assume a left back stance facing the opposite side while delivering an open-hand back-arm block with the right arm, bringing the left hand to the solar plexus.

5-A) Turning the head to the left, draw the left foot in toward the right foot to assume a natural posture (open V stance) while extending the right arm out in front of the body with the left hand positioned below the right underarm.

**5) *Shizentai/Hidari chūdan tate shutō-uke***

Draw the left hand out in front the chest to deliver a middle-level vertical knife-hand block while pulling the right fist back to above the right hip. When performing the block, the left hand travels along the far side of the right arm.

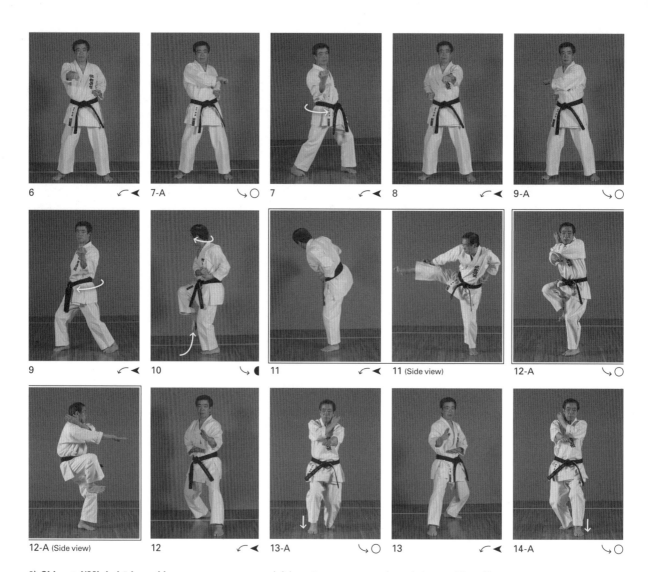

6    7-A    7    8    9-A

9    10    11    11 (Side view)    12-A

12-A (Side view)    12    13-A    13    14-A

### 6) *Shizentai/Migi chūdan zuki*
Deliver a middle-level straight punch with the right arm.

7-A) Pull the right fist back and across the front of the body to the left side.

### 7) *Migi chūdan uchi-uke*
Turning the hips sharply to the left, perform a right middle-level inside-to-outside block to the front. As the hips rotate, turn the right foot inward while extending the right leg sharply and bending the left knee.

### 8) *Shizentai/Hidari chūdan zuki*
Straighten the left leg to return to a natural posture while delivering a left middle-level straight punch.

9-A) Pull the left fist back and across the body to the right side.

### 9) *Hidari chūdan uchi-uke*
Turning the hips sharply to the right, deliver a left middle-level inside-to-outside block to the front.

### 10) *Kata-ashi-dachi/Koshi-gamae*
Turning the head to the right to face the rear, draw the sole of the right foot up to just above the inside of the left knee to assume a one-legged stance while pulling both fists back to above the left hip.

### 11) *Migi yoko ke-age/Migi yoko-mawashi uraken-uchi*
Deliver a right side snap kick to the right side while simultaneously executing a right side round back-fist strike in the same direction.

12-A) Turn the head to the left to face the opposite side (the same orientation as the original ready position) while retracting the kicking leg. At the same time, pull the left hand, formed into a knife hand with the back of the hand facing outward, up to above the right shoulder while thrusting the right hand, also formed into a knife hand, out across the chest to the left side with the palm facing the floor.

### 12) *Kōkutsu-dachi/Hidari chūdan shutō-uke*
Plant the right foot to the rear, assuming a right back stance facing the front while performing a left middle-level knife-hand block.

13-A) Step forward with the right foot, pulling the right knife hand up to above the left shoulder while thrusting the left knife hand out in front of the chest.

14

15-A

15

16-A

16-A (Rear view)

16

16 (Rear view)

17

17 (Rear view)

18-A

18

19

20-A

### 13) *Kōkutsu-dachi/Migi chūdan shutō-uke*

Complete the step forward with the right foot into a left back stance while performing a right middle-level knife-hand block.

14-A) Step forward with the left foot while simultaneously pulling the left knife hand back to above the right shoulder and thrusting the right knife hand out in front of the body.

### 14) *Kōkutsu-dachi/Hidari chūdan shutō-uke*

Complete the step forward with the left foot into a right back stance while executing a left middle-level knife-hand block.

### 15-A) *Hidari osae-uke*

Stepping forward with the right foot, drop the left hand along a circular course centered on the elbow to perform a left pressing block.

### 15) *Zenkutsu-dachi/Migi chūdan shihon-nukite*

Complete the step forward with the right foot into a right front stance, delivering a right middle-level spear hand with a *kiai*. The left hand is positioned beneath the right arm for added support.

16-A) Turn the head to the left to face the rear while shifting the left foot across the back to the opposite side. At the same time, draw the left hand, formed into a knife hand, back toward the left leg to deliver a knife-hand downward block while pulling the right elbow back sharply to the right side of the body.

### 16) *Zenkutsu-dachi/Migi jōdan shutō-uchi/Gyaku-hanmi*

Shift into a left front stance, turning the hips sharply to the left to *gyaku-hanmi* (45-degree angle to the front, with the hip on the side opposite to the front leg pushed forward) while delivering a right upper-level knife-hand strike. At the same time, draw the left hand up to the forehead with the palm of the hand facing outward and the elbow pulled back alongside the left ear.

### 17) *Migi jōdan mae-geri*

Maintaining the same upper body position, deliver an upper-level front snap kick with the right leg.

18-A) Upon retracting the kicking leg, turn the head to the left to face the opposite direction while thrusting the right arm back across the front of the body and downward, dropping the left elbow and drawing the left hand back to above the right shoulder.

### 18) *Kōkutsu-dachi/Manji-uke*

Plant the right foot on the floor in the direction of the preceding kick into a right back stance while simultaneously drawing the right arm back strongly and driving the left arm downward to execute a hi-low block. The right arm performs an upper-level inside-to-outside block to the rear while the left arm delivers a downward block to the front.

### 19) *Zenkutsu-dachi/Hidari nagashi-uke/Migi gedan nukite*

Slide the left foot out to the left and transfer the center of gravity forward into a left front stance while driving the right hand down at an angle in front of the body to deliver a downward spear-hand attack while pulling the left hand back toward the right shoulder to simultaneously perform a sweeping block.

20-A) Draw the left foot back toward the right foot while pulling the right fist toward the right hip and lowering the left arm toward the front of the body.

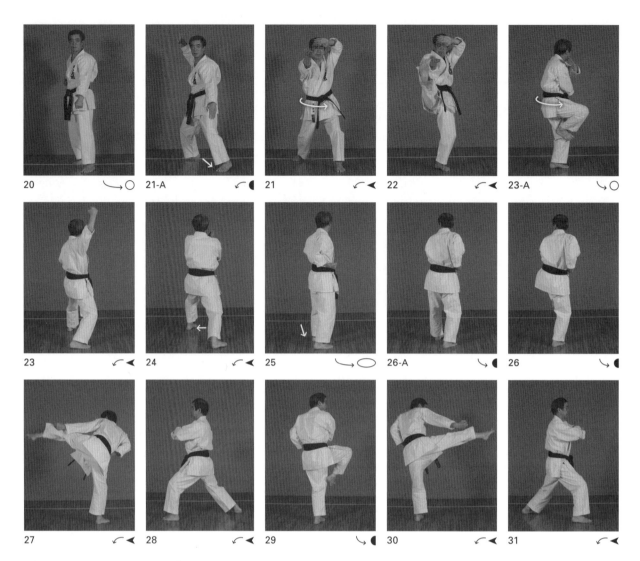

| | | | | |
|---|---|---|---|---|
| 20 | 21-A | 21 | 22 | 23-A |
| 23 | 24 | 25 | 26-A | 26 |
| 27 | 28 | 29 | 30 | 31 |

**20) *Renoji-dachi/Gedan-gamae***
Assuming an L stance, pull the right fist back to above the right hip and extend the left arm downward at an angle in the position of a completed downward block.

**21-A)** Shifting the left foot forward and out to the left at an angle, deliver a knife-hand downward block with the left hand while drawing the right elbow back sharply to the rear.

**21) *Zenkutsu-dachi/Migi jōdan shutō-uchi/Gyaku-hanmi***
Assuming a left front stance with the hips turned to *gyaku-hanmi*, deliver a right upper-level knife-hand strike while drawing the left hand up to the forehead.

**22) *Migi jōdan mae-geri***
Deliver an upper-level front snap kick with the right leg.

**23-A)** Retracting the kicking leg, turn the head to the left to face the opposite direction and extend the right arm across the front of the body and downward while drawing the left hand back to above the right shoulder.

**23) *Kōkutsu-dachi/Manji-uke***
Plant the right foot in the direction of the kick into a right back stance while pulling the right arm back strongly

and driving the left arm downward to execute a hi-low block.

**24) *Zenkutsu-dachi/Hidari nagashi-uke/Migi gedan nukite***
Slide the left foot out to the left, shifting into a left front stance while delivering a downward spear-hand attack with the right hand while executing a sweeping block with the left hand back toward the right shoulder.

**25) *Renoji-dachi/Gedan-gamae***
Draw the left foot back into an L stance while pulling the right fist to above the right hip and extending the left arm downward in front of the body.

**26-A)** Turning the head to the left, turn the hips 45 degrees in the same direction while drawing the left fist back toward the right hip, positioning it on top of the right fist.

**26) *Kata-ashi-dachi/Koshi-gamae***
Keeping both fists positioned above the right hip, lift the left knee, positioning the sole of the left foot just above the inside of the right knee into a one-legged stance with the left knee pointing toward the left side.

32-A ↘○

32 ↙◀

33 ↙◀

34-A ↘○

34 ↙◀

35 ↙◀

36-A ↘◗

36 ↙◀

37 ↙◀

38-A ↘○

### 27) *Hidari yoko ke-age/Hidari yoko-mawashi ura-ken-uchi*

Deliver a left side snap kick to the left side while executing a side round back-fist strike in the same direction with the left arm.

### 28) *Zenkutsu-dachi/Migi mae empi-uchi*

Plant the left foot in the direction of the kick into a left front stance while simultaneously delivering a right front elbow strike against the palm of the left hand.

### 29) *Kata-ashi-dachi/Koshi-gamae*

Keeping the left foot in place, lift the right knee to assume a one-legged stance, bringing the sole of the right foot to just above the inside of the left knee. At the same time, draw both fists down to above the left hip.

### 30) *Migi yoko ke-age/Migi yoko-mawashi uraken-uchi*

Deliver a right side snap kick to the right side while simultaneously executing a side round back-fist strike in the same direction with the right arm.

### 31) *Zenkutsu-dachi/Hidari mae empi-uchi*

Plant the right foot in the direction of the kick, assuming a right front stance while executing a left front elbow strike against the palm of the right hand.

32-A) Turning the head to the left, slide the left foot across the back in line with the right foot and extend the right arm across the chest toward the rear while pulling the left hand back to above the right shoulder.

### 32) *Kōkutsu-dachi/Hidari chūdan shutō-uke*

Turning the body 180 degrees to the left to face the opposite direction, shift into a right back stance while delivering a left middle-level knife-hand block.

### 33) *Kōkutsu-dachi/Migi chūdan shutō-uke*

Step forward with the right foot at a 45-degree angle to the right into a left back stance while performing a right middle-level knife-hand block.

34-A) Draw the right foot back at a 135-degree angle to the right while pulling the right knife hand up to above the left shoulder and thrusting the left knife hand out across the chest.

### 34) *Kōkutsu-dachi/Migi chūdan shutō-uke*

Shift into a left back stance while performing a right middle-level knife-hand block.

### 35) *Kōkutsu-dachi/Hidari chūdan shutō-uke*

Step forward with the left foot at a 45-degree angle to the left into a right back stance while performing a left middle-level knife-hand block.

36-A) Turning the head to the left, slide the left foot across to the left and draw the left hand down in the same direction to deliver a knife-hand downward block while pulling the right elbow back sharply toward the rear.

### 36) *Zenkutsu-dachi/Migi jōdan shutō-uchi/Gyaku-hanmi*

Shifting into a left front stance, deliver a right upper-level knife-hand strike, turning the hips sharply to the left to *gyaku-hanmi* while drawing the left hand up to the forehead.

### 37) *Migi jōdan mae-geri*

Deliver an upper-level front snap kick with the right leg.

38-A) Retract the kicking leg and thrust forward off the left foot while pulling the right hand, closed into a fist, up to above the head. At the same time, drop the left hand out in front of the body to execute a middle-level pressing block.

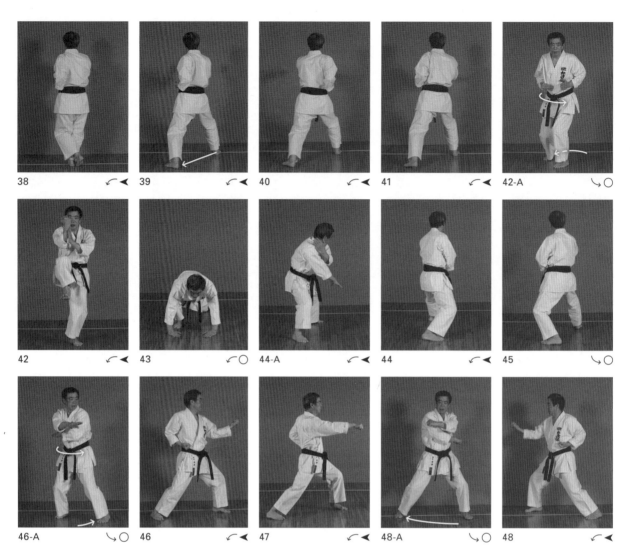

38    39    40    41    42-A

42    43    44-A    44    45

46-A    46    47    48-A    48

### 38) Kōsa-dachi/Migi chūdan uraken-uchi

Plant the right foot on the floor and immediately draw the left leg behind it into a cross-legged stance while driving the right fist down in front of the body to deliver a middle-level back-fist strike.

### 39) Zenkutsu-dachi/Migi chūdan uchi-uke

Draw the left foot back into a right front stance while performing a middle-level inside-to-outside block with the right arm.

### 40) Zenkutsu-dachi/Hidari chūdan gyaku-zuki

Deliver a middle-level reverse punch with the left arm.

### 41) Zenkutsu-dachi/Migi chūdan zuki

Deliver a middle-level straight punch with the right arm.

42-A) Pivoting on the left foot, turn the body 180 degrees to the left while drawing the right knee forward alongside the left leg and up in front of the body. At the same time, guide the right fist out in front of the chest, keeping the right forearm in contact with the right side of the body as it travels forward.

### 42) Kata-ashi-dachi/Migi ura-zuki/Hiza-gamae

Assuming a one-legged stance, lift the right knee in front of the body while delivering a right close punch with the right arm, supported by the open left hand, which is positioned along the inner forearm just below the right wrist.

### 43) Ryōte-fuse

Plant the right foot forward and drop the upper body down to the floor, landing on the hands, which are positioned approximately shoulder-width apart and turned inward at an angle.

44-A) Keeping the feet in place, immediately raise the upper body and turn to the left to face the opposite direction while drawing the left hand up to above the right shoulder and extending the right arm downward across the front of the body.

### 44) Kasei kōkutsu-dachi/Morote gedan shutō-uke

Assuming a right back stance with the hips positioned lower than a conventional back stance, deliver a two-handed downward knife-hand block.

49

50

51

52

52 (Side view)

53-A

53-A (Side view)

53

54

55-A

### 45) *Kōkutsu-dachi/Migi chūdan shutō-uke*
Step forward with the right foot into a standard left back stance while performing a right middle-level knife-hand block.

46-A) Draw the left leg around to the left, turning the hips in the same direction while driving the left fist back toward the right-hand side of the body.

### 46) *Zenkutsu-dachi/Hidari chūdan uchi-uke*
Completing a 270-degree rotation of the body to the left, shift into a left front stance while performing a middle-level inside-to-outside block with the left arm.

### 47) *Zenkutsu-dachi/Migi chūdan gyaku-zuki*
Deliver a middle-level reverse punch with the right arm.

48-A) Turning the head to the right, shift the right foot across the rear to the opposite side and extend the left arm across the chest to the right side of the body. At the same time, draw the right fist back beneath the left arm and across the midsection to the left side of the body.

### 48) *Zenkutsu-dachi/Migi chūdan uchi-uke*
Shift into a right front stance facing the opposite direction while executing a right middle-level inside-to-outside block.

### 49) *Zenkutsu-dachi/Hidari chūdan gyaku-zuki*
Deliver a left middle-level reverse punch.

### 50) *Zenkutsu-dachi/Migi chūdan zuki*
Deliver a right middle-level straight punch.

### 51) *Koshi-gamae*
Turning the head to the right, draw the left foot forward one half-step while pulling the right fist back to above the left hip, positioning it above the left fist.

### 52) *Migi yoko ke-age/Migi yoko-mawashi uraken-uchi*
Deliver a right side snap kick to the right while executing a right side round back-fist strike in the same direction

53-A) Turning the head to the left to face the opposite direction, retract the kicking leg while pulling the left hand, opened into a knife hand, up to above the right shoulder while thrusting the right hand out across the chest to the left.

### 53) *Kōkutsu-dachi/Hidari chūdan shutō-uke*
Plant the right foot to the rear, shifting into a right back stance while performing a left middle-level knife-hand block.

### 54) *Zenkutsu-dachi/Migi chūdan shihon-nukite*
Step forward with the right foot into a right front stance, dropping the left hand to perform a pressing block followed by a right middle-level spear hand, which travels above the back of the left hand.

55-A) In response to an opponent grasping the right wrist, twist the right hand clockwise and raise the right forearm in front of the face with the back of the hand facing outward. At the same time, draw the left foot forward and behind the right foot, turning the body to the left. The left hand remains positioned below the right upper arm during the initial part of this motion.

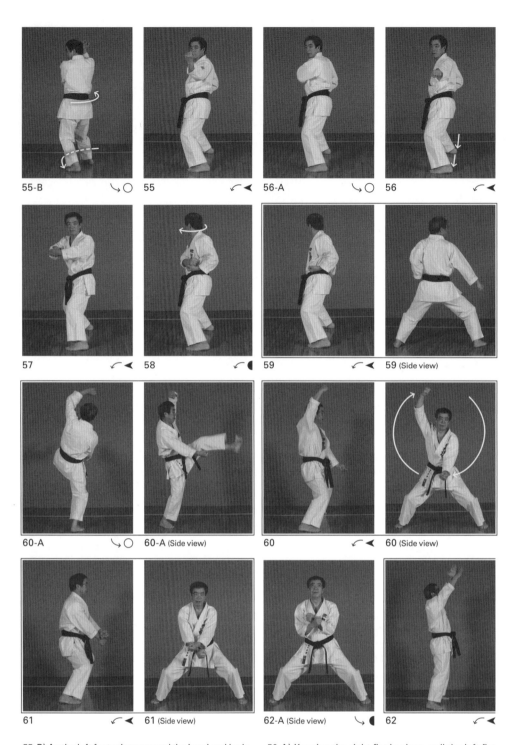

55-B)   ↘○   55   ↙◀   56-A   ↘○   56   ↙◀

57   ↙◀   58   ↙◑   59   ↙◀   59 (Side view)

60-A   ↘○   60-A (Side view)    60   ↙◀   60 (Side view)

61   ↙◀   61 (Side view)    62-A (Side view)   ↘◑   62   ↙◀

55-B) As the left foot advances and the head and body turn to the left, the right hand remains behind the head and the left hand travels upward in front of the face while closing into a fist.

### 55) *Kiba-dachi/Hidari jōdan uraken-uchi*
Complete the rotation of the body, assuming a straddle-leg stance while delivering a left upper-level backfist strike, simultaneously pulling the right fist down to above the right hip.

56-A) Keeping the right fist in place, pull the left fist across the front of the body to the left side.

### 56) *Kiba-dachi/Hidari chūdan tettsui-uchi*
Thrusting off the right foot, slide the left foot out to the left, immediately followed by the right foot, while driving the left fist out to the left side of the body to deliver a middle-level hammer-fist strike.

### 57) *Kiba-dachi/Migi sokumen empi-uchi*
Deliver a right elbow strike to the left side, striking the elbow against the palm of the left hand.

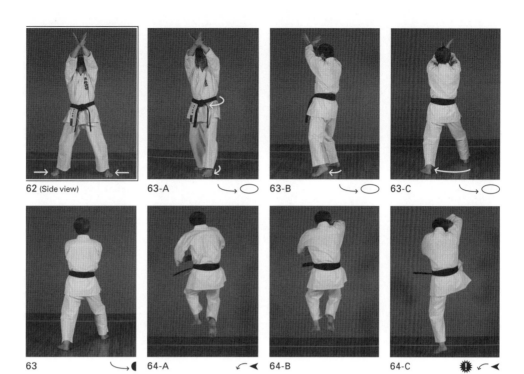

62 (Side view)  63-A  63-B  63-C

63  64-A  64-B  64-C

**58) *Kiba-dachi/Koshi-gamae***
Turn the head to the right while dropping both fists down to above the left hip.

**59) *Kiba-dachi/Migi sokumen gedan-barai***
Deliver a right downward block to the right side.

60-A) Pivoting on the right foot, turn the body 180 degrees to the right and draw the left foot up sharply in front of the body while pulling the left fist up to above the head. The right arm remains extended downward in front of the body.

**60) *Kiba-dachi/Ryō-ude mawashi-uke***
Plant the left foot into a straddle-leg stance while simultaneously swinging the left arm downward around the left side of the body and the right arm upward around the right side to execute a double-armed circular block. The left and right arms move in synchronization with the fists describing a large circle around the body as if both hands were positioned on opposite sides of a large steering wheel.

**61) *Kiba-dachi/Migi otoshi-zuki***
Thrust the right fist downward behind the wrist of the left arm to deliver a dropping punch.

62-A) Pull both elbows back to the body while raising the forearms toward the chest so that the fists point upward at an angle.

**62) *Shizentai/jōdan haishu jūji-uke***
Thrusting off the legs to propel the body upward, drive both hands straight up, opening them as they rise to deliver an upper-level back-hand X-block while assuming a natural posture (open V stance).

**63-A) *Tenshin***
Pivoting on the right foot, draw the left foot around the front of the body, employing *tenshin* (body rotation) to turn the body toward the right.

63-B) Continue turning the body, keeping the arms crossed at the wrists in an X-block formation above the head.

63-C) Upon completing a 270-degree turn to the right, position the left leg behind the right foot to assume a slightly shortened right front stance (*moto-dachi*).

**63) *Moto-dachi/Jūji-gamae***
Maintaining the slightly shortened front stance, draw the elbows down toward the chest while closing the hands into fists, keeping the arms crossed at the wrists in an X-block formation with the backs of the hands facing each other.

**64-A) *Hidari tobi-geri***
Keeping the arms formed into an X-block, leap into the air, leading with the left leg to deliver a left jumping kick.

**64-B, C) *Migi tobi-geri* (*Nidan geri*)**
Immediately execute a right jumping kick with a *kiai* to complete a double kick. During the second kick, pull the right hand, closed into a fist, up to above the head.

64

Yame-A

Yame-B

Yame-C

Yame-D

Yame-E

Yame

### 64) *Zenkutsu-dachi/Migi chūdan uraken-uchi*

Land on the floor into a right front stance while driving the right fist down in front of the body to deliver a middle-level back-fist strike.

*Yame*-A) Keeping the arms in the same position, draw the left foot around the front of the right foot and to the opposite side, turning the body to the right while leaning the upper body forward slightly.

*Yame*-B) Completing a 180-degree turn of the body to the right, plant the left foot in line with the right so that the distance between the feet is approximately double the width of the shoulders. Extend the left arm downward directly behind the right arm at the instant that the left foot arrives at its destination.

*Yame*-C) Draw the arms out to the sides, describing a large circle with the fists while raising the upper body and pulling the left leg in toward the right leg.

*Yame*-D) Continue drawing the arms upward above the head while assuming a natural posture (open V stance).

### *Yame*-E) *Heishin*

Follow through with the motion of the arms, crossing them in front of the chest with the right arm positioned above the left. In contrast with the opening movement (*kaishin*, see step 2-B), this movement is called *heishin*, meaning to close the mind (or heart).

### *Yame*

Continue drawing the fists down to the front of the hips, returning to the initial ready position assumed prior to starting the *kata*.

## TECHNICAL ANALYSIS
### Movements 54–56

In response to an opponent grabbing the right wrist following a spear hand attack (photo 1), bend the right arm upward and pivot on the right foot to turn the hips to the left while closing the left hand into a fist in preparation for a back-fist strike (photo 2). Snap the left fist out to deliver the back-fist strike to the opponent's face (photo 3) and follow through with a hammer-fist strike to the midsection (photo 4).

1

2

3

4

## TECHNICAL ANALYSIS
### Movements 60–63

Block an opponent's kicking attack with a double-armed circular block (photo 1) and immediately counter with a dropping punch to the foot (photo 2). When the opponent responds with a punch to the face, block with an upper-level back-hand X-block (photo 3), seizing the opportunity to grab the wrist and turn the body to face the opposite direction, forcing the opponent into submission by locking the arm over the shoulder (photo 4).

1

2

3

4

# Kankū Shō

As mentioned in the previous chapter, Kankū Dai, a representative *kata* within the Shōtōkan style, is also known by the name Kūshankū. It is said to have been introduced by Kōsōkun, a special envoy from China proficient in Chinese martial arts during the Ming Dynasty.

The sibling *kata* to Kankū Dai, Kankū Shō was created by Master Yasutsune Itosu. Although there are other variations based on these two *kata*, such as Shihō Kūshankū, only Kankū Dai and Kankū Shō have been passed down within the Shōtōkan style.

The name, Kankū, meaning "viewing the sky," supposedly derives from the opening movement of Kankū Dai, in which the practitioner directs his gaze toward the sky through his hands. Despite the name, no corresponding movement exists in Kankū Shō. There are, however, similarities in the performance lines (*embusen*) of the two *kata*.

While the opening of Kankū Shō—three consecutive augmented middle-level inside-to-outside blocks, first to the left, then to the right, then to the front—may not appear as flamboyant as the opening of Kankū Dai, it demands a high level of technical skill.

Instructor Asanobu Chihana, an advanced disciple of Master Itosu's, is credited with having effectively preserved Kūshankū Shō (Kankū Shō), passing it down to future generations by teaching it to his students.

## Kankū Shō

Yōi     1-A ↘○     1 ◿◀ 2-A ↘○

**Yōi (Ready position)**
*Soto hachiji-dachi* (open V stance) with both fists positioned in front of the hips.

1-A) Turn the head to the left while pulling the left fist back sharply across the body toward the right-hand side.

**1) Kōkutsu-dachi/Hidari chūdan morote-uke**
Thrusting off the left foot, drive the hips to the right, sliding the right foot out to the right-hand side of the body, immediately followed by the left foot, assuming a right back stance while executing an augmented middle-level inside-to-outside block to the left with the left arm.

2-A) Turning the head to the right to face the opposite direction, lower the left arm and drive the right fist over the left elbow toward the left-hand side.

**2) Kōkutsu-dachi/Migi chūdan morote-uke**
Thrusting off the right foot, drive the hips back toward the left-hand side of the body, sliding the left foot out to the left, immediately followed by the right foot, shifting into a left back stance while executing an augmented middle-level inside-to-outside block to the right with the right arm.

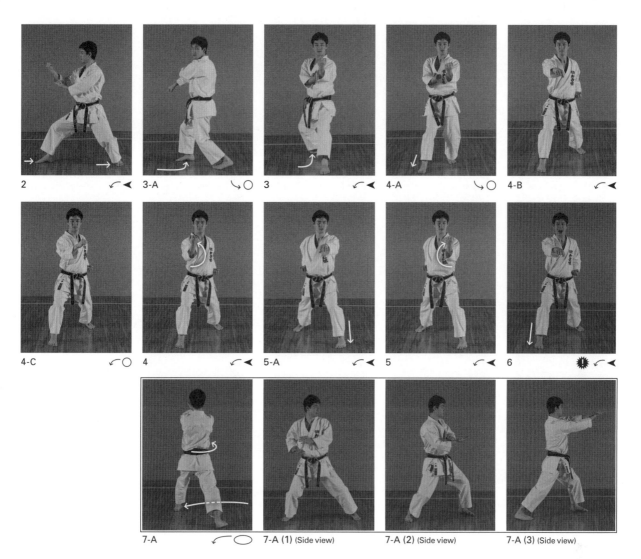

2    3-A    3    4-A    4-B

4-C    4    5-A    5    6

7-A    7-A (1) (Side view)    7-A (2) (Side view)    7-A (3) (Side view)

3-A) Turning the head to the left, draw the right foot back toward the left foot while extending the right arm out to the right-hand side of the body and driving the left fist in the same direction above the right elbow.

### 3) *Kōkutsu-dachi/Hidari chūdan morote-uke*

Thrusting off the left foot, drive the hips to the rear, sliding the right foot back, immediately followed by the left foot, assuming a right back stance while executing an augmented middle-level inside-to-outside block to the front with the left arm.

4-A) Keeping the left arm in place, step forward with the right foot.

### 4-B) *Zenkutsu-dachi/Migi chūdan oi-zuki*

Complete the step forward into a right front stance while delivering a right middle-level lunge punch.

4-C) Pull the right elbow back sharply toward the body while rotating the forearm to execute a twist return.

### 4) *Zenkutsu-dachi/Hineri-kaeshi*

Complete the motion of the arm, bending the elbow approximately 90 degrees.

### 5-A) *Zenkutsu-dachi/Hidari chūdan oi-zuki*

Step forward with the left foot into a left front stance while delivering a left middle-level lunge punch.

### 5) *Zenkutsu-dachi/Hineri-kaeshi*

Pull the left elbow back sharply, rotating the forearm to execute a twist return.

### 6) *Zenkutsu-dachi/Migi chūdan oi-zuki*

Step forward with the right foot into a right front stance while delivering a right middle-level lunge punch with a *kiai*.

7-A) Turning the head to the left to face the rear, draw the left foot across the back, turning the hips 180 degrees to the left to assume a slightly shortened left front stance facing the opposite direction. At the same time, draw the right hand, formed into a knife hand, out in front of the body at a slight angle to the left with the palm facing upward. The left hand, which is also open with the palm facing downward, rests on top of the right wrist.

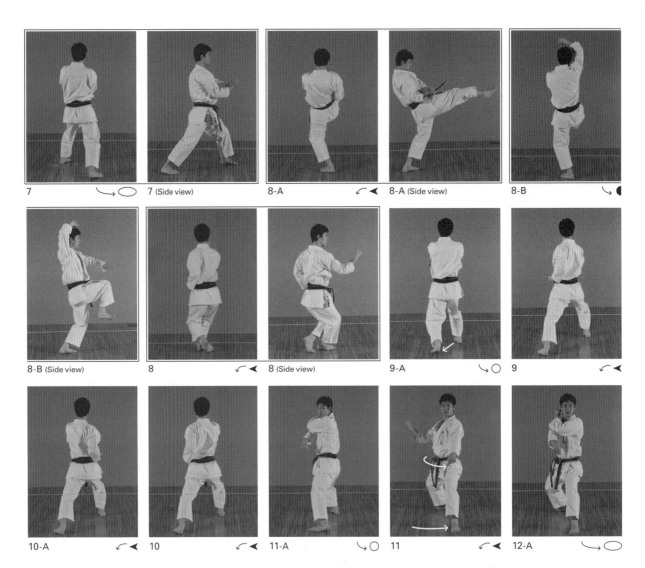

7    7 (Side view)    8-A    8-A (Side view)    8-B

8-B (Side view)    8    8 (Side view)    9-A    9

10-A    10    11-A    11    12-A

### 7) *Moto-dachi/Soete kake-dori*

As the right arm reaches full extension, rotate the hand counter-clockwise and pull the right elbow back toward the right hip, grasping the right wrist with the left hand to perform an augmented hooking grasp. Curl the fingers of the right hand during the motion, forming the hand as if holding a large cup.

### 8-A) *Tsukami-dori/Migi mae-geri*

Pull the right hand back to the right hip, closing it into a fist to perform a grasping clutch while simultaneously delivering a right front snap kick.

### 8-B) *Hidari chūdan hirate osae-uke*

Retracting the right leg following the kick, drop the left hand out in front of the body to perform a middle-level pressing block while drawing the right fist up to above the head.

### 8) *Kōsa-dachi/Migi tate uraken-uchi*

Thrusting forward off the left foot, plant the right foot on the floor and immediately draw the left foot behind it into a cross-legged stance while delivering a right vertical back-fist strike.

9-A) Drive the left foot back at an angle to the left while extending the left arm out in front of the body and drawing the right fist back to below the left underarm.

### 9) *Zenkutsu-dachi/Migi chūdan uchi-uke*

Assuming a right front stance, execute a middle-level inside-to-outside block with the right arm.

### 10-A) *Zenkutsu-dachi/Hidari chūdan gyaku-zuki*

Deliver a left middle-level reverse punch.

### 10) *Zenkutsu-dachi/Migi chūdan jun-zuki*

Deliver a right middle-level front punch.

11-A) Turning the head to the left, draw the right arm across the front of the body to the left-hand side while pulling the left fist up to above the right shoulder. At the same time, slide the left foot across the back to the left while turning the hips in the same direction to face the opposite side, keeping the center of gravity toward the right leg.

12-B    12    13-A    13-B    13

14-A    14-B    14    15-A    15

### 11) *Kōkutsu-dachi/Kasui-ken (Hidari gedan-barai/ Migi chūdan uchi-uke)*

Assuming a right back stance, drive the left fist down to deliver a downward block while simultaneously pulling the right fist back to execute a middle-level inside-to-outside block to the right side of the body. This technique is known as *kasui-ken* (fire and water fists).

12-A) Without moving the lower body, extend the right arm downward in front of the body while pulling the left fist back to above the right shoulder.

12-B) Draw the left foot back toward the right foot while lowering the left arm and pulling the right fist back towards the hip.

### 12) *Shizentai/Gedan-gamae*

Moving in synchronization with the left foot, raise the hips into a natural-posture L stance while assuming a left downward-block posture.

13-A) Step forward with the left foot into a slightly shortened left front stance while drawing the right hand, formed into a knife hand, out in front of the body with the palm facing upward. At the same time, open and raise the left hand to meet the right arm as it travels upward in front of the chest.

13-B) With the left hand resting on top of the right wrist, extend the right arm upward and out in front of the body at a slight angle to the left.

### 13) *Moto-dachi/Soete kake-dori*

As the right arm reaches full extension, rotate the hand counter-clockwise and pull the right elbow back toward the right hip, grasping the right wrist with the left hand to perform an augmented hooking grasp.

### 14-A) *Tsukami-dori/Migi mae-geri*

Pull the right hand back to the right hip, closing it into a fist to perform a grasping clutch while delivering a right front snap kick.

### 14-B) *Hidari chūdan hirate osae-uke*

Retracting the kicking leg, drop the left hand out in front of the body to perform a left middle-level pressing block while drawing the right fist up to above the head.

### 14) *Kōsa-dachi/Migi tate uraken-uchi*

Thrusting forward off the left foot, plant the right foot on the floor and immediately draw the left foot behind it into a cross-legged stance while executing a right vertical back-fist strike.

15-A) Thrusting the left foot back at an angle to the left, extend the left arm out in front of the body while drawing the right fist back to below the left underarm.

### 15) *Zenkutsu-dachi/Migi chūdan uchi-uke*

Assuming a right front stance, execute a right middle-level inside-to-outside block.

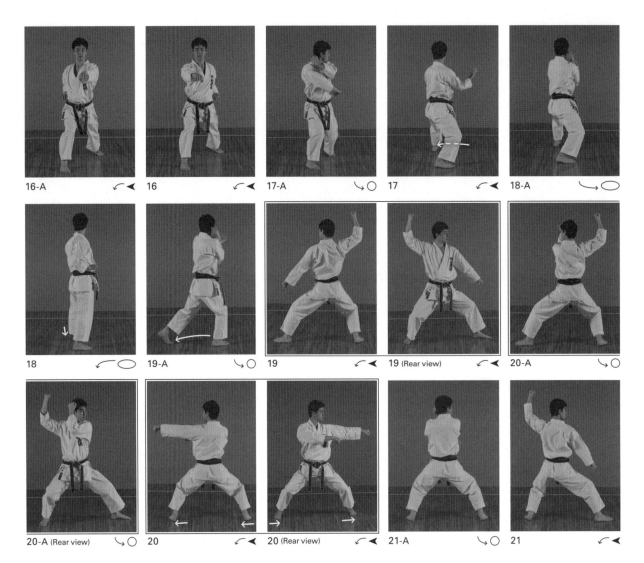

**16-A) *Zenkutsu-dachi/Hidari chūdan gyaku-zuki***
Deliver a left middle-level reverse punch.

**16) *Zenkutsu-dachi/Migi chūdan jun-zuki***
Deliver a right middle-level front punch.

17-A) Turning the head to the left, draw the right arm across the front of the body to the left-hand side while pulling the left fist up to above the right shoulder.

**17) *Kōkutsu-dachi/Kasui-ken* (*Hidari gedan-barai/ Migi chūdan uchi-uke*)**
Slide the left foot across the back and turn the hips to the left to assume a right back stance facing the opposite direction while simultaneously executing a left downward block and right middle-level inside-to-outside block to the right.

18-A) Maintaining a strong back stance, extend the right arm downward in front of the body while pulling the left fist back to above the right shoulder.

**18) *Renoji-dachi/Gedan-gamae***
Draw the left foot back into an L stance while assuming a left downward-block posture.

19-A) Turning the head to the left, draw the left foot out to the left-hand side while extending the right arm downward across the front of the body and pulling the left fist up to above the right shoulder.

**19) *Kōkutsu-dachi/Manji-uke***
Turning 90 degrees to the left, assume a right back stance while drawing the right arm back strongly and driving the left arm downward to execute a hi-low block.

**20-A) *Kōkutsu-dachi/Hidari chūdan ude-uke***
Maintaining a strong back stance, draw the left fist back, pulling the forearm across the front of the body to execute a middle-level forearm block.

**20) *Kiba-dachi/Sokumen morote-zuki***
Thrusting off the right foot, drive the left foot to the left with a gliding step (*suri-ashi*), immediately followed by the right foot, assuming a straddle-leg stance while executing a side double-fist punch to the left.

21-A) Turning the head to the right to face the opposite side, extend the left arm across the front of the body to the right while pulling the right fist up to above the left shoulder.

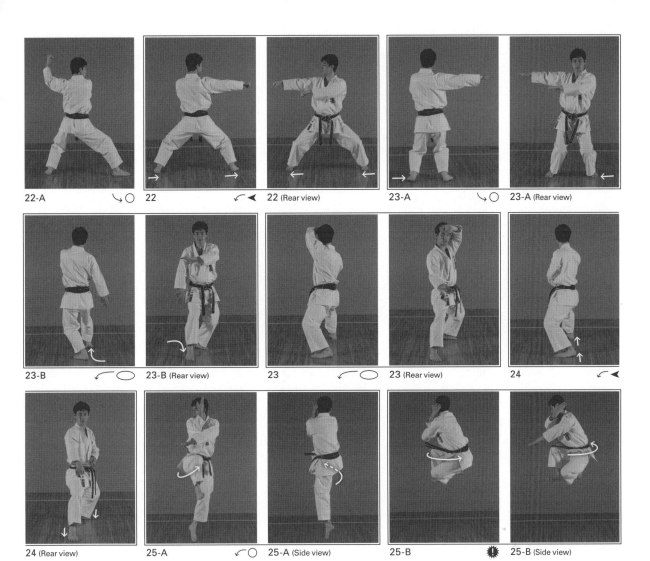

**22-A** ↘○ | **22** ↙◀ | **22** (Rear view) | **23-A** ↘○ | **23-A** (Rear view)

**23-B** ↙○ | **23-B** (Rear view) | **23** ↙○ | **23** (Rear view) | **24** ↙◀

**24** (Rear view) | **25-A** ↙○ | **25-A** (Side view) | **25-B** ✹ | **25-B** (Side view)

### 21) *Kōkutsu-dachi/Manji-uke*
Pull the hips back toward the left leg to assume a left back stance while drawing the left arm back and driving the right arm downward to execute a hi-low block.

### 22-A) *Kōkutsu-dachi/Migi chūdan ude-uke*
Draw the right arm back across the front of the chest to execute a middle-level forearm block.

### 22) *Kiba-dachi/Sokumen morote-zuki*
Thrust off the left foot toward the right, shifting into a straddle-leg stance while delivering a side double-fist punch to the right-hand side.

23-A) Turn the head to the left while simultaneously opening the hands and drawing the left foot in toward the right foot without raising the hips.

23-B) Slide the right foot forward, drawing the right hand in the same direction in a low scooping motion while raising the left elbow.

### 23) *Kōkutsu-dachi/Morote jō-uke*
Assuming a left back stance, raise the right hand to approximately waist level and the left hand to above the forehead to deliver a two-handed block against a

*jō* (stick, or staff) attack. The right elbow is positioned against the right hip while the left forearm is above the head with the left elbow pulled back to the rear.

### 24) *Kōkutsu-dachi/Jō-zukami tsuki-otoshi*
Thrusting off the left foot, drive the body forward while maintaining a back stance, driving both hands, closed into fists, downward at an angle in front of the body to execute a *jō* grab. Thrust the right fist forward with the back of the hand facing upward while drawing the left fist down to the midsection with the inside of the left wrist resting against the lower abdomen.

25-A) Pivoting on the left foot, rapidly turn the hips to the left, raising the right knee while drawing the right hand up toward the left shoulder and extending the left arm across the front of the chest to the right-hand side of the body.

### 25-B) *Tenshin/Tobi-gaeshi*
Launching off the left leg, drive the right knee upward to leap into the air with a *kiai* while turning the body to the left. While in midair, the right hand is positioned above the left shoulder while the left arm extends across the front of the body.

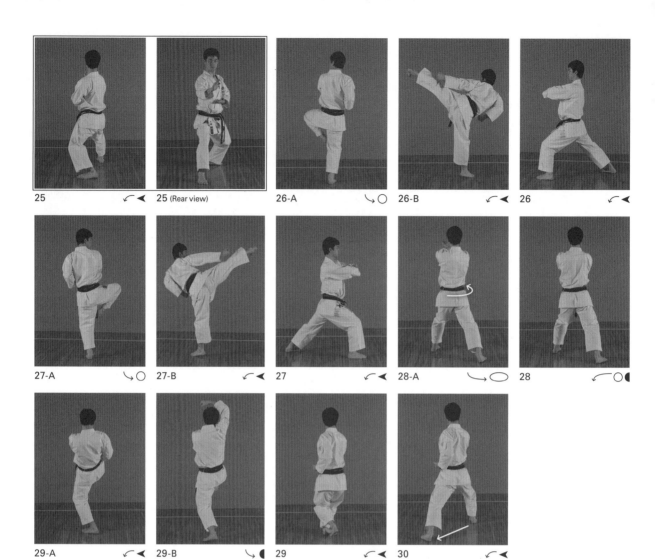

25     25 (Rear view)     26-A     26-B     26

27-A     27-B     27     28-A     28

29-A     29-B     29     30

### 25) *Kōkutsu-dachi / Migi chūdan shutō-uke*

Completing a 360-degree turn (to face the same orientation as prior to the jump), plant both feet at the same time into a left back stance while simultaneously executing a right middle-level knife-hand block.

### 26-A) *Kata-ashi-dachi / Koshi-gamae*

Turning the head to the left, draw the sole of the left foot up to just above the inside of the right knee to assume a one-legged stance while pulling both fists back to above the right hip.

### 26-B) *Hidari yoko ke-age / Hidari yoko-mawashi uraken-uchi*

Deliver a left side snap kick to the left while executing a side round back-fist strike in the same direction with the left arm.

### 26) *Zenkutsu-dachi / Migi mae empi-uchi*

Plant the left foot in the direction of the kick into a left front stance while simultaneously delivering a right front elbow strike against the palm of the left hand.

### 27-A) *Kata-ashi-dachi / Koshi-gamae*

Turning the head to the right to face the opposite direction, lift the right knee to assume a one-legged stance,

bringing the sole of the right foot up to just above the inside of the left knee while drawing both fists to above the left hip.

### 27-B) *Migi yoko ke-age / Migi yoko-mawashi uraken-uchi*

Deliver a right side snap kick to the right while simultaneously executing a side round back-fist strike in the same direction with the right arm.

### 27) *Zenkutsu-dachi / Hidari mae empi-uchi*

Plant the right foot in the direction of the kick, assuming a right front stance while executing a left front elbow strike against the palm of the right hand.

28-A) Without moving the location of the feet, rotate the hips to the left while drawing the right elbow in toward the body and then extending the right arm out in front of the body at a slight angle upward to the left with the left hand resting on top of the right wrist.

### 28) *Moto-dachi / Soete kake-dori*

Pull the right elbow back to the right hip, grasping the right wrist with the left hand to perform an augmented hooking grasp.

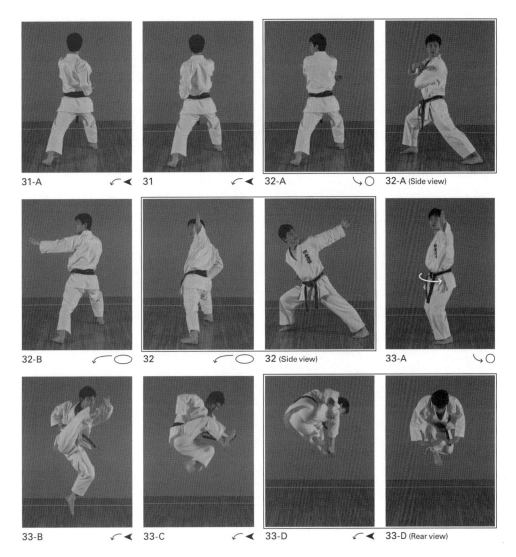

31-A    31    32-A    32-A (Side view)

32-B    32    32 (Side view)    33-A

33-B    33-C    33-D    33-D (Rear view)

**29-A)** *Tsukami-dori/Migi mae-geri*
Pull the right hand back to the right hip, closing it into a fist to perform a grasping clutch while delivering a right front snap kick.

**29-B)** *Hidari chūdan hirate osae-uke*
Retracting the kicking leg, execute a left middle-level pressing block while drawing the right fist up to above the head.

**29)** *Kōsa-dachi/Migi tate uraken-uchi*
Thrusting forward off the left foot, assume a cross-legged stance while delivering a right vertical back-fist strike.

**30)** *Zenkutsu-dachi/Migi chūdan uchi-uke*
Step back with the left foot into a right front stance while performing a right middle-level inside-to-outside block.

**31-A)** *Zenkutsu-dachi/Hidari chūdan gyaku-zuki*
Deliver a left middle-level reverse punch.

**31)** *Zenkutsu-dachi/Migi chūdan jun-zuki*
Deliver a right middle-level front punch.

32-A) Turning the head to the left, extend the left arm across the front of the body while pulling the right hand back toward the left shoulder.

32-B) Open and draw the left hand around the left-hand side of the body in a large arcing motion while pulling the right fist back to the right hip.

**32)** *Zenkutsu-dachi/Hidari ushiro jōdan haishu-uke*
Leaning forward slightly with the upper body, complete the motion of the left hand to deliver an upper-level back-hand block to the rear.

33-A) Pivoting on the left foot, turn the hips sharply to the left while drawing the right foot back toward the left foot.

33-B) Thrusting off the left leg, bring the right foot around in a sweeping motion toward the left hand.

**33-C)** *Jōdan tobi ashi-barai*
Deliver an upper-level jumping leg sweep with the right foot, slapping the palm of the left hand with the sole of the right foot.

**33-D)** *Tobi ushiro-geri*
Thrust the left leg back to deliver a jumping back kick.

33    33 (Side view)    34-A (Side view)    34

34 (Side view)    35    36-A    36

37    38-A    38    39

### 33) *Ryōte-fuse*

Completing a 360-degree turn to the left, drop to the floor with the upper body extended over the bent right leg and the left leg extended to the rear. The hands are positioned approximately shoulder-width apart and turned inward at an angle.

34-A) Raising the upper body sharply, rapidly interchange the locations of the feet, pulling the right foot back while drawing the left foot forward. At the same time, pull the left hand back to above the right shoulder.

### 34) *Kasei kōkutsu-dachi/Morote gedan shutō-uke*

Assume a right back stance with the hips positioned lower than a conventional back stance while delivering a two-handed downward knife-hand block.

### 35) *Kōkutsu-dachi/Migi chūdan shutō-uke*

Step forward with the right foot into a standard left back stance while performing a right middle-level knife-hand block.

36-A) Draw the left leg around the body to the left, turning the body in the same direction while thrusting the left hand back toward the right-hand side of the body.

### 36) *Zenkutsu-dachi/Hidari chūdan uchi-uke*

Completing a 270-degree rotation to the left, shift into a left front stance while performing a middle-level inside-to-outside block with the left arm.

### 37) *Zenkutsu-dachi/Migi chūdan oi-zuki*

Step forward with the right foot into a right front stance while delivering a right middle-level lunge punch.

38-A) Turning the head to the right, pull the right foot back and across to the opposite side of the left foot, turning the hips to the right while simultaneously pulling the right fist across the chest to below the left underarm and thrusting the left fist out across the chest toward the right.

### 38) *Zenkutsu-dachi/Migi chūdan uchi-uke*

Complete a 180-degree turn of the hips to the right into a right front stance facing the opposite direction while executing a middle-level inside-to-outside block with the right arm.

### 39) *Zenkutsu-dachi/Hidari chūdan oi-zuki*

Step forward with the left foot into a left front stance while delivering a left middle-level lunge punch.

Yame-A

Yame

*Yame*-A) Draw the left foot back, placing it alongside the right foot in an open V stance while crossing the arms in front of the body with the left arm above the right.

### Yame

Extend the arms downward in front of the body so that the fists are positioned in front of the hips as in the original starting ready position and maintain a state of physical and mental readiness (*zanshin*).

**TECHNICAL ANALYSIS**
## Movements 4-B–4

In response to an opponent grabbing the wrist (photo 1), break the hold by pulling the elbow back sharply while turning the forearm inward (photo 2).

1

2

**TECHNICAL ANALYSIS**
## Movements 7–10

After blocking an attacker's lunge punch and grabbing his wrist (photos 1 and 2), first deliver a front snap kick while pulling the opponent forward (photo 3), then deflect the punching arm while retracting the kicking leg (photo 4), following through with a back-fist strike to the face (photo 5). As the attacker responds with a reverse punch, step back and block with an inside-to-outside block (photo 6), and then counter with a two-punch combination to the midsection (photos 7 and 8).

1

2

3

4

5

6

7

8

A wooden statue of the legendary Indian monk Bodhidharma, known as Daruma Taishi in Japan, who is credited with having established the Zen (Chan) sect of Buddhism. Some scholars believe that karate's roots can be traced back to the teachings of Bodhidharma.

# Jion

Jion, Jitte and Jiin, which belong to the same family of *kata*, are all believed to have come from the Tomari region.

Long ago, it was commonly thought that these *kata* had come from China. This assumption was based on the appearance in ancient documents from China of the characters used to write *jion* (慈恩), a Buddhist term. Further reinforcing this view was a Buddhist temple bearing the name Jionji (慈恩寺, literally "Jion Temple"), which was known for its tradition of martial arts. Today, however, the correct assumption appears to be that these *kata* originated at Jionji and, from there, were conveyed to the Tomari region. As the characters in its name implies, the Jion *kata* features movements suggesting maturity and tranquility, which conceal an inner vigorous spirit.

While Jion has only been passed down within the Shōtōkan and Wadō-ryū styles, it is not a particularly difficult *kata* and could be thought of as a compilation of various elements from the Heian series of *kata*. As such, for anyone capable of properly performing Heian Nos. 1 to 5, Jion would be a fairly easy *kata* to learn. It would only be necessary to acquire a proper understanding of the meanings of the various techniques contained in the *kata*. It contains several techniques deserving of close study, such as those appearing at the end of the *kata*—deflecting an attacker's punch while grabbing his wrist, then pulling him in while delivering a punch to the side of the body—which make use of the opponent's strength to deliver an effective counterattack. Combining a variety of basic stances, including straddle-leg stances, front stances and back stances, Jion is a representative *kata* of the Shōtōkan style and a compulsory *kata* for the Japan Karatedo Federation. As such, it is a *kata* that should be practiced frequently.

## Jion

Shizentai

Yōi

Yōi (Detail)

1-A

1

### *Shizentai* (Natural posture)
*Soto hachiji-dachi* (open V stance) with both fists positioned in front of the hips.

### *Yōi* (Ready position)/*Jiai no kamae*
Slide the left foot in toward the right foot to assume a closed parallel stance (*heisoku-dachi*) while bending the arms and drawing the hands together in front of the chin. The left hand opens and wraps around the right fist with the elbows tucked closely to the sides of the body. This posture is known as *jiai no kamae* (posture of benevolence).

1-A) Stepping back with the left foot, drive the right fist downward at an angle in front of the body while pulling the left hand back to above the right shoulder.

### 1) *Zenkutsu-dachi/Kōsa-uke*
Completing the step backward with the left foot into a right front stance, execute a cross block with the right arm delivering a middle-level inside-to-outside block while the left arm performs a downward block.

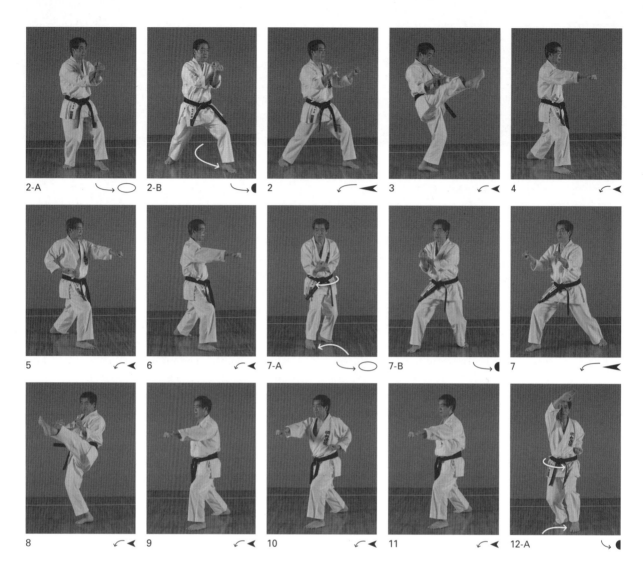

| | | | | |
|---|---|---|---|---|
| 2-A | 2-B | 2 | 3 | 4 |
| 5 | 6 | 7-A | 7-B | 7 |
| 8 | 9 | 10 | 11 | 12-A |

2-A) Drawing the left foot forward past the right foot and then out at a 45-degree angle to the left, bend the left elbow to raise the left forearm, crossing the arms at the wrists with the back of the right fist resting against the underside of the left fist and the backs of the hands facing outward.

2-B) Stepping forward with the left foot, draw the forearms up slightly and outward in preparation to execute the subsequent blocking technique.

### 2) *Zenkutsu-dachi/Chūdan kakiwake-uke*
Complete the step forward with the left foot into a left front stance while pulling the elbows back to the body and drawing the fists apart to perform a middle-level separating block, paying special attention to keep the elbows tucked in near the body

### 3) *Migi mae-geri*
Keeping the arms in place, deliver a front snap kick with the right leg.

### 4) *Zenkutsu-dachi/Migi chūdan oi-zuki*
Plant the right foot forward into a right front stance while executing a right middle-level lunge punch.

### 5) *Zenkutsu-dachi/Hidari chūdan gyaku-zuki*
Deliver a middle-level reverse punch with the left arm.

### 6) *Zenkutsu-dachi/Migi chūdan zuki*
Deliver a middle-level punch with the right arm.

7-A) Turning the head to the right, draw the right foot back halfway toward the left foot and across to the right-hand side, turning the body 90 degrees in the same direction. At the same time, pull the right elbow in toward the body and raise the left forearm in front of the chest, crossing the arms at the wrists in front of the body.

7-B) Stepping forward with the right foot, draw the forearms up slightly and outward.

### 7) *Zenkutsu-dachi/Chūdan kakiwake-uke*
Complete the step forward with the right foot into a right front stance, pulling the elbows back and drawing the fists apart to perform a reverse wedge block.

### 8) *Hidari mae-geri*
Keeping the arms in place, deliver a front snap kick with the left leg.

12

13

14-A

14

15

16-A

16

17

18-A

18

18 (Rear view)

**9) *Zenkutsu-dachi/Hidari chūdan oi-zuki***
Plant the left foot forward into a left front stance while executing a middle-level lunge punch with the left arm.

**10) *Zenkutsu-dachi/Migi chūdan gyaku-zuki***
Deliver a right middle-level reverse punch.

**11) *Zenkutsu-dachi/Hidari chūdan zuki***
Deliver a left middle-level punch.

12-A) Draw the left foot back and to the left approximately one half-step while turning the hips sharply to the left. At the same time, pull the left fist back to above the left hip while extending the right arm upward at an angle in front of the body.

**12) *Zenkutsu-dachi/Hidari jōdan age-uke***
Step forward with the left foot into a left front stance while delivering an upper-level rising block with the left arm.

**13) *Zenkutsu-dachi/Migi chūdan gyaku-zuki***
Deliver a right middle-level reverse punch.

14-A) Stepping forward with the right foot, pull the right fist back to above the right hip and extend the left arm upward at an angle in front of the body.

**14) *Zenkutsu-dachi/Migi jōdan age-uke***
Complete the step forward with the right foot into a right front stance while executing a right upper-level rising block.

**15) *Zenkutsu-dachi/Hidari chūdan gyaku-zuki***
Deliver a reverse punch with the left arm.

16-A) Step forward with the left foot while pulling the left fist back to above the left hip and extending the right arm upward.

**16) *Zenkutsu-dachi/Hidari jōdan age-uke***
Complete the step forward with the left foot into a left front stance while delivering a left upper-level rising block.

**17) *Zenkutsu-dachi/Migi chūdan oi-zuki***
Step forward with the right foot into a right front stance while delivering a right middle-level lunge punch with a *kiai*.

18-A) Draw the left foot across the rear to the right-hand side, pivoting on the right foot to turn 270 degrees to the left (to face toward the right side). At the same time, pull the left fist up to above the right shoulder and thrust the right fist across the front of the body and downward.

**18) *Kōkutsu-dachi/Manji-uke***
Assuming a right back stance, draw the right arm back strongly while driving the left arm downward to execute a hi-low block. The right arm performs an upper-level inside-to-outside block to the rear while the left arm delivers a downward block to the front.

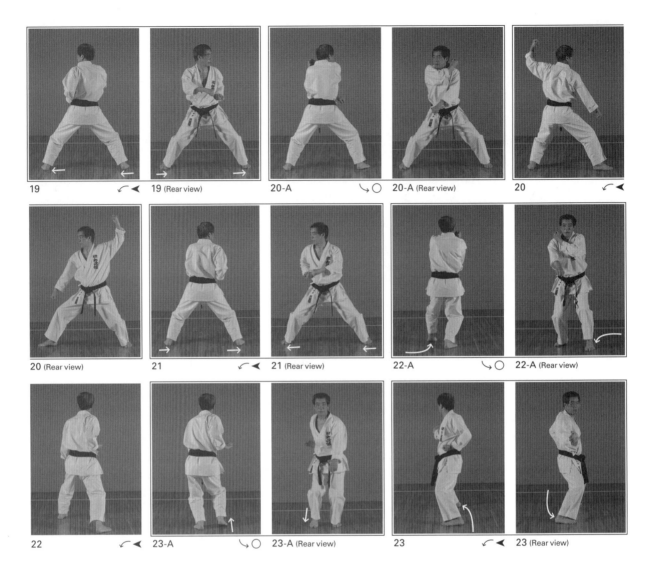

19) *Kiba-dachi/Migi chūdan kagi-zuki*

Thrusting off the right foot, shift into a straddle-leg stance sliding slightly to the left while driving the right arm downward and across the front of the chest to deliver a middle-level hook punch.

20-A) Turn the head to the right while pulling the right fist back to above the left shoulder and driving the left fist across the front of the body to the right side.

20) *Kōkutsu-dachi/Manji-uke*

Transferring the center of gravity toward the left leg, shift into a left back stance while drawing the left arm back strongly and driving the right arm downward to execute a hi-low block.

21-A) Thrust off the left foot into a straddle-leg stance, sliding slightly to the right while executing a middle-level hook punch with the left arm.

22-A) Draw the left foot in toward the right foot while pulling the left fist up to above the right shoulder and extending the right arm downward in front of the body.

22) *Zenkutsu-dachi/Hidari gedan-barai*

Step forward with the left foot into a left front stance while delivering a downward block with the left arm.

23-A) Drawing the right foot forward, open the right hand into a palm heel, keeping it positioned above the right hip.

23) *Kiba-dachi/Migi teishō-uchi*

Waiting until the last possible instant to turn the hips, complete the step forward with the right foot into a straddle leg stance while delivering a palm-heel strike with the right hand.

24-A) Stepping forward with the left foot, open the left hand in preparation to deliver a palm-heel strike.

24) *Kiba-dachi/Hidari teishō-uchi*

Complete the step forward with the left foot into a straddle-leg stance while executing a palm-heel strike with the left hand

25-A) Step forward with the right foot while preparing the right hand to deliver a palm-heel strike.

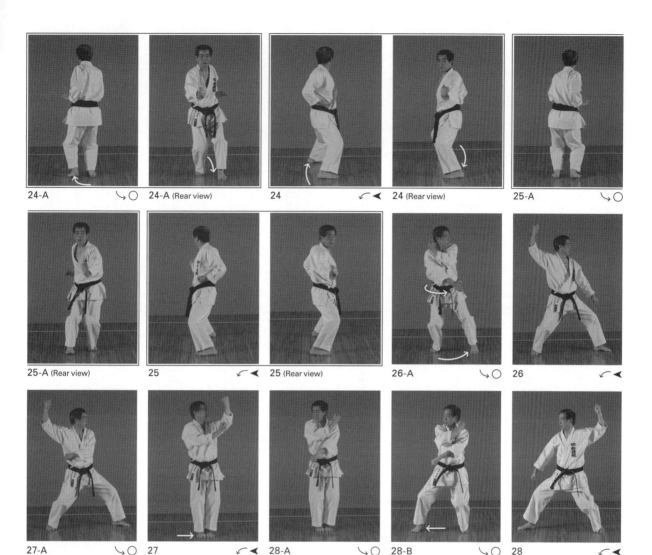

24-A    24-A (Rear view)    24    24 (Rear view)    25-A

25-A (Rear view)    25    25 (Rear view)    26-A    26

27-A    27    28-A    28-B    28

29-A

29

### 25) *Kiba-dachi/Migi teishō-uchi*
Follow through with the right leg into a straddle-leg stance while delivering a palm-heel strike with the right hand.

26-A) Draw the left foot back, pivoting on the right foot to turn the body 90 degrees to the left while pulling the left fist up to above the right shoulder and extending the right arm downward in front of the body.

### 26) *Kōkutsu-dachi/Manji-uke*
Assuming a right back stance, draw the right arm back strongly while driving the left arm downward to execute a hi-low block.

27-A) Maintaining a solid back stance, drive the left fist across the front of the body to the right-hand side while keeping the right arm in place.

### 27) *Heisoku-dachi/Jōdan morote-uke*
Thrusting off the right foot, drive the right leg in toward the left leg to assume a closed parallel stance while executing an upper-level augmented block to the left-hand side of the body. In the completed position, the

knees are straight and the left elbow is positioned at a 45-degree angle to the body with the eyes directed toward the left wrist.

28-A) Turning the head to the right, pull the right fist up to above the left shoulder while driving the left arm downward across the front of the body.

28-B) Draw the right foot out directly to the right side.

### 28) *Kōkutsu-dachi/Manji-uke*
Complete the step outward with the right foot into a left back stance while drawing the left arm back strongly and driving the right arm downward to execute a hi-low block.

29-A) Maintaining a strong back stance, pull the right fist across the front of the body to the left-hand side.

### 29) *Heisoku-dachi/Jōdan morote-uke*
Thrust off the left foot to drive the left leg in toward the right leg into a closed parallel stance while executing an upper-level augmented block to the right-hand side of the body, directing the eyes toward the right wrist.

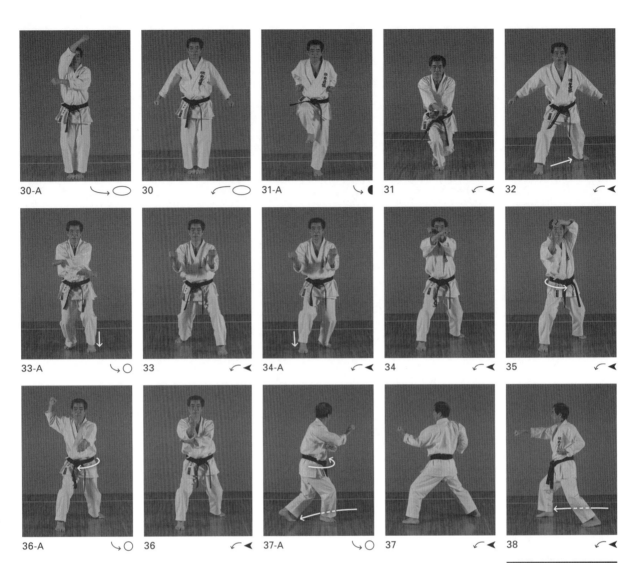

30-A) Keeping the left arm in position, draw the right arm up and over toward the left-hand side in a large sweeping motion.

### 30) Heisoku-dachi/Ryōwan-gamae
As the right fist reaches the level of the left fist on the opposite side, draw both arms downward and out to the sides of the body.

31-A) Raise the right knee sharply while pulling the elbows straight back, drawing the fists to above the hips.

### 31) Kōsa-dachi/Gedan jūji-uke
Thrust forward off the left foot, dropping the hips into a cross-legged stance while delivering a downward X-block with the right fist above the left.

### 32) Zenkutsu-dachi/Ryōwan gedan kakiwake-uke
Thrusting off the right foot, extend the left leg back sharply, keeping the right knee bent to assume a right front stance while driving the fists directly back to the sides of the body to execute a double downward separating block. Keep the arms as straight as possible when executing the technique.

33-A) Stepping forward with the left foot, draw the fists across the front of the body, crossing the left arm over the right.

### 33) Zenkutsu-dachi/Ryōwan uchi-uke
Complete the step forward with the left foot into a left front stance while delivering a double inside-to-outside block.

34-A) Keeping the arms in place, step forward with the right foot.

### 34) Zenkutsu-dachi/Jōdan jūji-uke
Complete the step forward with the right foot into a right front stance while driving the arms upward to execute an upper-level X-block with the right arm positioned on the far side of the left.

### 35) Zenkutsu-dachi/Migi ura-uchi zuki/Hidari age-uke
Turning the hips to the left, drive the right arm forward to deliver a close punch while pulling the left arm back to perform a rising block.

### 36-A) Zenkutsu-dachi/Migi jōdan nagashi-uke
Turning the hips to the right, pull the right elbow back past the side of the head to perform an upper-level sweeping block while extending the left arm directly out in front of the body.

40

41-A

41

41 (Rear view)

42-A

42-A (Rear view)

42

42 (Rear view)

43-A

43-A (Rear view)

43

44-A

44

### 36) *Zenkutsu-dachi/Migi jōdan ura-uchi zuki*

Drawing the left fist back toward the body, drive the right fist forward to execute an upper-level close punch, using the back of the left fist to support the right elbow.

37-A) Draw the left foot around the body to the left, turning the hips in the same direction while thrusting the left fist back toward the right-hand side of the body.

### 37) *Zenkutsu-dachi/Hidari chūdan uchi-uke*

Completing a 270-degree rotation of the body to the left, assume a left front stance while performing a middle-level inside-to-outside block with the left arm.

### 38) *Zenkutsu-dachi/Migi chūdan oi-zuki*

Step forward with the right foot into a right front stance while delivering a right middle-level lunge punch.

39-A) Turning the head to the right, pull the right foot back and across to the opposite side of the left foot to turn the body 180 degrees to the right. At the same time, pull the right fist back to the left side of the body below the left underarm while extending the left arm across the front of the chest toward the opposite side.

### 39) *Zenkutsu-dachi/Migi chūdan uchi-uke*

Assume a right front stance while executing a middle-level inside-to-outside block with the right arm.

### 40) *Zenkutsu-dachi/Hidari chūdan oi-zuki*

Step forward with the left foot into a left front stance while delivering a left middle-level lunge punch.

41-A) Turn the head to the left while drawing the left foot across to the left, pivoting on the right foot to turn the body 90 degrees to the left. At the same time, pull the left fist back to above the right shoulder and extend the right arm out at angle toward the left.

### 41) *Zenkutsu-dachi/Hidari gedan-barai*

Assume a left front stance while performing a left downward block.

42-A) Keeping the left arm in place, swing the right leg up sharply in front of the body while raising the right fist to above the head.

### 42) *Kiba-dachi/Fumikomi/Migi otoshi-uke*

Deliver a stamping kick in front of the body, assuming a straddle-leg stance while executing a dropping block to the right side of the body. In the completed position, the right elbow is approximately one fist's width from the side of the body with the forearm parallel to the floor and extending at a 45-degree angle to the left relative to the position of the feet.

43-A) Swing the left leg up and across the front of the body to the right-hand side while drawing the left fist up to above the head.

### 43) *Kiba-dachi/Fumikomi/Hidari otoshi-uke*

Deliver a stamping kick with the left leg into a straddle-leg stance while executing a dropping block with the left arm.

44-A) Swing the right leg up and across the front of the body to the left-hand side while raising the right fist to above the head.

### 44) *Kiba-dachi/Fumikomi/Migi otoshi-uke*

Deliver a stamping kick with the right leg into a straddle-leg stance while driving the right arm down to perform a dropping block.

45-A    45-B    45    46-A

46    Yame-A    Yame    Shizentai

### 45-A) *Jōdan tsukami-uke*

Turning the hips 90 degrees to the left, pull the left foot in toward and alongside the right foot while drawing the right hand upward and across to the left-hand side. When extending the right arm, open the right hand as if to grab an opponent's arm.

45-B) Sliding the left foot out to the left-hand side, draw the left fist out in the same direction while closing the right hand into a fist and pulling the right elbow back to the right-hand side.

### 45) *Kiba-dachi/Hidari yumi-zuki*

Assume a straddle-leg stance while delivering a left bow punch, with the left arm delivering a straight punch to the left-hand side of the body and the right elbow pulled back in the opposite direction.

### 46-A) *Kiba-dachi/Jōdan tsukami-uke*

Turn the head to the right and draw the left hand upward and across to the right-hand side as if to grab an opponent's arm. At the same time, pull the right elbow back and lower the right fist to above the right hip.

### 46) *Kiba-dachi/Migi yumi-zuki*

Thrust off the left foot to slide the right foot, followed by the left foot, out to the right-hand side, maintaining a straddle-leg stance while executing a right bow punch with a *kiai*. The right arm performs a straight punch to the right while the left elbow travels back in the opposite direction.

Yame-A) Turning the head to the left to face the front, draw the right foot in toward the left foot and bring the right fist back toward the front of the body while lowering the left elbow and opening the left hand

Yame-B) Aligning the feet into a closed parallel stance, pull the right fist back to in front of the chin while raising the left hand to the same location, wrapping the left hand over the right fist to assume the same ready position in which the *kata* began.

### Yame

Draw the left foot out to the left side into an open V stance while lowering both fists to the front of the hips, the same natural-posture stance assumed prior to starting the *kata*.

---

**TECHNICAL ANALYSIS**
## Movements 18–19

Block a reverse-punch attack from the side with a hi-low block (photo 1), immediately followed by a hook-punch counterattack to the midsection (photo 2).

1

2

## TECHNICAL ANALYSIS
### Movements 26–27

Upon blocking a front snap kick with a hi-low block (photo 1), the subsequent augmented block lends itself to several applications. It can be used to deflect a follow-up reverse-punch attack (photo 2) or, in response to a lunge punch, as an augmented back-fist strike (photo 3) or a simultaneous sweeping block/back-fist strike (photo 4).

1

2

3

4

## TECHNICAL ANALYSIS
### Movements 28–30

Following the second hi-low block/augmented block combination (photos 1 and 2), the downward sweeping motion of the arms can be used to deliver a hammer-fist strike counterattack to the opponent's midsection (photos 3 and 4).

1

2

3

4

## TECHNICAL ANALYSIS
### Movements 34–36

Block an opponent's lunge-punch attack with an upper-level X-block (photo 1). Follow through with the motion of the arms, turning the hips to deflect the punch while delivering a back-fist strike counterattack (photo 2). As the attacker responds with a reverse punch, sweep his fist past the head while simultaneously launching a punch to the

1

1 (Reverse-angle view)

midsection (photo 3), followed by an augmented back-fist strike to the face (photo 4).

2

2 (Reverse-angle view)

3

3 (Reverse-angle view)

4

4 (Reverse-angle view)

**TECHNICAL ANALYSIS**
## Movements 45-A–46

The closing techniques in Jion assume a grabbing block in response to a lunge punch from the side (photos 1 and 3), followed by a bow punch counterattack (photos 2 and 4).

1

2

3

4

# Jiin

Jiin is believed to be a Tomari-te *kata*. It was said to have been assigned the name Shōkyō by Master Gichin Funakoshi at the time that he changed the characters used to write "karate." Now, however, even within the Shōtōkan style, this *kata* is called Jiin and details regarding its history between then and now remain unclear.

Jiin, commonly grouped in the same family as Jitte and Jion, is not a particularly advanced *kata*. It is considered a *kata* to be learned by karate students progressing from a fundamental level toward a higher stage of proficiency. Straddle-leg stances, front stances and back stances occur frequently throughout Jiin. Unique characteristics include the footwork required to assume a straddle-leg stance following body rotation, sharp rotations of the hips, and maintaining a consistent stepping distance. Accordingly, it demands tenacity and the ability to maintain a proper center of gravity on the part of the practitioner. Jiin is a *kata* rich in variety with such techniques as simultaneous inside and downward blocks, and kick/double punch combinations.

Today, Jiin has become a *kata* that is not often encountered within the Shōtōkan style. This can probably be attributed to the fact that, because it is a *kata* from the Tomari region and Master Yasutsune Itosu did not introduce any modifications to it, Master Funakoshi did not actively teach it to his students.

With some exceptions, it appears that this *kata* has not been passed down within other styles of karate. To prevent Jiin from becoming lost forever, it should be included as a compulsory component of *kata* study to ensure that it gets passed on to future generations of karate practitioners. Accordingly, this *kata* could be considered an essential area of focus within the field of karate research.

## Jiin

Shizentai

Yōi

1-A

1

### *Shizentai* (Natural posture)
*Soto hachiji-dachi* (open V stance) with both fists positioned in front of the hips.

### *Yōi* (Ready position)/*Jiai no kamae*
Slide the left foot in toward the right foot to assume a closed parallel stance (*heisoku-dachi*) while bending the elbows to draw the hands together in front of the chin. The left hand opens and wraps around the right fist with the elbows tucked closely to the sides of the body. This posture is known as *jiai no kamae* (posture of benevolence).

1-A) Stepping back with the left foot, drive the left hand downward at an angle in front of the body while pulling the right fist back to above the left shoulder.

### 1) *Zenkutsu-dachi/Kōsa-uke*
Completing the step back with the left foot into a right front stance, execute a cross block with the right arm delivering a downward block while the left arm performs a middle-level inside-to-outside block.

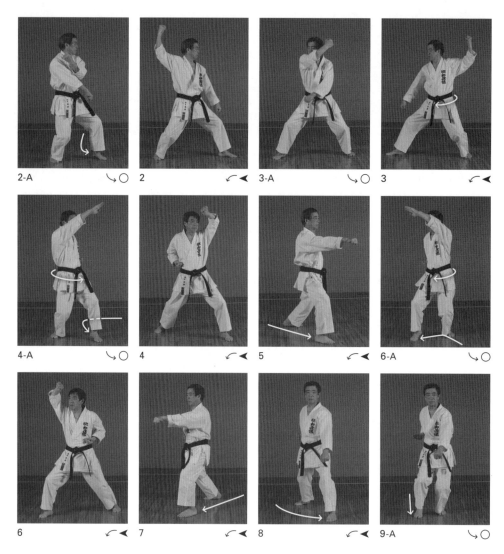

2-A) Turning the head to the left, draw the left foot forward alongside the right foot and then out to the left, pulling the left fist up to above the right shoulder while extending the right arm across the front of the body and downward at an angle.

### 2) *Kōkutsu-dachi/Manji-uke*
Sliding the left foot out to the left side into a right back stance, draw the right arm back strongly while driving the left arm downward to execute a hi-low block. The right arm performs an upper-level inside-to-outside block to the rear while the left arm delivers a downward block to the front.

3-A) Turning the head to the right to face the opposite direction, draw the right fist back to above the left shoulder while extending the left arm across the front of the body.

### 3) *Kōkutsu-dachi/Manji-uke*
Shifting the center of gravity toward the left leg, assume a left back stance facing the opposite direction while drawing the left arm back and driving the right arm downward to execute a hi-low block.

4-A) Turning the head to the left, pull the left foot back toward the right foot while drawing the left fist down to above the left hip and extending the right arm upward at an angle toward the left-hand side.

### 4) *Zenkutsu-dachi/Hidari jōdan age-uke*
Step forward with the left foot at a 45-degree angle to the left into a left front stance while performing an upper-level rising block with the left arm.

### 5) *Zenkutsu-dachi/Migi chūdan oi-zuki*
Step forward with the right foot into a right front stance while delivering a right middle-level lunge punch.

6-A) Turning the head to the right, draw the right foot back toward the left foot and across to the right-hand side, turning the hips 90 degrees in the same direction while pulling the right fist back to the right hip and extending the left arm upward at an angle to the right.

### 6) *Zenkutsu-dachi/Migi jōdan age-uke*
Step forward with the right foot into a right front stance while executing a right upper-level rising block.

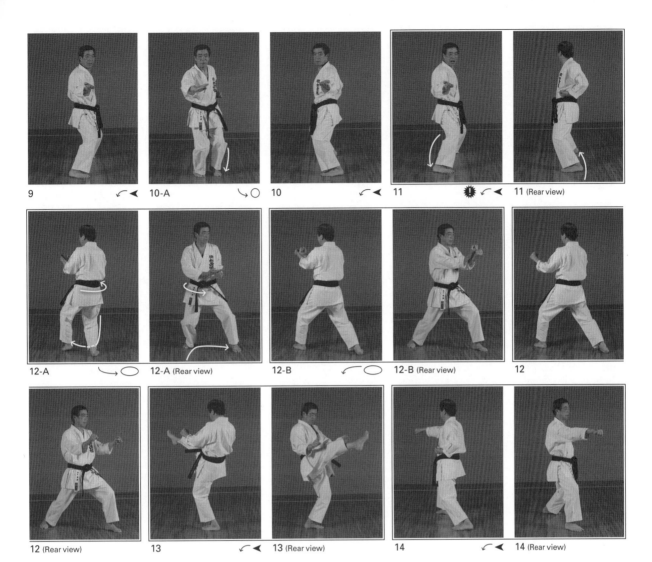

9    10-A    10    11    11 (Rear view)

12-A    12-A (Rear view)    12-B    12-B (Rear view)    12

12 (Rear view)    13    13 (Rear view)    14    14 (Rear view)

### 7) *Zenkutsu-dachi/Hidari chūdan oi-zuki*
Step forward with the left foot into a left front stance while delivering a middle-level lunge punch with the left arm.

### 8) *Zenkutsu-dachi/Hidari gedan-barai*
Draw the left foot across to the left, turning 45 degrees in the same direction into a left front stance while delivering a downward block.

9-A) Step forward with the right foot, extending the left arm out in front of the body while preparing to launch a knife-hand strike with the right arm.

### 9) *Kiba-dachi/Migi chūdan shutō-uchi*
Complete the step forward with the right foot into a straddle-leg stance while delivering a middle-level knife-hand strike with the right arm.

10-A) Keeping the right arm extended out in front of the body, step forward with the left foot while preparing the left hand to deliver a knife-hand strike.

### 10) *Kiba-dachi/Hidari chūdan shutō-uchi*
Complete the step forward with the left foot into a straddle-leg stance while executing a left middle-level knife-hand strike.

### 11) *Kiba-dachi/Migi chūdan shutō-uchi*
Step forward again with the right leg into a straddle-leg stance, delivering a right middle-level knife-hand strike with a *kiai*.

12-A) Draw the left foot in toward the right foot and then back at a 45-degree angle to the rear, turning the hips 135 degrees to the left while bringing the forearms together level with the waist, crossing them at the wrists with the right fist resting on top of the left fist and the backs of the hands facing downward.

12-B) Stepping forward with the left leg, draw the forearms upward in front of the chest.

### 12) *Zenkutsu-dachi/Chūdan kakiwake-uke*
Assuming a left front stance, draw the fists apart to perform a middle-level separating block, keeping the elbows tucked in near the body.

### 13) *Migi mae-geri*
Keeping the arms in place, deliver a front snap kick with the right leg.

### 14) *Zenkutsu-dachi/Migi chūdan oi-zuki*
Plant the right foot forward into a right front stance while executing a right middle-level lunge punch.

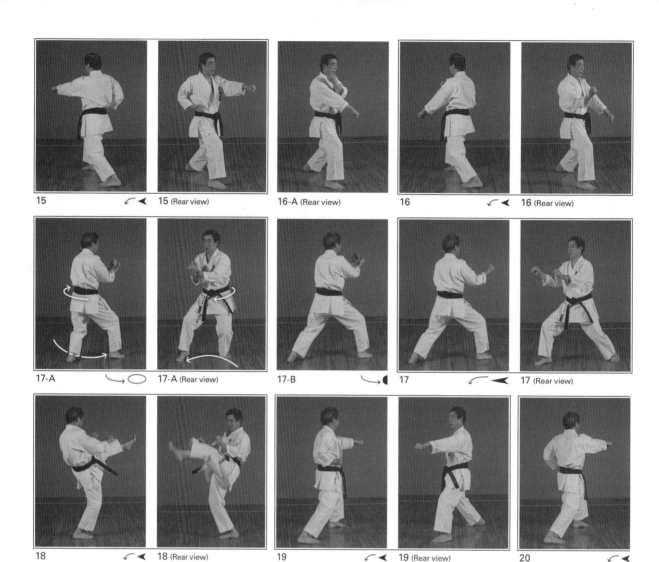

15    15 (Rear view)    16-A (Rear view)    16    16 (Rear view)

17-A    17-A (Rear view)    17-B    17    17 (Rear view)

18    18 (Rear view)    19    19 (Rear view)    20

**15) *Zenkutsu-dachi/Hidari chūdan gyaku-zuki***
Deliver a middle-level reverse punch with the left arm.

16-A) Pull the left fist back to above the right shoulder while extending the right arm downward across the body to the left-hand side.

**16) *Zenkutsu-dachi/Kōsa-uke***
Perform a cross block, with the right arm executing a middle-level inside-to-outside block while the left arm delivers a downward block.

17-A) Draw the right foot back slightly toward the left foot and across to the right-hand side, turning 90 degrees in the same direction while raising the left fist and drawing both elbows back toward the body.

17-B) Stepping forward with the right foot, bring the arms up in front of the chest, crossing them at the wrists with the back of the left fist resting against the right fist.

**17) *Zenkutsu-dachi/Chūdan kakiwake-uke***
Complete the step forward with the right foot into a right front stance while drawing the fists apart to perform a middle-level separating block.

**18) *Hidari mae-geri***
Deliver a front snap kick with the left leg.

**19) *Zenkutsu-dachi/Hidari chūdan oi-zuki***
Plant the left foot forward into a left front stance while delivering a left middle-level lunge punch.

**20) *Zenkutsu-dachi/Migi chūdan gyaku-zuki***
Execute a middle-level reverse punch with the right arm.

20 (Rear view)

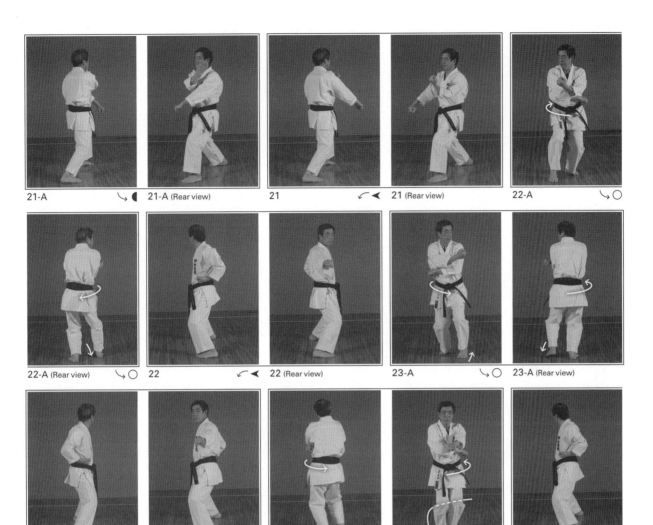

| | | | | |
|---|---|---|---|---|
| 21-A | 21-A (Rear view) | 21 | 21 (Rear view) | 22-A |
| 22-A (Rear view) | 22 | 22 (Rear view) | 23-A | 23-A (Rear view) |
| 23 | 23 (Rear view) | 24-A | 24-A (Rear view) | 24 |

24 (Rear view)

25-A

21-A) Pull the right fist back toward the left shoulder while extending the left arm across the front of the body to the right-hand side.

### 21) *Zenkutsu-dachi/Kōsa-uke*

Execute a cross block, with the left arm performing an inside-to-outside block while the right arm delivers a downward block.

22-A) Pivoting on the left foot, draw the right foot toward the left foot, turning the hips to the right while simultaneously pulling the left fist back toward the right shoulder and drawing the right arm across the front of the body to the left-hand side.

### 22) *Kiba-dachi/Migi chūdan tettsui-uchi*

Assume a straddle-leg stance while executing a middle-level hammer-fist strike with the right arm.

23-A) Turning the head to the left, look over the left shoulder while drawing the left foot back behind the right foot, pivoting on the right foot to turn the hips to the left. At the same time, extend the left arm across the front of the body while drawing the right arm across the chest above the left arm.

### 23) *Kiba-dachi/Hidari chūdan tettsui-uchi*

Completing a 180-degree turn to the left, assume a straddle-leg stance while delivering a middle-level hammer-fist strike with the left arm.

24-A) Pivoting on the left foot, draw the right foot toward the left foot, turning the hips to the left while drawing the right fist across the front of the body and under the left arm, which remains extended in the same direction as the preceding hammer-fist strike.

### 24) *Kiba-dachi/Migi chūdan tettsui-uchi*

Completing a 180-degree turn to the left, assume a straddle-leg stance while executing a right middle-level hammer-fist strike.

25-A) Draw the left foot in toward the right foot and forward at a 45-degree angle to the left, directing the right fist in the same direction while pulling the left hand, formed into a knife hand, across the front of the body and under the right arm.

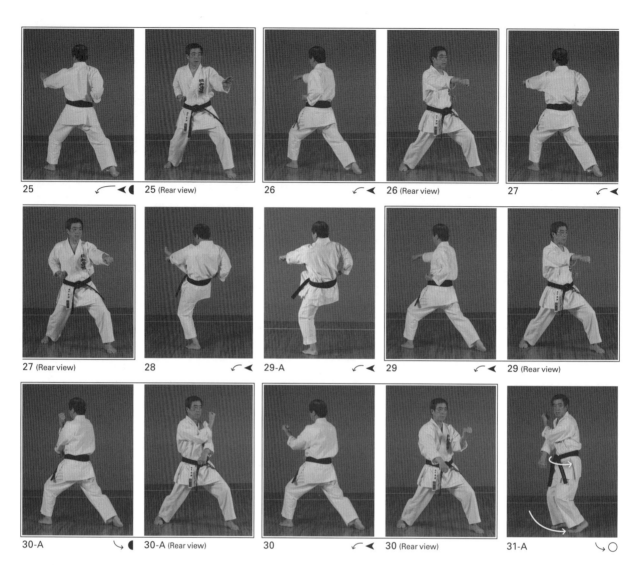

25     25 (Rear view)     26     26 (Rear view)     27

27 (Rear view)     28     29-A     29     29 (Rear view)

30-A     30-A (Rear view)     30     30 (Rear view)     31-A

**25) Zenkutsu-dachi/Hidari chūdan tate shutō-uke**
Complete the step forward with the left foot into a left front stance while performing a vertical knife-hand block with the left arm.

**26) Zenkutsu-dachi/Migi chūdan gyaku-zuki**
Deliver a right middle-level reverse punch.

**27) Zenkutsu-dachi/Hidari chūdan zuki**
Deliver a middle-level punch with the left arm.

**28) Migi mae-geri**
Keeping the arms in place, deliver a front snap kick with the right leg.

29-A) Maintaining the same upper-body position, retract the kicking leg.

**29) Zenkutsu-dachi/Migi chūdan gyaku-zuki**
Step back with the right foot into a left front stance while delivering a right middle-level reverse punch.

30-A) Pull the right fist back toward the left shoulder while drawing the left arm across the front of the body to the right.

**30) Zenkutsu-dachi/Kōsa-uke**
Execute a cross block, with the left arm performing an inside-to-outside block while the right arm delivers a downward block.

31-A) Draw the left foot back along a course in front of the right foot, turning the hips to the left while pulling the left fist up to above the right shoulder and extending the left arm across to the left side of the body.

**31) Kiba-dachi/Kōsa-uke**
Plant the left foot in line with the right foot into a straddle-leg stance while simultaneously performing a right inside-to-outside block and a left downward block.

**32) Kiba-dachi/Morote gedan-uke**
Keeping the left arm in place, swing the right forearm down to execute a downward block.

33-A) Keeping the elbows in place, draw both forearms inward and up simultaneously, crossing them as they pass in front of the chest.

**33) Kiba-dachi/Morote chūdan kōsa-uke**
Complete the motion of the arms to execute a middle-level cross block with both arms performing inside-to-outside blocks.

31    32    33-A    33

34    35    Yame-A    Yame

### 34) *Kiba-dachi/Hidari jōdan zuki*
Deliver an upper-level punch with the left arm, launching the fist directly from the previous blocking position.

### 35) *Kiba-dachi/Migi chūdan zuki*
Deliver a right middle-level punch with a *kiai*.

*Yame*-A) Draw the left foot in toward the right foot, aligning the feet into a closed parallel stance. At the same time, pull the right fist back to in front of the chin while raising the left hand to the same location, wrapping the left hand over the right fist to assume the same ready position in which the *kata* began.

### *Yame*
Draw the left foot out to the left side into an open V stance while lowering both fists to the front of the hips, the same natural-posture stance assumed prior to starting the *kata*.

---

### TECHNICAL ANALYSIS
## Movement 1

The cross block performed at the opening and elsewhere in Jiin can be used in response to a simultaneous front snap kick/middle-level punch attack (photo 1). Utilizing the momentum initiated by the block, the opponent can then be forced off balance (photo 2), lifted (photo 3), and thrown to the ground.

1

2

3

# Empi

According to the most widely accepted theory regarding its origin, this *kata* was introduced by the Chinese envoy Wanshū. It was said to have been passed down to the Tomari region of Japan, combining elements of both Chinese and Okinawan martial arts and, from there, was believed to have developed along two paths, one in which it was passed on from Shin'unjō Sanaeda to Kōsaku Matsumora, the other in which modifications to the *kata* were introduced by Master Yasustune Itosu.

In his book *Ryūkyū Kempō Karate*, Master Gichin Funakoshi describes this *kata*, called Wanshū (Shōrei-ryū), as having a total of 40 steps, providing evidence that it is a Tomari-based *kata*. Within the Shōtōkan style, around the time Master Funakoshi changed the characters used to write "karate" from 唐手 (meaning "Chinese hand") to 空手 (meaning "empty hand"), he also renamed this *kata* Empi (meaning "swallow in flight").

Distinguished by techniques that call to mind a flying swallow, the *kata* includes body reversals and movements that are light and rapid. According to an essay by Master Chōki Motobu, until Japan's Meiji government abolished feudal domains and established a centralized prefectural system in 1871, the two *kata* Wanshū and Rōhai (Meikyō) had spread only within Tomari and were both deemed representative *kata* of the region. Motobu goes on to explain that neither *kata* had been seen in Shuri or Naha.

Among the seven traditional *kata* introduced in Master Chōtoku Kiyatake's Shōrin-school Kiyatake-faction compilation of Shuri-te and Tomari-te karate, Wanshū and Nankō are included as basic *kata*, a clear indication of their importance.

Bearing the names Wanshū and Empi (the latter used within the SKIF organization) and written using a variety of Chinese character combinations, this is an extremely old *kata*. Due to the complex nature of how the *kata* has been passed down, it is believed that its appellation and history have been subject to change over time.

## Empi

Shizentai

Yōi

**Shizentai (Natural posture)**
*Soto hachiji-dachi* (open V stance) with both fists positioned in front of the hips.

**Yōi (Ready position)**
Draw the left foot in toward the right foot to assume a closed parallel stance (*heisoku-dachi*) while raising the right fist up to above the left hip. At the same time, draw the left hand up to above the left hip while opening the hand into a knife hand. In the completed ready position, the front of the right fist presses against the palm-side of the open left hand.

1-A) Turning the hips to the left, draw the left foot out one half-step to the left side while driving the right fist downward in front of the body.

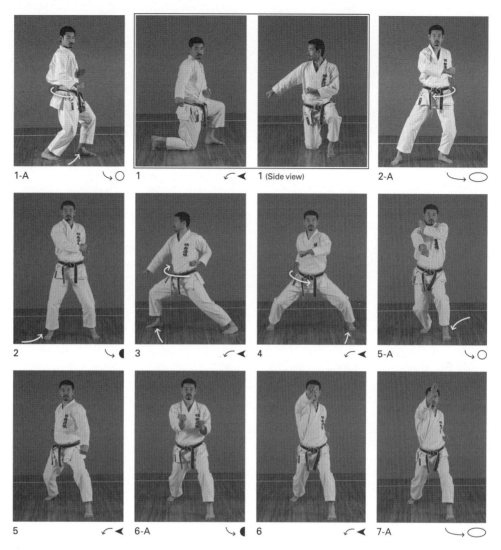

1-A     1     1 (Side view)     2-A

2     3     4     5-A

5     6-A     6     7-A

### 1) *Tachi-hiza/Gedan-barai*

Following through with the motion, lower the hips, bringing the right knee to the floor while delivering a strong downward block to the front with the right arm. At the same time, the left hand closes into a fist and travels across the midsection toward the right side of the body. When viewed from the side, the distance between the right knee and the heel of the left foot is approximately the width of one or two fists.

2-A) Standing up, draw the right foot back in line with the left foot while pulling the left fist back to above the left hip. The right fist also moves toward the left hip.

### 2) *Shizentai/Koshi-gamae*

Assume an open V stance with the right fist resting on top of the left fist above the left hip.

### 3) *Zenkutsu-dachi/Migi gedan-barai*

Thrusting off the left foot, turn the head to the right and drive the right foot out and back at an angle to the right into a right front stance facing the right while delivering a right downward block.

### 4) *Kiba-dachi/Hidari kagi-zuki*

Pull the left foot back, shifting into straddle-leg stance facing the front while delivering a hook punch with the left arm.

5-A) Drawing the left foot along a course inward toward the right foot and then out in front of the body, pull the left fist back to above the right shoulder while extending the right arm downward in front of the body.

### 5) *Zenkutsu-dachi/Hidari gedan-barai*

Complete the step forward into a left front stance while executing a left downward block.

6-A) Launch the right fist as if delivering a middle-level reverse punch, but as soon as the right elbow passes the side of the body, raise the arm so that the fist travels upwards.

### 6) *Zenkutsu-dachi/Migi jōdan age-zuki*

Complete the motion to execute a rising punch with the right arm.

7-A) Without moving the rest of the arm, open the right hand and rotate it in a clockwise motion so that the tips of the fingers describe a small circle.

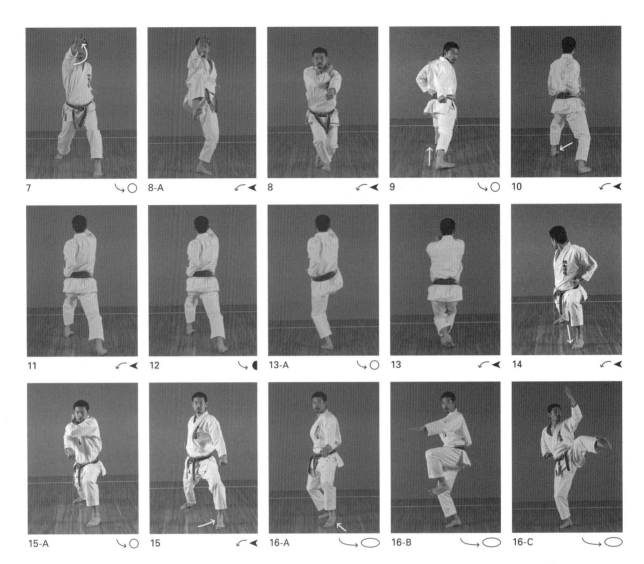

| | | | | |
|---|---|---|---|---|
| 7 ↘○ | 8-A ↙◄ | 8 ↙◄ | 9 ↘○ | 10 ↙◄ |
| 11 ↙◄ | 12 ↘◗ | 13-A ↘○ | 13 ↙◄ | 14 ↙◄ |
| 15-A ↘○ | 15 ↙◄ | 16-A ↘◯ | 16-B ↘◯ | 16-C ↘◯ |

**7) *Zenkutsu-dachi/Kami-zukami***

Complete the motion of the hand to perform a hair grab.

8-A) Drive the right knee up in front of the body while thrusting the right hip forward.

**8) *Kōsa-dachi/Fumikomi/Nagashi-uke/Otoshi-zuki***
Execute a stamping kick with the right leg, immediately drawing the left leg forward into a cross-legged stance. At the same time, drop the hips while delivering a downward punch with the left arm, pulling the right fist back to above the right shoulder to simultaneously perform a sweeping block.

**9) *Zenkutsu-dachi/Migi ushiro gedan-barai***
Thrusting off the right foot, step straight back with the left foot into a narrow elongated left front stance, leaning the upper body over the left leg while executing a downward block to the rear with the right arm. Throughout the movement, the head faces the same direction, with the eyes directed toward the downward block.

**10) *Zenkutsu-dachi/Hidari gedan-barai***
Raising the upper body, pull the left fist up to above the

right shoulder while extending the right arm downward in front of the body. Then slide the left foot back slightly and out to left side into a left front stance while executing a downward block with the left arm.

**11) *Zenkutsu-dachi/Migi jōdan age-zuki***
Deliver a rising punch with the right arm.

**12) *Zenkutsu-dachi/Kami-zukami***
Rotate the right hand to perform a hair grab.

13-A) Drive the right knee up in front of the body while thrusting the right hip forward.

**13) *Kōsa-dachi/Fumikomi/Nagashi-uke/Otoshi-zuki***
Deliver a stamping kick with the right leg, immediately pulling the left leg forward into a crossed-leg stance while simultaneously performing a left downward punch and a right sweeping block.

**14) *Zenkutsu-dachi/Migi ushiro gedan-barai***
Step to the rear with the left foot into a narrow elongated left front stance, leaning over the left leg while delivering a back downward block with the right arm in the direction of the right leg.

16    17    18-A    18    19-A

19    20-A    20    21    22

23-A

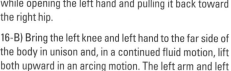

23

15-A) Raising the upper body, draw the left fist up to above the right shoulder while extending the right arm downward in front of the body.

**15) *Zenkutsu-dachi/Hidari gedan-barai***
Slide the left foot back slightly and out to left side into a left front stance while executing a downward block with the left arm.

16-A) Keeping the right fist firmly in place above the right hip, draw the left foot in toward the right foot while opening the left hand and pulling it back toward the right hip.

16-B) Bring the left knee and left hand to the far side of the body in unison and, in a continued fluid motion, lift both upward in an arcing motion. The left arm and left leg move together as if the elbow and knee were connected by a steel rod.

16-C) Continue to draw the left arm and left leg up and across the front of the body to the left. After the left arm passes in front of the face, follow the path of the left hand with the eyes.

**16) *Kiba-dachi/Jōdan haishu-uke***
The left foot lands on the floor into a straddle-leg stance as the left arm settles into place with the forearm extending upward and the elbow positioned at a 45-degree angle to the left at shoulder level. The back of the left hand faces outward and the eyes are directed at the left wrist.

**17) *Kata-ashi-dachi/Empi-uchi***
Keeping the left hand in place, deliver a right elbow strike against the palm of the left hand with a *kiai* while driving the right knee toward the left leg to generate momentum. As the elbow approaches its target, extend the left leg to raise the hips and hook the right foot behind the left knee at the moment of impact.

18-A) Return the right foot to its previous location while drawing the left hand across the front of the chest and beneath the right arm.

**18) *Kiba-dachi/Hidari chūdan tate shutō-uke***
Resuming a straddle-leg stance, draw the left arm out in front of the body to perform a middle-level vertical knife-hand block.

**19-A) *Kiba-dachi/Migi chūdan-zuki***
Deliver a right middle-level punch

**19) *Kiba-dachi/Hidari chūdan-zuki***
Deliver a left middle-level punch

20-A) Turning the head to the left, slide the left foot back one half-step, drawing the left fist up to above the right shoulder while extending the right arm downward across the front of the body.

**20) *Zenkutsu-dachi/Hidari gedan-barai***
Assuming a left front stance facing the left-hand side, execute a left downward block.

**21) *Zenkutsu-dachi/Migi jōdan age-zuki***
Deliver a rising punch with the right arm.

**22) *Kōkutsu-dachi/Migi chūdan shutō-uke***
Step forward with the right foot into a left back stance while performing a right middle-level knife-hand block.

23-A) Draw the right foot back, positioning it alongside the left foot while pulling the left hand back to above the right shoulder and extending the right arm out in front of the chest.

**23) *Kōkutsu-dachi/Hidari chūdan shutō-uke***
Step forward with the left foot into a right back stance while delivering a left middle-level knife-hand block.

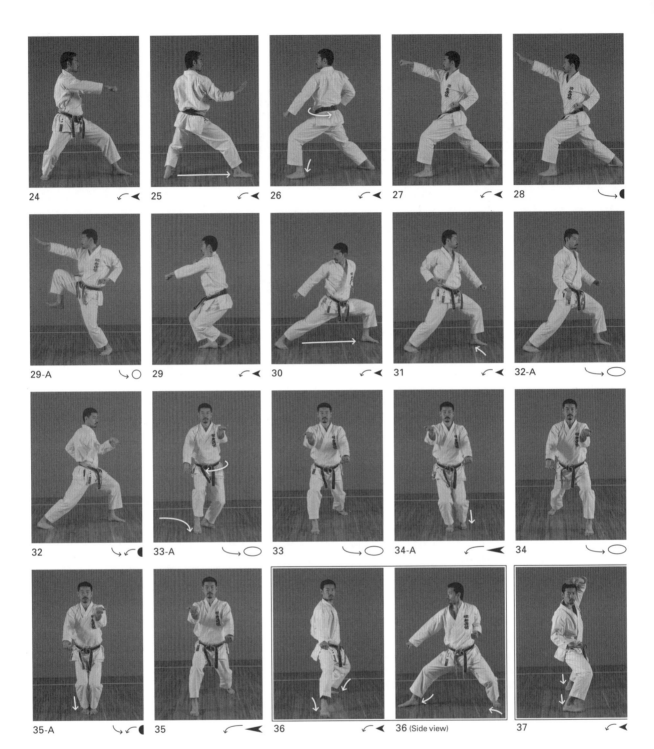

**24) Kōkutsu-dachi/Migi chūdan gyaku-zuki**
Maintaining a strong back stance, execute a right middle-level reverse punch.

**25) Kōkutsu-dachi/Migi chūdan shutō-uke**
Step forward with the right foot into a left back stance while delivering a right middle-level knife-hand block.

**26) Zenkutsu-dachi/Hidari gedan-barai**
Slide the left across the rear to the right-hand side and turn the body 180 degrees to the left, shifting into a left front stance facing the opposite direction while executing a left downward block.

**27) Zenkutsu-dachi/Migi jōdan age-zuki**
Deliver a right rising punch.

**28) Zenkutsu-dachi/Kami-zukami**
Rotate the right hand to perform a hair grab.

37 (Side view)  38-A  ↘○  38-B  ↘○  38-C  ✹ ↙◀  38  ↙◀

29-A) Drive the right knee up in front of the body while thrusting the right hip forward.

### 29) Kōsa-dachi/Fumikomi/Nagashi-uke/Otoshi-zuki
Deliver a stamping kick with the right leg, immediately assuming a crossed-leg stance while simultaneously executing a downward punch with the left arm and a sweeping block with the right arm.

### 30) Zenkutsu-dachi/Migi ushiro gedan-barai
Step to the rear with the left foot into a narrow elongated left front stance, leaning over the left leg while delivering a back downward block with the right arm in the direction of the right leg.

### 31) Zenkutsu-dachi/Hidari gedan-barai
Raising the upper body, shift into a left front stance while executing a downward block with the left arm.

32-A) Open the right hand and push it downward, heel first, at a 45-degree angle to the right in front of the right hip while pulling the left fist back toward the left hip.

### 32) Zenkutsu-dachi/Migi teishō-uke
Raise the right hand, formed into a palm heel, to complete a palm-heel block while turning the hips to the left and pulling the left fist back to above the left hip.

33-A) Turn the head to the right and slide the right foot in toward the left foot, turning the hips to the right while directing the right palm heel downward and drawing the left hand, also formed into a palm heel, upward in front of the body.

### 33) Zenkutsu-dachi/Teishō morote-uke
Step forward with the right foot into a right front stance while delivering a double palm-heel block with the right palm heel moving upward as the left palm heel travels downward. Both hands travel along straight vertical paths.

34-A) Keeping the hands in place, step forward with the left foot. The hands do not move until the left leg passes the right leg.

### 34) Zenkutsu-dachi/Teishō morote-uke
Complete the step forward with the left foot into a left front stance, performing a double palm-heel block with the left hand delivering an upward palm-heel block and the right hand a downward palm-heel block.

35-A) Keeping the hands in place, step forward with the right foot.

### 35) Zenkutsu-dachi/Teishō morote-uke
Complete the step forward with the right foot into a right front stance, delivering a double palm-heel block with the right palm heel traveling upward and the left palm heel descending.

### 36) Kōkutsu-dachi/Migi gedan-barai
Pull the right hand back to above the left shoulder and then thrust off the left foot, driving the right foot forward while sliding the left foot across to the right side in line with the right foot into a left front stance. At the same time, drive the right fist down in front of the body to deliver a right downward block.

### 37) Kiba-dachi/Morote kokō-gamae
Thrusting again off the left foot, slide both feet forward in the direction of the right foot while shifting into a straddle-leg stance. At the same time, drive the right hand forward at approximately waist level with the palm of the hand facing upward while launching the left hand along a course upward and forward to just in front of the forehead, also with the palm of the hand facing upward. Upon completing the motion, the right elbow rests against the right hip while the left elbow is positioned just behind and above the head.

38-A) Pivoting on the left foot, turn the hips sharply to the left, drawing the right hand up toward the left shoulder and extending the left arm across the front of the chest toward the right side of the body.

38-B) Continue with the motion initiated in the previous step while raising the right knee to generate momentum in preparation for a leap upward.

### 38-C) Jōhō kaiten-tobi
Launching off the left leg, drive the right knee upward to leap into the air with a *kiai*, tucking the legs up under hips while turning the body 360 degrees to face the same direction as prior to the jump. While in midair, the right hand is positioned above the left shoulder while the right arm extends across the front of the body.

### 38) Kōkutsu-dachi/Migi chūdan shutō-uke
Land with both feet at the same time into a left back stance while executing a right middle-level knife-hand block.

39

Yame-A

Yame

**39) *Kōkutsu-dachi/Hidari chūdan shutō-uke***

Step back with the right foot into a right back stance while delivering a left middle-level knife-hand block.

*Yame*-A) Draw the left foot back to alongside the right foot into a closed parallel stance, pulling the left hand to the left side of the body while closing the right hand into a fist and positioning it against the left hand as in the opening ready position at the start of the *kata*.

**Yame**

Slide the left foot out into an open V stance and lower the hands, closing the left hand into a fist and positioning the fists in front of the hips.

**TECHNICAL ANALYSIS**
**Movements 5–8-A**

Upon blocking a kicking attack with a downward block (photo 2), deliver a rising-punch counterattack (photo 3) and then grab the attacker's hair with the punching hand (photo 4), pulling his head downward while finishing with a knee strike to the face (photo 5).

1

2

3

4

5

## TECHNICAL ANALYSIS
### Movements 36–38

Deflect an opponent's kick with a downward block (photo 1) and immediately thrust forward off the rear foot, firmly grabbing hold of the attacker with both hands (photo 2). Proceed to lift and throw the attacker to the opposite side (photos 3 and 4) and, turning the hips in the same direction as the throw, jump over the his body (photos 5 and 6) and land in a back stance prepared to respond to any subsequent attacks (photo 7).

1

2

3

4

5

6

7

# Jitte

Within the Shōtōkan style, Jitte, a *kata* from the Tomari region, is recognized for the techniques it contains against stick attacks. It is a relatively short intermediate-level *kata* comprising 27 movements that, while generally weighty in nature, contains several subtle techniques involving the twisting of the wrists and reversals. Its name, written 十手 (literally "ten hands"), is commonly interpreted to mean that, by mastering this *kata*, the practitioner would be able to take on ten opponents. Another theory believed by some is that Jitte is so called because the mountain blocks that appear in the *kata* call to mind the shape of the traditional Japanese weapon called a jitte, a branched staff that could be used as a club or to defend against sword attacks.

Jitte is a very powerful *kata* containing offensive and defensive techniques against stick attacks. It incorporates many subtle "secret" techniques from which some of karate's more enigmatic aspects can be learned, as well as a series of reversal techniques.

In other styles of karate the Chinese characters 術手 ("technique hand") and 実手 ("actual hand") are used to write the name. Jitte belongs to the same family of *kata* as Jion and Jiin.

Jitte contains a variety of open-hand techniques, including ridge-hand blocks, a knife-hand block, and palm-heel strikes, and also features a move to cast off an opponent following a block delivered from a crossed-leg stance. Despite the diverse range of techniques it contains, one interesting characteristic of the *kata* is that it includes not a single kicking technique.

In other karate styles, this *kata* does not include blocks against stick attacks, which is believed to be due to differences in interpretation among past instructors by whom it has been passed down. In either case, because it is a short *kata*, most of the movements are similar regardless of the style.

## Jitte

Shizentai          Yōi          1-A          1-B

### *Shizentai* (Natural posture)
*Soto hachiji-dachi* (open V stance) with both fists positioned in front of the hips.

### *Yōi* (Ready position)/*Jiai no kamae*
Slide the left foot in toward the right foot to assume a closed parallel stance (*heisoku-dachi*) while bending the arms to draw the hands together in front of the chin. The left hand opens and wraps around the right fist with the elbows tucked closely to the sides of the

body. This posture is known as *jiai no kamae* (posture of benevolence).

1-A) Bend the knees while simultaneously opening and lowering the right hand in front of the body with the palm facing downward.

1-B) Keeping the right leg bent, slide the left foot straight back while lowering the right hand to approximately waist level. At the same time, draw the left hand out slightly from the body.

1-C       1-D       1       2-A

2-B       2       3       4-A

4       5-A       5-B

1-C) Sliding the left foot further to the rear, draw the right hand up along the front of the chest while simultaneously lowering the left along a slightly curved path in front of the body.

1-D) Settling into a right front stance, pull the left hand, closed into a fist, back to above the left hip while turning the right hand so the palm faces upward.

### 1) *Zenkutsu-dachi/Migi tekubi kake-uke*
Lowering the hips into a right front stance, draw the right arm downward to complete a wrist-hook block, with the hand positioned approximately level with the shoulder.

2-A) Turning the head to the left, slide the left foot forward alongside the right foot and direct the left hand, opened into a palm heel, downward toward the floor.

2-B) Stepping forward with the left foot at a 45-degree angle to the left, turn the left palm heel upward while turning the right palm heel over.

### 2) *Zenkutsu-dachi/Teishō morote-uke*
Complete the step forward with the left foot into a left front stance while delivering a double palm-heel block with the left palm heel moving upward as the left palm heel travels downward. Both hands move along straight vertical paths.

### 3) *Zenkutsu-dachi/Hidari haitō-uke*
Keeping the legs firmly in place, turn the head to the right and execute a sharp ridge-hand block with the left hand against the right arm. The right arm stays in place during the technique.

4-A) Shifting the weight of the body toward the left leg, draw the right hand, opened into a ridge hand, across to the left-hand side.

### 4) *Kiba-dachi/Migi haitō-uke*
Pushing off the left foot, drive the right foot out to the right-hand side, assuming a straddle-leg stance while delivering a ridge-hand strike with the right hand.

5-A) Turn the head to the left and, without raising the hips, draw the left foot in one half-step toward the right foot while thrusting the right elbow to the rear in preparation for the following strike.

5-B) Step forward with the right foot while driving the right hand, formed into a palm heel, forward.

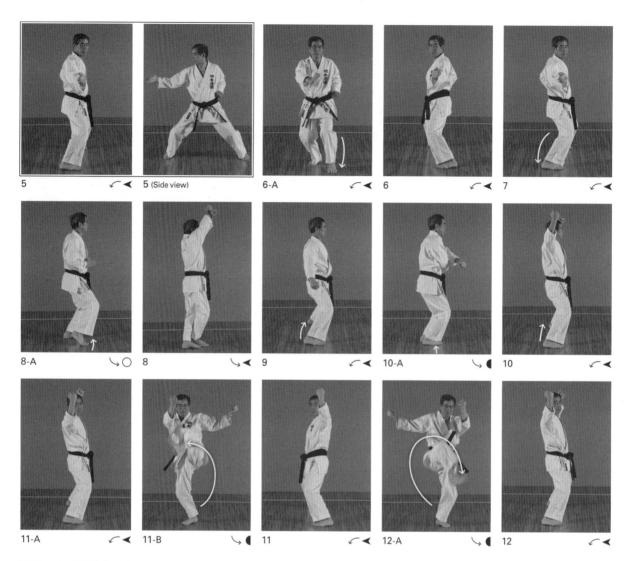

5

5 (Side view)

6-A

6

7

8-A

8

9

10-A

10

11-A

11-B

11

12-A

12

**5) *Kiba-dachi/Migi teishō-uchi***
Complete the step forward with the right foot into a straddle leg stance while delivering a palm-heel strike with the right hand.

6-A) Keeping the right hand in place, step forward with the left foot.

**6) *Kiba-dachi/Hidari teishō-uchi***
Complete the step forward into a straddle-leg stance while delivering a palm-heel strike with the left hand.

**7) *Kiba-dachi/Migi teishō-uchi***
Step forward with the right foot into a straddle leg stance while delivering a palm-heel strike with the right hand.

8-A) Turning the head to the left, draw the right foot in toward the left foot while pulling the right hand in toward the body.

**8) *Kōsa-dachi/Jōdan jūji-uke***
Bring the right foot to the far side of the left foot and fully extend both legs, assuming a crossed-leg stance while thrusting both fists upward to deliver an upper X-block.

**9) *Kiba-dachi/Ryōwan gedan kakiwake-uke***
Draw the left foot out to the left-hand side and drop the

hips into a straddle-leg stance while driving both arms down sharply to the sides of the body to deliver a double downward reverse-wedge block.

10-A) Keeping the hips at the same height, draw the right foot in alongside the left foot while driving the fists out to opposite sides of the body, crossing the arms in front of the chest with the left arm above the right arm.

**10) *Kiba-dachi/Yama kakiwake-uke***
Driving off the right foot, push the left foot out to the left-hand side into a straddle leg stance while thrusting the elbows up and back to execute a mountain separating block.

11-A) Turn the head to the right.

11-B) Keeping the fists in place, swing the left leg up sharply across the front of the body to the right-hand side.

**11) *Kiba-dachi/Fumikomi/Yama-uke***
Turning the body 180 degrees to the left, deliver a stamping kick with the left leg, assuming a straddle-leg stance while executing a mountain block. To ensure a powerful and dynamic block, the upper body, and especially the fists, should not begin turning until the latest possible instant before the left foot lands on the floor.

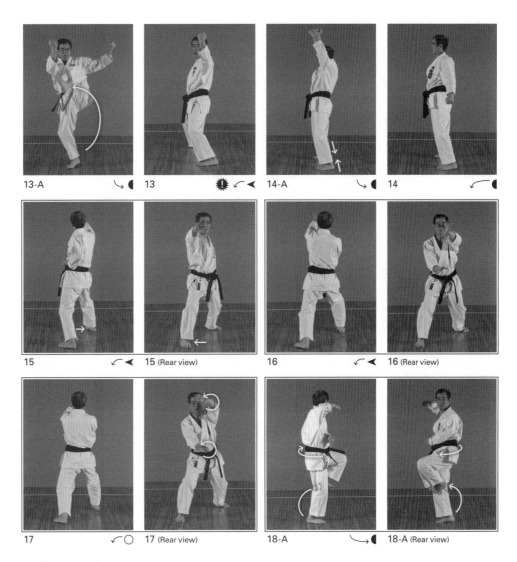

13-A    13    14-A    14

15    15 (Rear view)    16    16 (Rear view)

17    17 (Rear view)    18-A    18-A (Rear view)

12-A) Swing the right leg up sharply across the front of the body to the left-hand side.

### 12) Kiba-dachi/Fumikomi/Yama-uke
Turning 180 degrees to the right, deliver a stamping kick with the right leg into a straddle-leg stance while performing a mountain block.

13-A) Swing the left leg up sharply across the front of the body to the right-hand side.

### 13) Kiba-dachi/Fumikomi/Yama-uke
Turning 180 degrees to the left, deliver a stamping kick with the left leg, assuming a straddle-leg stance while executing a mountain block with a *kiai*.

14-A) Straighten the knees, drawing the feet together slightly into a natural posture while pushing both fists directly upward and then toward each other.

### 14) Shizentai/Ryōwan-gamae
Draw the arms down and out to the sides of the body, crossing them as they travel in front of the body.

### 15) Zenkutsu-dachi/Migi jōdan shutō-uke
Turn the head to the right and step out with the right foot at an angle to the right into a right front stance while

delivering an upper-level knife-hand block with the right arm.

### 16) Zenkutsu-dachi/Morote jō-uke
Draw the right hand straight down in front of the mid-section while thrusting the left hand out in front of the head to deliver a two-handed block against a *jō* (stick, or staff) attack.

### 17) Zenkutsu-dachi/Morote kokō-dori
Rotate both hands clockwise to reposition the hold on the *jō*.

### 18-A) Sagi-ashi-dachi/Morote jō-dori
Draw the left leg forward while turning the hips to the right, bringing the left foot to rest against the inside of the right knee in a heron-leg stance with the left knee pointing at a 45-degree angle to the right. At the same time, pull the right elbow back and up to behind the head, bringing the right hand to just behind the right ear while dropping the left elbow and drawing the left hand across the front of the body to the right-hand side. In the completed position, the hands should be aligned vertically, as if holding a stick alongside the right side of the body.

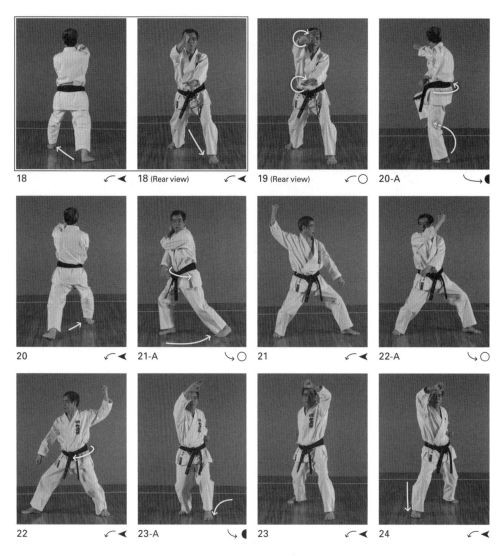

18    18 (Rear view)    19 (Rear view)    20-A

20    21-A    21    22-A

22    23-A    23    24

### 18) *Zenkutsu-dachi/Morote jō tsuki-dashi*

Step forward with the left foot into a left front stance while thrusting the left hand out in front of the midsection and the right hand out in front of the head to deliver a *jō* thrust.

19) Rotate both hands counter-clockwise to reposition the grasp on the *jō*.

### 20-A) *Sagi-ashi-dachi/Morote jō-dori*

Draw the right leg forward and turn the hips to the left, positioning the right foot against the inside of the left knee into a heron-leg stance while pulling the left elbow up and to the rear, and drawing the right hand down and back to the right-hand side of the body.

### 20) *Zenkutsu-dachi/Morote jō tsuki-dashi*

Step forward with the right foot into a right front stance, thrusting the right hand out in front of the midsection and the left hand out in front of the head to execute a *jō* thrust.

21-A) Draw the left foot across the rear to the right, pivoting on the right foot to turn 270 degrees to the left (to face toward the right side). At the same time, pull the left hand up to above the right shoulder and thrust the right arm across the front of the body and downward.

### 21) *Kōkutsu-dachi/Manji-uke*

Assuming a right back stance, draw the right arm back strongly while driving the left arm downward to execute a hi-low block. The right arm performs an upper-level inside-to-outside block to the rear while the left arm delivers a downward block to the front.

22-A) Turn the head to the right while pulling the right fist across to above the left shoulder and driving the left fist across the front of the body to the right-hand side.

### 22) *Kōkutsu-dachi/Manji-uke*

Transferring the center of gravity toward the left leg, shift into a left back stance while drawing the left arm back strongly and driving the right arm downward to execute a hi-low block facing the opposite direction.

23-A) Turning the head to the left, draw the left foot in toward the right foot and forward. At the same time, open the right hand and thrust it upward at an angle in front of the body while pulling the left fist back to above the left hip.

25     26     26 (Rear view)     27     Yame

### 23) *Zenkutsu-dachi/Hidari jōdan age-uke*
Complete the step forward with the left foot into a left front stance while performing a left upper-level rising block.

### 24) *Zenkutsu-dachi/Migi jōdan age-uke*
Step forward with the right foot into a right front stance while performing a right upper-level rising block.

### 25) *Zenkutsu-dachi/Hidari jōdan age-uke*
Shift the left leg across the back to the opposite side, pivoting on the right foot to turn the body 180 degrees to the left into a left front stance facing the opposite direction while executing an upper-level rising block with the left arm.

### 26) *Zenkutsu-dachi/Migi jōdan age-uke*
Step forward with the right foot into a right front stance while performing a right upper-level rising block with a *kiai*.

27) Pivoting on the right foot, turn the body 180 degrees to the left while drawing the left foot alongside the right foot into a closed parallel stance. At the same time, lower the right elbow and pull the right fist toward the chin while raising the left hand to the same location, wrapping the left hand over the right fist to assume the same ready position in which the *kata* began.

### *Yame*
Draw the left foot out to the left into an open V stance while lowering both fists to the front of the hips, the same natural-posture stance assumed prior to starting the *kata*.

---

### TECHNICAL ANALYSIS
### Movements 8–9

Upon blocking an upper level punching attack with an X-block (photo 1), drive the arms out to the sides of the body to throw the opponent off-balance (photos 2 and 3).

1

2

3

## TECHNICAL ANALYSIS
### Movements 10 and 11

The mountain block that appears several times in Jitte can be used to block a punching attack from the front (photo 1), as well as from either side (photos 2 and 3).

1

2

3

## TECHNICAL ANALYSIS
### Movements 15–17

In response to a *jō* attack, block the strike with a knife-hand block (photo 1) and immediately grab hold of the staff with both hands (photo 2). Rotate the hands clockwise to reposition the grasp and disarm the opponent while pulling him off-balance (photos 3–5).

1

2

3

4

5

# Hangetsu (Seishan)

According to Master Gichin Funakoshi's book *Ryūkyū Kempō Karate*, the *kata* Seishan (Shōrei-ryū style) comprises 41 movements, leading one to believe it is of Naha-te origins. Within the Shōtōkan style, this *kata* has been named Hangetsu (and, in this book, follows a rhythm of 32 movements).

The name Hangetsu, meaning half-moon, probably refers to the semicircular path that the feet describe when advancing during the *kata*. Today, the stance employed throughout the performance of Hangetsu is known as *hangetsu-dachi* (half-moon stance). When standing in a half-moon stance, the feet are shoulder-width apart when viewed from the front, and the distance between the front foot and rear foot is a little less than double the width of the shoulders when viewed from the side. The front foot points inward at a 45-degree angle and the rear foot points outward at a 45-degree angle. Both knees are bent and drawn inward as if being pulled together.

One of the characteristics of Hangetsu is the inclusion of numerous breathing techniques. While it goes without saying that proper breathing plays an important role in karate, among the various Shōtōkan-school *kata*, Hangetsu is the only one to include such a large number of these breathing techniques. As such, Hangetsu is a *kata* deserving of diligent practice.

In the section of *Ryūkyū Kempō Karate* introducing the Seishan *kata*, with regard to the swinging of the right leg from the side and kicking the left hand, Master Funakoshi writes, "This is called *mikazuki* (crescent moon)." This technique—now known as *mikazuki-geri* (crescent kick)—which is used to deflect middle-level attacks, represents another distinguishing feature of this *kata*.

By tightening the sides of the upper body and constricting the anus while in the half-moon stance, it is possible for male practitioners to retract the testicles into the lower abdomen, offering protection even in the event of a kick to the groin. As Hangetsu includes such advanced techniques that can be mastered through dedicated practice, it represents an indispensable training *kata*.

## Hangetsu

Yōi

1-A

1-B

**Yōi (Ready position)**
*Soto hachiji-dachi* (open V stance) with both fists positioned in front of the hips.

1-A) Draw the left foot in toward the right foot while raising the right fist toward the left shoulder and pulling the left fist across the midsection to the right-hand side of the body.

1-B) Step forward with the left foot at a 45-degree angle to the left while drawing the left fist out in front of the body and pulling the right fist back toward the right hip.

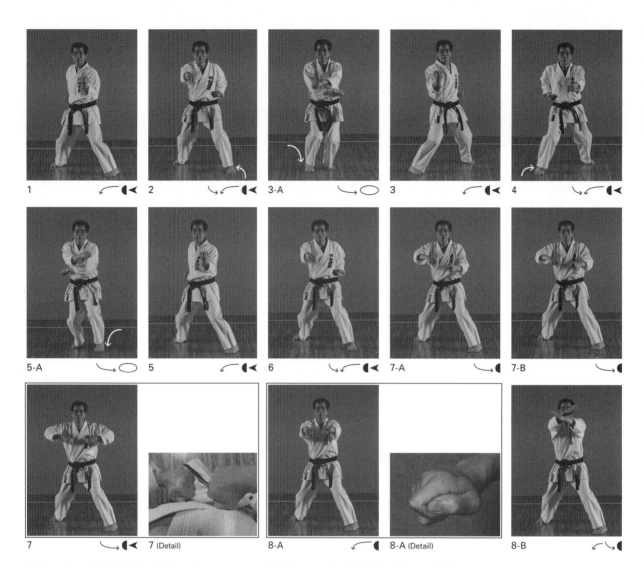

1     2     3-A     3     4

5-A     5     6     7-A     7-B

7     7 (Detail)     8-A     8-A (Detail)     8-B

### 1) *Hangetsu-dachi/Hidari chūdan uchi-uke*

Assuming a half-moon stance, complete the motion of the arms to execute a middle-level inside-to-outside block with the left arm. Upon completing the technique, immediately tighten the anus while drawing the testicles upward into the lower abdomen.

### 2) *Hangetsu-dachi/Migi chūdan gyaku-zuki*

Maintaining a strong half-moon stance, draw the right fist forward to deliver a middle-level reverse punch. Upon completing the technique, sharply expel the remaining breath, tightening the anus and drawing the testicles upward into the lower abdomen while pulling the left heel inward so that the toes point forward.

3-A) Draw the right foot forward toward the left foot while extending the left arm out in front of the body and pulling the right arm back across the midsection toward the left-hand side.

### 3) *Hangetsu-dachi/Migi chūdan uchi-uke*

Step forward with the right foot at a 45-degree angle to the right into a half-moon stance while drawing the right fist out in front of the body to deliver a middle-level inside-to-outside block. Upon completing the technique, again tighten the anus while drawing the testicles up into the body.

### 4) *Hangetsu-dachi/Hidari chūdan gyaku-zuki*

Deliver a middle-level reverse punch with the left arm, sharply expelling the remaining breath upon completing the technique while tightening the anus and drawing the testicles up into the lower abdomen. At the same time, pull the right heel inward so the toes point forward.

5-A) Draw the left foot forward toward the right foot while extending the right arm out in front of the body and pulling the left fist back toward the right-hand side.

### 5) *Hangetsu-dachi/Hidari chūdan uchi-uke*

Complete the step forward with the left foot into a half-moon stance while executing a middle-level inside-to-outside block with the left arm, again tightening the anus and drawing the testicles up immediately upon completion of the technique.

8-C

8

9-A

9-B

9

9 (Rear view)

10-A

10-A (Rear view)

10

10 (Rear view)

### 6) *Hangetsu-dachi/Migi chūdan gyaku-zuki*

Deliver a right middle-level reverse punch, tightening the anus and drawing the testicles up into the abdomen upon completing the technique.

7-A) Forming both fists into side fists (*yokoken*), draw the right fist back toward the chest while raising the left elbow, bringing the left fist up in front of the left side of the chest and away from the body.

7-B) Once the fists align with each other in front of the chest, begin pulling the left fist back toward the body in synchronization with the right fist while extending the elbows out to the sides.

### 7) *Hangestsu-dachi/Morote yokoken-ate*

Continue pulling the elbows out to the sides, drawing the fists back to the chest while keeping the arms parallel to the floor.

### 8-A) *Hangestsu-dachi/Heikō ippon-ken*

Draw both fists, formed into one-knuckle fists, out in front of the body level with the shoulders.

8-B) Keeping the arms straight, open the hands into knife hands while rotating the wrists slightly so that the backs of the hands face outward. At the same time, draw the arms together, crossing them at the wrists with the right arm positioned above the left.

8-C) Raise both arms and draw the elbows out to the sides as the arms approach the head.

### 8) *Hangestsu-dachi/Kaishu yama-gamae*

Continue to draw the elbows out to the sides, lowering them level with the shoulders into an open-hand mountain posture.

9-A) Raise the elbows and extend the arms upward.

9-B) Draw the arms together, crossing them above the head and then lowering them in front of the body.

### 9) *Hangestsu-dachi/Kaishu ryōwan-gamae*

Continue drawing the arms down and then out to the sides with the backs of the hands facing outward.

10-A) Pivoting on the left foot, draw the right foot forward past the left foot, turning the hips to the left while pulling the left hand up to above the right shoulder and extending the right arm downward across the front of the body.

### 10) *Hangestsu-dachi/Kaishu kōsa-uke*

Complete the step initiated by the right foot, turning the body 180 degrees to the left into a half-moon stance facing the opposite direction while executing an open-hand cross block with a *kiai*. The left arm delivers a downward block while the right arm performs an inside-to-outside block.

11-A) Without moving the left arm, rotate the right hand in a counter-clockwise motion.

11-A (Rear view)

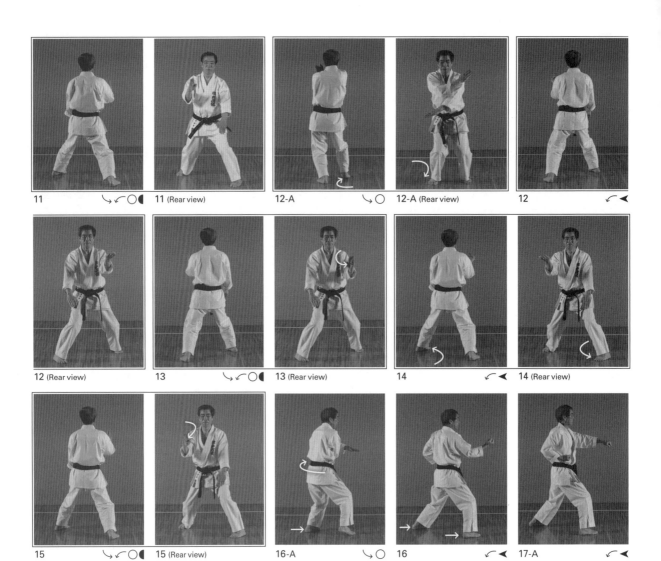

11      11 (Rear view)      12-A      12-A (Rear view)      12

12 (Rear view)      13      13 (Rear view)      14      14 (Rear view)

15      15 (Rear view)      16-A      16      17-A

### 11) *Hangestsu-dachi/Migi kake-dori*

Complete the rotation of the right hand to perform a hooking grasp.

12-A) Stepping forward with the right foot, pull the right hand back to above the left shoulder while drawing the left arm across the front of the body toward the right-hand side.

### 12) *Hangetsu-dachi/Kaishu kōsa-uke*

Complete the step forward with the right foot into a half-moon stance while executing an open-hand cross-arm block with the right arm delivering a downward block and the left arm an inside-to-outside block.

### 13) *Hangetsu-dachi/Hidari kake-dori*

Rotate the left hand in a clockwise motion to perform a hooking grasp.

### 14) *Hangetsu-dachi/Kaishu kōsa-uke*

Step forward with the left foot into a half-moon stance while executing an open-hand cross-arm block with the left arm performing a downward block and the right arm an inside-to-outside block.

### 15) *Hangetsu-dachi/Migi kake-dori*

Turn the right hand over to perform a hooking grasp.

16-A) Drawing the left foot in slightly toward the right foot, turn the hips to the right while pulling the right hand beneath the left arm toward the left side of the body. At the same time, extend the left arm out in front of the chest.

### 16) *Hangetsu-dachi/Migi chūdan uchi-uke*

Thrusting off the left foot, drive the right leg forward with a gliding step (*suri-ashi*), immediately followed by the left leg, assuming a half-moon stance while executing a right middle-level inside-to-outside block.

### 17-A) *Hangetsu-dachi/Hidari chūdan gyaku-zuki*

Deliver a left middle-level reverse punch.

### 17) *Hangetsu-dachi/Migi chūdan jun-zuki*

Deliver a right middle-level front punch.

18-A) Pivoting on the right foot, slide the left foot across the back to the opposite side to turn the body 180 degrees to the left. At the same time, pull the left fist back to the right side of the body while extending the right arm across the front of the body to the opposite side.

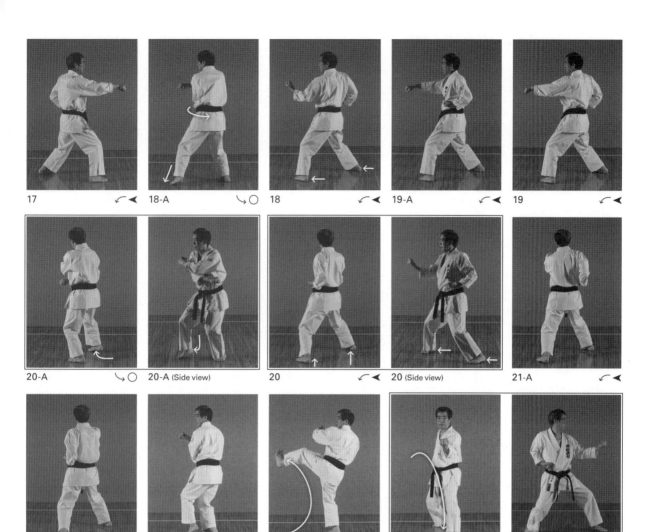

17    18-A    18    19-A    19

20-A    20-A (Side view)    20    20 (Side view)    21-A

21    22-A    22-B    22    22 (Side view)

23

**18) *Hangetsu-dachi/Hidari chūdan uchi-uke***

Thrusting off the right foot to drive the left foot forward into a half-moon stance, slide both feet using *suri-ashi* while executing a middle-level inside-to-outside block with the left arm.

**19-A) *Hangetsu-dachi/Migi chūdan gyaku-zuki***

Deliver a right middle-level reverse punch.

**19) *Hangetsu-dachi/Hidari chūdan jun-zuki***

Deliver a left middle-level front punch.

20-A) Drawing the right foot forward slightly, turn the hips to the right while pulling the right fist back toward the left side of the body and extending the left arm out in front of the body.

**20) *Hangetsu-dachi/Migi chūdan uchi-uke***

Thrusting off the left foot, drive the right leg forward using *suri-ashi* into a half-moon stance while executing a right middle-level inside-to-outside block.

**21-A) *Hangetsu-dachi/Hidari chūdan gyaku-zuki***

Deliver a left middle-level reverse punch.

**21) *Hangetsu-dachi/Migi chūdan jun-zuki***

Deliver a right middle-level front punch.

22-A) Turning the head to the left, draw the left foot forward, passing alongside the right foot and then up in front of the right knee. At the same time, pull the right fist across the front of the chest toward the left-hand side while extending left arm in the opposite direction.

**22-B) *Hidari engetsu-kaeshi***

Draw the left leg up and across the front of the body to the left in an arcing motion while raising the left elbow up and across the front of the head in the same direction.

**22) *Kōkutsu-dachi/Chūdan uraken-gamae***

Lower the left foot, assuming a middle-level back-fist-strike posture in a right back stance.

**23) *Hanmi sashi-ashi***

Maintaining the same upper-body position, draw the right foot forward, placing it in front of the left foot with the toes pointing out to the right. Lead with the left hip when drawing the right foot forward.

23 (Side view)

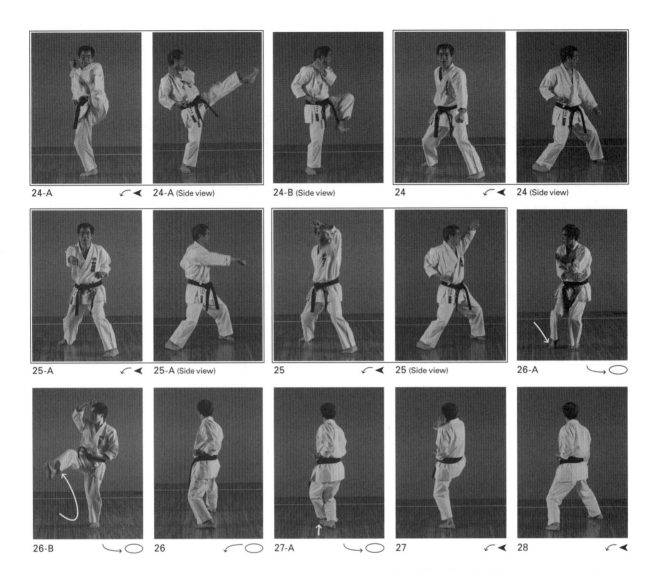

24-A ↙◄ 24-A (Side view)  24-B (Side view)  24 ↙◄ 24 (Side view)

25-A ↙◄ 25-A (Side view)  25 ↙◄ 25 (Side view)  26-A ↘○

26-B ↘○ 26 ↙○ 27-A ↘○ 27 ↙◄ 28 ↙◄

**24-A) *Hidari mae-geri/Hazushi-te***
Deliver a front snap kick with the left leg while pulling the left fist back sharply to above the right shoulder as if to release it from an opponent's grasp.

24-B) Keeping the left fist in place, retract the kicking leg.

**24) *Hangetsu-dachi/Hidari gedan-barai***
Plant the left foot forward into a half-moon stance while simultaneously executing a left downward block.

**25-A) *Hangetsu-dachi/Migi chūdan gyaku-zuki***
Deliver a right middle-level reverse punch.

**25) *Hangetsu-dachi/Hidari jōdan age-uke***
Maintaining a strong half-moon stance, perform an upper-level rising block with the left arm.

26-A) Turning the head to the right, draw the right foot forward to beside the left foot and then up in front of the left knee. At the same time, draw the left fist across the front of the chest to right-hand side while extending right arm in the opposite direction.

**26-B) *Migi engetsu-kaeshi***
Draw the right leg up and across the front of the body

in an arcing motion to the right while raising the right elbow up and across the front of the head in the same direction.

**26) *Kōkutsu-dachi/Chūdan uraken-gamae***
Lower the right foot, assuming a middle-level back-fist-strike posture in a left back stance.

**27) *Hanmi sashi-ashi***
Leading with the right hip, draw the left foot forward, placing it in front of the right foot with the toes pointing out to the left.

**28-A) *Migi mae-geri/Hazushi-te***
Deliver a right front snap kick while pulling the right fist back sharply to above the left shoulder.

**28) *Hangetsu-dachi/Migi gedan-barai***
Plant the right foot forward into a half-moon stance while simultaneously executing a downward block with the right arm.

**29-A) *Hangetsu-dachi/Hidari chūdan gyaku-zuki***
Deliver a left middle-level reverse punch.

**29) *Hangetsu-dachi/Migi jōdan age-uke***
Deliver an upper-level rising block with the right arm.

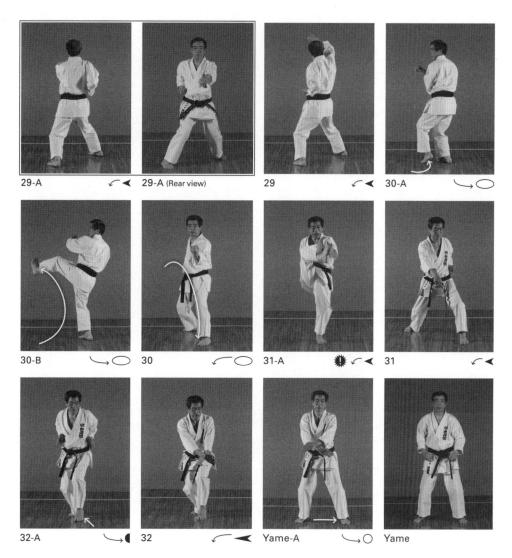

29-A    29-A (Rear view)    29    30-A

30-B    30    31-A    31

32-A    32    Yame-A    Yame

**30-A)** Turning the head to the left, draw the left foot in toward the right foot and then upward while pulling the right fist across the front of the chest and extending left arm in the opposite direction.

### 30-B) *Hidari engetsu-kaeshi*
Draw the left leg up and across in an arcing motion to the left while raising the left elbow up and across the front of the head.

### 30) *Kōkutsu-dachi/Chūdan uraken-gamae*
Lower the left foot, assuming a middle-level back-fist-strike posture in a right back stance.

### 31-A) *Migi mikazuki-geri*
Swing the right leg up across the front of the body to deliver a crescent kick with a *kiai*, striking the open palm of the left hand with the sole of the right foot. The right fist remains in place above the right hip.

### 31) *Zenkutsu-dachi/Migi gedan gyaku-zuki*
Plant the right leg back and to the right at an angle into a left front stance while delivering a downward reverse punch with the right arm. This technique is performed with a "silent *kiai*."

**32-A)** Centering the body's weight over the right leg, draw the left foot back toward the right foot while raising the heel of the left foot. At the same time, pull the right hand back to above the right hip while opening both hands in preparation for the subsequent blocking technique.

### 32) *Neko-ashi-dachi/Teishō awase gedan-uke*
Assuming a cat stance with the left knee directed squarely to the front, drive both hands, formed into palm heels, downward at a 45-degree to the left, drawing the hands together at the wrists as they descend to deliver a two-handed downward palm-heel block.

*Yame*-A) Draw the left foot back and out to the left-hand side, positioning it in line with the right foot in an open V stance. At the same time, extend the left arm across the chest to the right side of the body and above the right arm, which extends to the left side of the body.

### Yame
Return to a natural-posture stance with the arms extended downward in front of the body, maintaining a state of physical and mental readiness (*zanshin*).

## TECHNICAL ANALYSIS
### Movements 7–9

In response to an opponent grabbing from behind (photo 1), raise both arms to break the hold (photo 2), and counter with a downward knife-hand strike (photo 3).

1

2

3

## TECHNICAL ANALYSIS
### Movements 10–11

Upon blocking an opponent's reverse punch with an open-handed inside-to-outside block (photo 1), immediately perform a hooking grasp with the blocking hand (photo 2), pulling the attacker forward and off-balance.

1

2

## TECHNICAL ANALYSIS
### Movements 21–25

As an opponent prepares to strike from the rear with a stamping kick (photo 1), draw the leg out of the path of the attack (photo 2) and counter with a back-fist strike to the face (photo 3). As the attacker grabs hold of the wrist (photo 4), launch a front snap kick while pulling the fist back sharply to break his grasp (photo 5). When the attacker retaliates with a reverse punch, block the attack with a downward block (photo 6) followed by a reverse punch (photo 7). This exchange is followed by an upper-level punch from the opponent, which is deflected with a rising block (photo 8).

1

2

3

4

5     6

7     8

**TECHNICAL ANALYSIS**
## Movements 30–32

Deflect an attacker's middle-level punch using a powerful crescent kick (photos 1 and 2), knocking the attacker off balance and creating an opportunity to counter with a downward punch (photo 3). The following two-handed downward palm-heel block can then be used in response to a front-snap-kick attack (photo 4).

1     2

3     4

# Gankaku (Chintō)

This *kata*, known as Gankaku in the Shōtōkan style, was formerly called Chintō. According to the writings of Master Gichin Funakoshi, it includes combinations from the Shōrei-ryū style.

Chintō is an old Tomari-based *kata* that has been passed down to the Shōtōkan and Shitō-ryū styles. While details regarding its creator and origins are not well known, historical evidence indicates that it was passed down to the early Tomari-te master Kōsaku Matsumora, after which modifications were introduced by Masters Chōtoku Kiyatake and Yasutsune Itosu. As such, three versions of Chintō are recognized today: Tomari no Chintō, Kiyatake no Chintō, and Itosu no Chintō. The *kata* practiced within the Shōtōkan school is the version that incorporates the changes introduced by Itosu.

Nevertheless, all three versions are characterized by a straight performance line, or *embusen* (vertical, horizontal or, in the case of the Kiyatake version, diagonal), and the inclusion of techniques performed while standing on one leg in a heron-leg stance. Within the Shōtōkan style, the name Gankaku (written using the characters 岩鶴, meaning "rock" and "crane") was selected based on the image that the heron-leg stance evokes of a crane poised on a rock preparing to spring upon a foe.

Accordingly, when standing on one leg, it is essential to convey intimidating power and a boldness capable of stopping an opponent in his tracks. Gankaku also requires the development of specialized skills, including the ability to maintain proper balance when standing on one leg, followed by the execution of a simultaneous side snap kick and back-fist strike. Among the various advanced techniques appearing in the *kata* is a sequence involving the blocking of an opponent's attack, grasping the wrist, and then lifting it over the head with both hands while turning the body to lock the opponent's arm over the shoulder.

The Shōtōkan style of today distinguishes between the heron-leg stance (*sagi-ashi dachi*) and crane-leg stance (*tsuru-ashi dachi*). In the heron-leg stance, the instep of the raised foot rests against the inside of the supporting leg, while in the crane-leg stance, the raised foot is hooked behind the supporting leg.

## Gankaku

### *Yōi* (Ready position)
*Soto hachiji-dachi* (open V stance) with both fists positioned in front of the hips.

1-A) Driving the right hip to the rear, open the hands while drawing them back to behind the right hip.

1-B) Stepping back with the right foot, swing both hands around toward the front of the body, bringing the backs of the hands together with the right arm positioned above the left arm.

Yōi

1-A

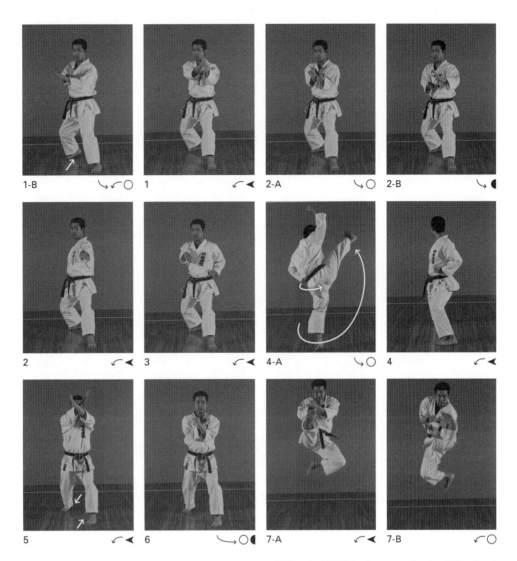

1-B    1    2-A    2-B

2    3    4-A    4

5    6    7-A    7-B

### 1) *Kōkutsu-dachi/Haishu awase-uke*
Complete the step back with the right foot into a right back stance while executing a two-handed upper-level back-hand block, sweeping the hands from right to left.

2-A) Keeping the wrists crossed, drop the right hand down toward the left-hand side while rotating the left hand so that the palm faces upward.

### 2-B) *Gyaku te-dori*
Swing the left hand back toward the right hand using the wrist as a pivot while drawing the right hand back along the same path to perform a reverse hand grasp.

### 2) *Kōkutsu-dachi/Hidari chūdan-zuki*
As the hands drop level with the chest, immediately deliver a middle-level punch with the left arm while pulling the right hand, formed into a fist, back to above the right hip.

### 3) *Kōkutsu-dachi/Migi chūdan gyaku-zuki*
Maintaining a strong back stance, deliver a right middle-level reverse punch with the right arm.

4-A) Swing the right leg up in front of and around the body to the left while driving the right fist up above the head.

### 4) *Kiba-dachi/Migi sokumen gedan-barai/Fumikomi*
Completing a 360-degree turn to the left, deliver a stamping kick with the right leg, planting the right foot into a straddle-leg stance facing the opposite direction while delivering a downward block with the right arm.

### 5) *Moto-dachi/Jōdan haishu jūji-uke*
Turning the hips 90 degrees to the left, draw the legs together slightly, sliding the left foot back and the right foot forward to assume a narrow front stance (*moto-dachi*) while thrusting the arms upward to deliver an upper-level back-hand X-block with the right arm positioned above the left arm.

6) Pull the elbows down toward the chest while closing the hands into fists.

### 7-A) *Nidan-geri (Migi tobi mae-geri)*
Maintaining the same upper-body position, deliver a double jump kick. First thrust off the left leg to deliver a jumping front kick with the right leg.

### 7-B) *Nidan-geri (Hidari tobi mae-geri)*
Deliver a jumping front kick with the left leg.

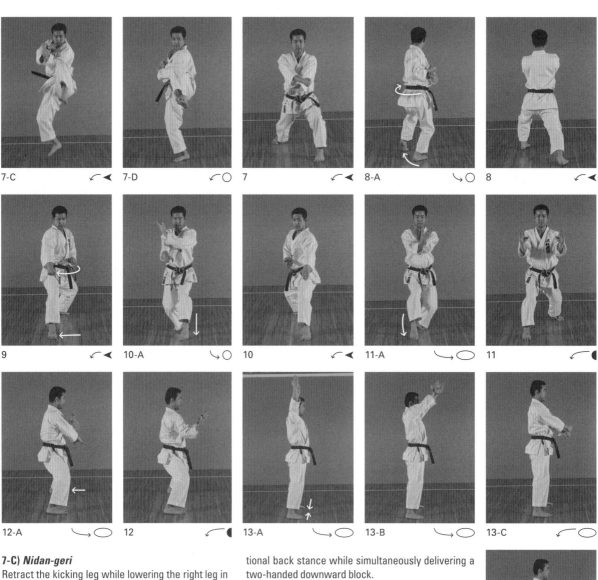

7-C ↙◀   7-D ↙○   7 ↙◀   8-A ↘○   8 ↙◀

9 ↙◀   10-A ↘○   10 ↙◀   11-A ↘○   11 ↶●

12-A ↘○   12 ↶●   13-A ↘○   13-B ↘○   13-C ↶○

### 7-C) *Nidan-geri*
Retract the kicking leg while lowering the right leg in preparation for the landing.

### 7-D) *Nidan-geri*
Plant the right foot on the floor, pulling the hands back toward the right hip in preparation for the following blocking technique.

### 7) *Zenkutsu-dachi/Gedan jūji-uke*
Plant the left foot in front of the right foot into a left front stance while delivering a downward X-block.

8-A) Turning 180 degrees to the right, draw the left foot back alongside and past the right foot while pulling the fists back to above the right hip.

### 8) *Zenkutsu-dachi/Gedan jūji-uke*
Follow through with the left foot, stepping forward into a left front stance while executing a downward X-block facing the opposite direction.

### 9) *Kasei kōkutsu-dachi/Morote gedan-uke*
Turning the head to the right to face the opposite direction, shift the right foot across the back while turning the body 180 degrees to the right, assuming a left back stance with the hips positioned lower than a conven-

tional back stance while simultaneously delivering a two-handed downward block.

10-A) Step forward with the left foot, opening both hands into knife hands while pulling the left hand back to above the right shoulder.

### 10) *Kasei kōkutsu-dachi/Morote gedan shutō-uke*
Complete the step forward with the left foot into a lower-than-usual left back stance while executing a two-handed downward knife-hand block

11-A) Step forward with the right foot while crossing the arms at the wrists in front of the chest. The left arm is positioned above the right arm with the palms of the hands facing upward.

### 11) *Zenkutsu-dachi/Shutō kakiwake-uke*
Complete the step forward with the right foot into a right front stance while rotating the hands outward to perform a knife-hand separating block.

12-A) Turning 90 degrees to the left, slide the left foot across the back, aligning it with the right foot into a straddle-leg stance while lowering and crossing the arms in front of the body.

13 ↶○

14-A

14

15

15 (Rear view)

15 (Side view)

16-A

16-B

16

17-A

17

18-A

### 12) *Kiba-dachi/Haitō kakiwake-uke*

From the straddle leg stance, draw the forearms upward and out to the sides while turning the hands outward to perform a ridge-hand separating block.

13-A) Straighten the knees while drawing the feet together into a natural posture. At the same time, extend both arms directly out to the sides and then upward.

13-B) Draw the arms toward each other and downward in front of the body in large circular motions, crossing them as they travel downward in front of the chest.

13-C) Close the hands into fists as the arms travel downward in front of the chest.

### 13) *Shizentai/Ryōwan-gamae*

Complete the motion of the arms, extending them downward and out to the sides of the body.

14-A) Turn the head sharply to the left and draw the left foot out to the left-hand side while pulling the left fist back to above the right shoulder and thrusting the right fist across the front of the body and downward.

### 14) *Kōkutsu-dachi/Manji-uke*

Shift into a right back stance while drawing the right arm back strongly and driving the left arm downward to execute a hi-low block. The right arm performs an upper-level inside-to-outside block to the rear while the left arm delivers a downward block to the front.

### 15) *Kōkutsu-dachi/Manji-uke*

Step forward with the right foot into a left front stance while again delivering a hi-low block facing the same direction. The left arm executes an upper-level inside-to-outside block as the right arm performs a downward block.

16-A) Turning the head to the left, draw the left foot

back to toward the right foot, rotating the hips to the left while pulling the left fist across to the right-hand side of the body and the extending the right arm in the opposite direction.

16-B) Continue drawing the left foot back behind the right foot while pulling the left fist toward the right shoulder and extending the right arm across the front of the body and downward.

### 16) *Kōkutsu-dachi/Manji-uke*

Completing a 180-degree rotation of the hips, plant the left foot forward into a right back stance while delivering a third hi-low block, with the right arm performing an upper-level inside-to-outside block to the rear as the left arm executes a downward block to the front.

17-A) Drawing the right foot in toward the left foot and to the rear, bend the left knee to lower the hips while pulling both elbows back and upward.

### 17) *Katahiza-dachi/Gedan jūji-uke*

Lowering the hips into a kneeling posture with the right knee on the floor, drive the fists downward in front of the body to execute a downward X-block.

18-A) Raising the hips, draw the right foot out to the right side while extending the right arm to the left-hand side of the body and the left arm in the opposite direction.

### 18) *Kiba-dachi/Ryōwan uchi-uke*

Assuming a straddle-leg stance, execute a double inside-to-outside block.

19-A) Straightening the knees, draw the feet together into a natural posture while driving both fists upward.

19-A

x

18

| 19-B | 19 | 20 | 21 | 22 |

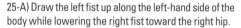

| 23-A | 23 | 24-A | 24-B | 24 |

19-B) Draw the arms toward each other and downward in front of the body in large circular motions, crossing them as they travel downward in front of the chest.

### 19) *Shizentai/Ryōwan-gamae*
Complete the motion of the arms until they extend downward and out to the sides of the body.

### 20) *Shizentai/Ryōken koshi-gamae*
Pull both fists in toward the body, positioning them above the hips with the elbows extending out to the sides.

### 21) *Moto-dachi/Migi hiji-barai*
Rotate the hips sharply to the left into a shortened front stance facing the left to deliver a sweeping elbow block to the front with the right arm.

### 22) *Moto-dachi/Hidari hiji-barai*
Rotate the hips sharply to the right, assuming a shortened front stance facing the right while executing a sweeping elbow block to the front with the left arm.

23-A) Turn the hips to the right and, pivoting on the right foot, draw the left foot in toward and behind the right foot while drawing the fists out to opposite sides of the body, crossing the arms in front of the chest with the left arm positioned above the right arm.

### 23) *Kōsa-dachi/Morote chūdan kōsa-uke*
Bend the knees and lower the hips, assuming a cross-legged stance while drawing the forearms upward and out to the sides to deliver a middle-level cross block, with both arms performing inside-to-outside blocks.

24-A) Without moving the lower body, turn the head to the left and pull the left fist back to above the right shoulder while extending the right arm across the front of the body and downward.

24-B) Raising the hips, lift the left foot up along the back of the right leg while pulling the right arm back and upward toward the right-hand side of the body and drawing the left arm downward across the front of the body.

### 24) *Gankaku-gamae*
With the left foot hooked behind the right knee, straighten the supporting leg and the back to assume a crane-leg stance, positioning the upper body as if having completed a hi-low block with the right arm behind the head and the left arm extending downward toward the left-hand side of the body. This position, unique to the Ganakaku *kata*, is known as the Gankaku posture.

25-A) Draw the left fist up along the left-hand side of the body while lowering the right fist toward the right hip.

25-B) Bring the left fist upward and across to the right-hand side of the body in a large arcing motion.

### 25) *Tsuru-ashi-dachi/Koshi-gamae*
Bring the left fist down to above the right hip, placing it on top of the right fist. As the left fist approaches the hip, bend the right knee slightly and lower the hips.

### 26-A) *Hidari yoko ke-age/Hidari yoko-mawashi ura-ken-uchi*
Deliver a left side snap kick while simultaneously executing a left side round back-fist strike.

26-B) Leaving the left arm extended, snap the left foot back following the kick.

26-C) Plant the left foot in the direction of the kick and step forward in the same direction with the right foot.

25-A

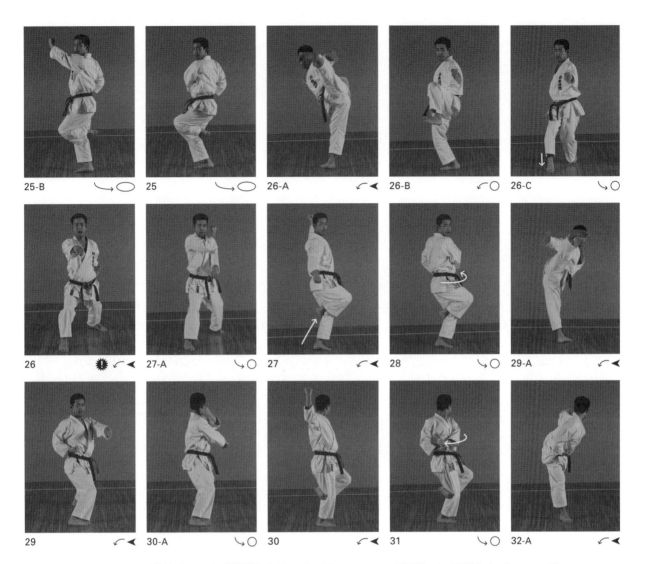

**26) *Zenkutsu-dachi/Migi chūdan oi-zuki***

Complete the step forward with the right foot into a right front stance while delivering a right middle-level lunge punch with a *kiai*.

27-A) Drawing the right foot back toward the left foot, pull the right fist back to above the left shoulder while extending the left arm downward across the front of the body.

**27) *Gankaku-gamae***

Pull the right foot back, hooking it behind the left knee and raising the hips into a crane-leg stance while pulling the left arm back and extending the right arm downward to the right to assume a Gankaku posture.

**28) *Tsuru-ashi-dachi/Koshi-gamae***

Bending the left knee slightly, pull both fists back to above the left hip. The right fist moves in front of the midsection, traveling in a direct path to the left hip.

**29-A) *Migi yoko ke-age/Migi yoko-mawashi uraken-uchi***

Deliver a right side snap kick while simultaneously executing a right side round back-fist strike.

**29) *Kiba-dachi/Hidari sokumen-zuki***

Plant the right foot in the direction of the kick, assuming a straddle-leg stance while delivering a side punch with the left arm.

30-A) Turn the head to the left and pull the left fist back to above the right shoulder while extending the right arm across the front of the body and downward.

**30) *Gankaku-gamae***

Pull the left foot back, hooking it behind the right knee and raising the hips into a crane-leg stance while pulling the right arm back behind the head and extending the left arm downward to the left-hand side of the body.

**31) *Tsuru-ashi-dachi/Koshi-gamae***

Bending the right knee slightly, pull both fists back to above the right hip.

**32-A) *Hidari yoko ke-age/Hidari yoko-mawashi uraken-uchi***

Deliver a left side snap kick while simultaneously executing a left side round back-fist strike.

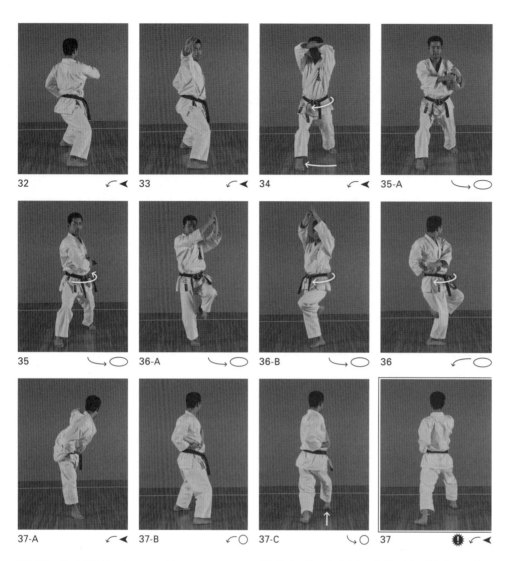

**32) *Kiba-dachi/Migi sokumen-zuki***

Plant the left foot in the direction of the kick, assuming a straddle-leg stance while executing a side punch with the right arm.

**33) *Kiba-dachi/Jōdan shutō-uchi***

Turning the head to the right, deliver an upper-level knife-hand block to the right-hand side of the body.

**34) *Zenkutsu-dachi/Tate empi-uchi***

Slide the right foot back while turning the hips 90 degrees to the right, shifting into a right front stance while delivering an upward elbow strike with the left arm against the open right hand.

35-A) Lower both arms, pulling the left elbow down along the left side of the body and to the rear while opening the left hand and closing the right hand into a fist.

**35) *Zenkutsu-dachi/Soete koshi-gamae***

Turning the hips to the left, draw both hands back to above the left hip, pressing the front of the right fist into the palm of the left hand.

36-A) Draw the left foot forward, raising the left knee while extending both arms upward. Keep the hands in contact with each other while moving the arms.

36-B) Hooking the left foot behind the right knee, pivot on the right foot to rotate the hips to the right while raising the hands above the head.

**36) *Tsuru-ashi-dachi/Koshi-gamae***

Completing a 270-degree rotation of the hips, pull both hands down to above the right hip, closing the left hand into a fist and positioning it on top of the right fist.

**37-A) *Hidari yoko ke-age/Hidari yoko-mawashi ura-ken-uchi***

Deliver a left side snap kick while simultaneously executing a left side round back-fist strike.

37-B) Plant the left foot forward in the direction of the kick.

37-C) Step forward with the right foot in the same direction.

**37) *Zenkutsu-dachi/Migi chūdan oi-zuki***

Complete the step forward with the right foot into a right front stance while delivering a right middle-level lunge punch with a *kiai*.

*Yame*-A) Pivoting on the right foot, turn the body 180 degrees to the left while drawing the left foot in align-

37 (Rear view)

Yame-A

Yame-B

Yame

ment with the right foot. At the same time, bring the right fist out to the left-hand side of the body while extending the left arm in the opposite direction beneath the right arm.

Yame-B) Assume an open V stance with the arms crossed in front of the body.

### Yame
Return to a natural-posture stance with the arms extended downward in front of the body, maintaining a state of physical and mental readiness (*zanshin*).

---

**TECHNICAL ANALYSIS**
### Movements 1–3

Deflect an opponent's punching attack using a two-handed back-hand block (photo 1). Grasping the attacker's punching arm, twist and pull it downward to throw him off-balance (photo 2) and counter with a reverse punch (photo 3).

1

2

3

---

**TECHNICAL ANALYSIS**
### Movements 21–22

Block an opponent's lunge punch with a sweeping elbow block using the right arm (photo 1), responding to a follow-up reverse punch by twisting the hips in the opposite direction to block with a subsequent sweeping elbow block using the left arm (photo 2).

1

2

## TECHNICAL ANALYSIS
### Movements 27–29

Block an opponent's front snap kick with a downward block from a crane-leg stance (photo 1). When the attacker launches a subsequent punching attack, use a back fist strike to deflect the assault while simultaneously countering with a side snap kick (photo 2) and follow through with a side punch to the midsection.

1

2

3

## TECHNICAL ANALYSIS
### Movements 33–36

Upon sidestepping an opponent's lunge-punch attack while simultaneously countering with a ridge-hand strike (photo 1), grab the attacker's wrist and use it as leverage when following through with an upper elbow strike to the head (photo 2). As the opponent then delivers a reverse punch, respond with a pressing block and grab the wrist (photo 3). Then bring the attacker's arm upward while turning the body (photo 4), using the opportunity to lock his arm over the shoulder (photo 5).

1

2

3

4

5

# Chinte

Chinte is believed to belong to the same family of *kata* as Chintō (called Gankaku in the Shōtōkan style).

Around the time that Master Funakoshi changed the Chinese characters used to write "karate" from 唐手 to 空手, he assigned the name Shōin to this *kata*, but the reason why is not well known.

Distinguishing characteristics of Chinte include circular-motion strikes centered on the shoulder, which employ centrifugal force to generate speed and power, two-finger spear hand attacks to the eyes, scissors strikes, and palm-heel blocks. Incorporating only one kicking technique, it is a *kata* made up almost exclusively of hand-based techniques, many of which are performed with the hands open. Accordingly, many of the sequences serve as self-defense applications for close-range combat.

Because Chinte includes repeated use of techniques that do not rely on strength to be effective, such as attacks to the eyes and elbow strikes, it is increasingly being practiced as a *kata* ideally suited for women.

In addition to vertical-fist strikes and such dynamic techniques as large circular scooping blocks, Chinte also incorporates intricate maneuvers, such as a downward separating block performed while standing on one leg. As such, Chinte could be rightly considered to be an advanced *kata*.

While Chinte is largely believed to be a Shuri-te *kata*, little is known about who created it or how it has been passed down. It is currently practiced in the Shōtōkan and Shitō-ryū styles of karate.

While the vast majority of Shōtōkan *kata* comprise techniques of a linear nature, Chinte features a significant number of techniques employing circular movements. These techniques, unique to China, make the *kata* something of an oddity within the Shōtōkan style. This is believed to be the reason behind the name Chinte, which is written using the characters 珍手, meaning "unusual hand" or "unusual techniques."

## Chinte

Shizentai

Yōi

1-A

### *Shizentai* (Natural posture)
*Soto hachiji-dachi* (open V stance) with both fists positioned in front of the hips.

### *Yōi* (Ready position)
Draw the right foot in toward the left foot to assume a closed parallel stance (*heisoku-dachi*) while pulling both fists up to the abdomen. The right fist rests against the solar plexus with the back of the fist facing the front. The left fist is positioned underneath the right fist with the back of the fist facing downward.

1-A) Gradually raise the right arm, "rolling" the right fist up the chest while slowly turning the head toward the right.

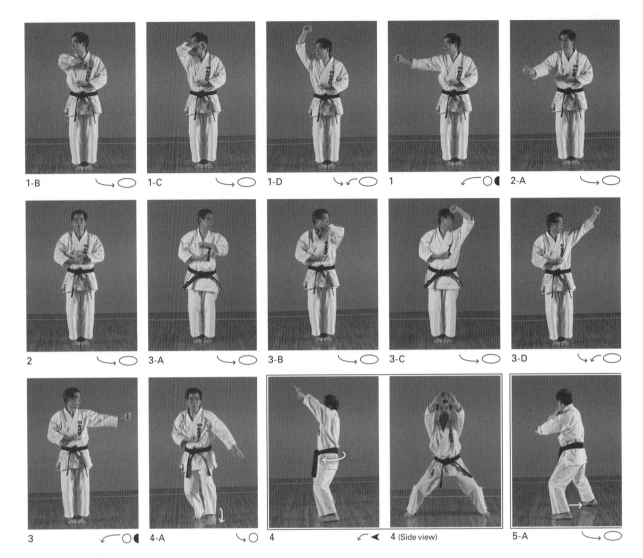

1-B    1-C    1-D    1    2-A

2    3-A    3-B    3-C    3-D

3    4-A    4    4 (Side view)    5-A

1-B) Continue raising the right arm, leading with the elbow while turning the head toward the right.

1-C) Draw the right fist upward past the left side of the head.

1-D) Once the right forearm passes the side of the head, move the right fist out along a curved path to the right side of the body.

**1) *Heisoku-dachi/Migi tettsui-uchi***
Lower the right arm, bringing the right fist level with the right shoulder to deliver a hammer-fist strike.

2-A) Draw the right fist back toward the abdomen, turning the head to the left in synchronization with the movement of the right arm. As the right fist moves, begin "rolling" the left fist upward so that the back of the fist faces the front.

2) Bring the right fist to the abdomen with the back of the fist facing downward. The left fist rests above the right fist with the back of the fist facing the front.

3-A) Gradually turning the head to the left, raise the left arm while "rolling" the left fist up the chest.

3-B) Continue raising the left arm while turning the head to face the left-hand side.

3-C) Draw the left fist up past the right side of the head

3-D) Bring the left fist out and downward to the left side of the body.

**3) *Heisoku-dachi/Hidari tettsui-uchi***
Follow through with the motion of the left arm, bringing the fist level with the shoulder to deliver a hammer-fist strike.

4-A) Stepping forward with the left foot, swing the left arm downward and out in front of the body while opening the left hand.

**4) *Kiba-dachi/Awase shutō age-uke***
Complete the step forward with the left foot, turning the hips 90 degrees to the right into a straddle-leg stance facing the right. At the same time, extend the right arm upward at a roughly 45-degree angle above the head with the right hand open while following through with the swinging motion of the left arm, bringing the back of the left hand up to meet the palm side of the right hand to execute a two-handed knife-hand rising block.

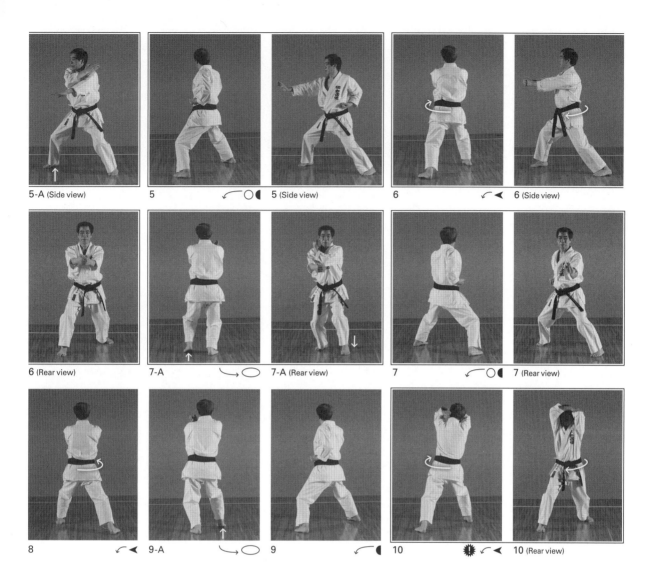

5-A (Side view)  5  5 (Side view)  6  6 (Side view)

6 (Rear view)  7-A  7-A (Rear view)  7  7 (Rear view)

8  9-A  9  10  10 (Rear view)

5-A) Turning the head to the right, draw the right foot back while pulling the right knife hand to above the left shoulder and extending the left arm across the front of the body.

### 5) *Fudō-dachi/Migi tate shutō-uke*
Turning the hips to the right, shift into a rooted stance while delivering a vertical knife-hand block with the right arm.

### 6) *Zenkutsu-dachi/Hidari tate-ken gyaku-zuki*
Keeping the feet in place, thrust off the left foot, shifting into a front stance while delivering a left vertical-fist reverse punch against the palm of the right hand, wrapping the fingers of the right hand around the left fist.

7-A) Maintaining the curved shape of the right hand, step forward with the left foot while pulling the left hand, opened into a knife hand, back to above the right shoulder.

### 7) *Fudō-dachi/Hidari tate shutō-uke*
Complete the step forward with the left foot into a rooted stance while performing a vertical knife-hand block with the left arm.

### 8) *Zenkutsu-dachi/Migi tate-ken gyaku-zuki*
Thrusting off the right foot, shift into a front stance while delivering a vertical-fist reverse punch with the right arm against the palm of the left hand.

9-A) Step forward with the right foot while drawing the right hand back to above the left shoulder, keeping the fingers of the left hand curved.

### 9) *Fudō-dachi/Migi tate shutō-uke*
Complete the step forward with the right foot into a rooted stance while delivering a right vertical knife-hand block.

### 10) *Zenkutsu-dachi/Hidari tate empi-uchi*
Thrusting off the left foot, shift into a front stance while executing a left upward elbow strike against the open right hand with a *kiai*.

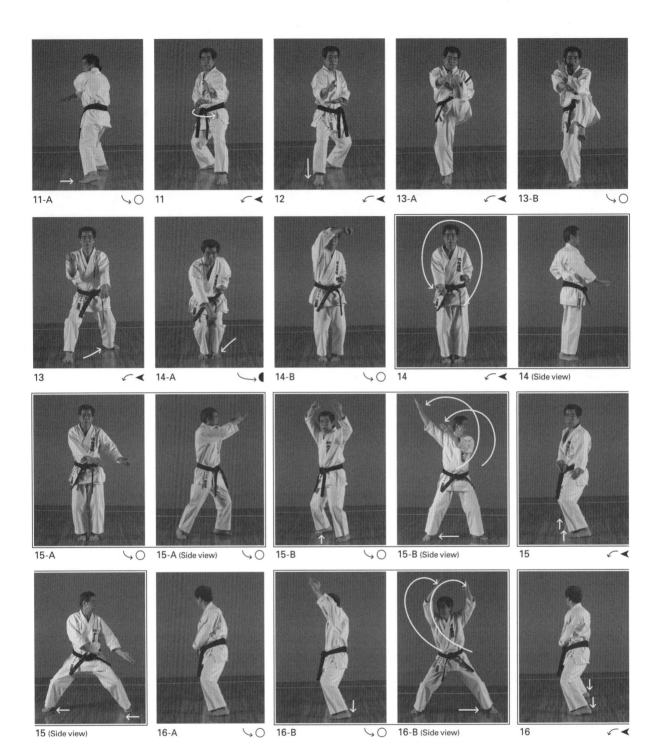

11-A  ↘○  11  ↙◀  12  ↙◀  13-A  ↙◀  13-B  ↘○

13  ↙◀  14-A  ↘◖  14-B  ↘○  14  ↙◀  14 (Side view)

15-A  ↘○  15-A (Side view)  ↘○  15-B  ↘○  15-B (Side view)  15  ↙◀

15 (Side view)  16-A  ↘○  16-B  ↘○  16-B (Side view)  16  ↙◀

**11-A)** Turning the head to the left, slide the left foot across the back and extend the right arm across the chest toward the rear while pulling the left hand back to above the right shoulder.

### 11) *Kōkutsu-dachi/Hidari chūdan shutō-uke*
Turning the hips to the left, shift into a right back stance facing the opposite direction while delivering a left middle-level knife-hand block.

### 12) *Kōkutsu-dachi/Migi chūdan shutō-uke*
Step forward with the right foot into a left back stance while performing a right middle-level knife-hand block.

### 13-A) *Hidari mae-geri*
Keeping the arms in place, deliver a front snap kick with the left leg.

**13-B)** While retracting the kicking leg, pull the left hand up to above the right shoulder and extend the right arm downward across the front of the body.

16 (Side view)

17-A          ↘ ○

17-A (Side view)

17          ↙ ◀

17 (Side view)

18-A          ↘ ○

18-A (Side view)

18-B          ↘ ○

18-B (Side view)

18-C          ↙ ○

18-C (Side view)

### 13) *Zenkutsu-dachi/Kōsa-uke*

Plant the left foot to the rear into a right front stance while executing a cross block with the right arm performing an inside-to-outside block as the left arm delivers a downward block.

### 14-A) *Heisoku-dachi/Naiwan sukui-nage*

Sliding the left foot forward into a closed parallel stance, bend the knees and lean forward at the waist while driving the right fist across the front of the knees to the left to execute an inner-arm scooping throw.

14-B) Straighten the legs and raise the hips to stand upright while drawing the right fist around and up over the head.

### 14) *Heisoku-dachi/Gedan tettsui-uchi*

Drive the right fist around the right side of the body in a large circular motion to deliver a lower-level hammer-fist strike in front of the body.

15-A) Thrusting strongly off the left foot, step straight back with the right foot while thrusting both hands, open with the palms facing upward, out to the left-hand side of the body.

15-B) Drive the right foot straight back, followed by a gliding step with the left foot in the same direction, assuming a straddle-leg stance while swinging both arms up above the head and around in a large circular motion to the right side of the body.

### 15) *Kiba-dachi/Morote enshin haitō-barai*

Follow through with the circular motion of the arms to deliver a two-handed centrifugal ridge-hand sweep. Upon completion, both arms extend outward toward the left-hand side of the body with the hands at waist level and the palms facing upward.

16-A) Turning the head to the right, thrust both arms across to the opposite side of the body.

16-B) Driving off the right foot, slide the left foot out to the left, followed by a gliding step with the right foot in the same direction, assuming a straddle-leg stance while swinging both arms up over the head and around in a large circular motion to the left side of the body.

### 16) *Kiba-dachi/Morote enshin haitō-barai*

Complete the motion of the arms to deliver a two-handed centrifugal ridge-hand sweep to the right-hand side of the body.

17-A) Turning the head to face forward, drive off of the right foot, sliding the left foot out to the left-hand side while extending the right arm over the left arm and across the front of the body to the left-hand side.

### 17) *Kiba-dachi/Ryōwan uchi-uke*

Following the motion of the left foot to the left side, slide the right foot in the same direction, maintaining a straddle-leg stance while performing a double inside-to-outside block.

18-A) Extend both fists straight out to the sides of the body and then upwards while drawing the right foot in toward the left foot and straightening the left knee.

18-B) Hooking the right foot behind the left knee to assume a crane-leg stance, continue raising the arms upward above the head.

18-C) Draw both arms downward in front of the body, crossing them at the wrists with the right arm positioned above the left arm.

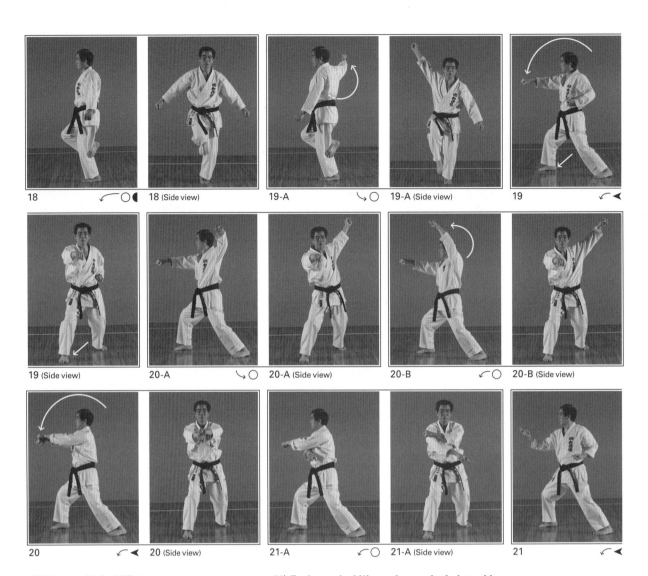

18    ⌒○◗    18 (Side view)    19-A    ↘○    19-A (Side view)    19    ⌒◀

19 (Side view)    20-A    ↘○    20-A (Side view)    20-B    ⌒○    20-B (Side view)

20    ⌒◀    20 (Side view)    21-A    ⌒○    21-A (Side view)    21    ⌒◀

**18) *Tsuru-ashi-dachi/Ryōwan-gamae***

Complete the motion of the arms until they extend downward and out to the sides of the body.

19-A) Keeping the right arm extended, draw the right fist, formed into a one-knuckle fist, back and upward in a large sweeping motion.

**19) *Zenkutsu-dachi/Ippon-ken furi-otoshi***

Draw the right foot forward into a right front stance while swinging the right arm sharply out in front of the body to deliver a swinging one-knuckle fist drop.

20-A) Draw the left fist, formed into a one-knuckle fist, back behind the body.

20-B) Swing the left arm upward along a large circular path pivoting on the shoulder.

**20) *Zenkutsu-dachi/Ippon-ken gyaku furi-otoshi***

Bring the left arm around and down, dropping the left fist on top of the right fist to deliver a follow-up swinging one-knuckle fist drop.

21-A) Pull the right hand, formed into a two-finger spear hand, back to below the left underarm.

**21) *Zenkutsu-dachi/Migi uchi-uke***

Turn the hips 45 degrees to the left while drawing the right arm out to deliver an inside-to-outside block. The right hand remains as a two-finger spear hand during the technique.

**22) *Zenkutsu-dachi/Hidari jōdan nihon-nukite***

Step forward with the left foot into a left front stance while executing an upper-level two-finger spear hand attack with the left hand.

23-A) Turning the head to the left to face the opposite direction, draw the left foot back while driving the right fist up to above the left shoulder and extending the left arm across the front of the body.

21 (Side view)  22  23-A  23  24

25-A  25  25 (Rear view)  26-A  26-A (Rear view)

26  26 (Rear view)  27  28-A  28

**23) *Zenkutsu-dachi/Hidari uchi-uke***
Turning the hips 180 degrees to the left, shift into a left front stance while drawing the left arm out to execute an inside-to-outside block. The left hand remains formed into a two-finger spear hand throughout the move.

**24) *Zenkutsu-dachi/Migi jōdan nihon-nukite***
Step forward with the right foot into a right front stance while delivering a right upper-level two-finger spear hand attack.

25-A) Pivoting on the left foot, draw the right foot across toward the left-hand side of the body, turning the hips to the left while pulling the right hand, formed into a palm heel, back behind the body.

**25) *Fudō-dachi/Migi chūdan teishō furi-uchi***
Plant the right foot into a rooted stance while driving the right hand around the body toward the front to deliver a middle-level swinging palm-heel strike.

26-A) Extend the left arm toward the rear while opening the left hand into a palm heel.

**26) *Zenkutsu-dachi/Hidari chūdan teishō furi-uchi***
Shifting into a front stance, drive the left hand around the body to the front to deliver a middle-level swinging palm-heel strike. The left palm heel comes into contact with the right palm heel in front of the chest.

**27) *Zenkutsu-dachi/Haimen hasami-uchi* (*Nakadaka ippon-ken*)**
Drive both hands, formed into one-knuckle fists, behind the body to deliver a scissors strike to the rear.

28-A) Shift the left leg across the back to the opposite side, pivoting on the right foot to turn the body 180 degrees to the left while extending the arms to the sides of the body.

**28) *Fudō-dachi/Hasami-uchi* (*Nakadaka ippon-ken*)**
Assuming a rooted stance, deliver a one-knuckle-fist scissors strike to the front with a *kiai*.

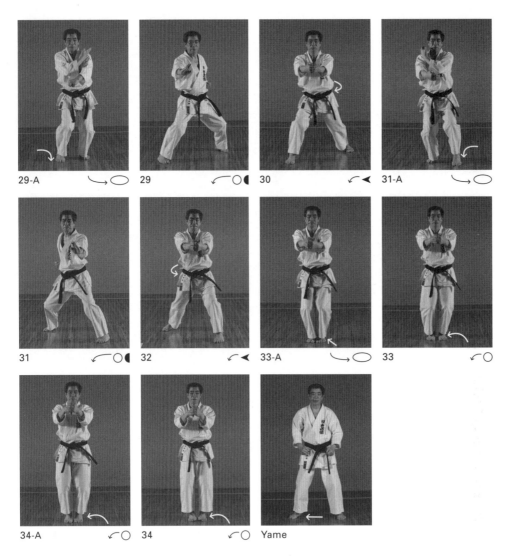

29-A      29      30      31-A

31      32      33-A      33

34-A      34      Yame

29-A) Step forward with the right foot while drawing the right hand back to above the left shoulder and extending the left arm forward.

### 29) Fudō-dachi/Migi tate shutō-uke
Complete the step forward with the right foot into a rooted stance while delivering a right vertical knife-hand block.

### 30) Zenkutsu-dachi/Hidari tate-ken gyaku-zuki
Thrusting off the left foot, shift into a front stance while delivering a left vertical-fist reverse punch against the palm of the right hand.

31-A) Step forward with the left foot while pulling the left hand back to above the right shoulder.

### 31) Fudō-dachi/Hidari tate shutō-uke
Complete the step forward with the left foot into a rooted stance while performing a vertical knife-hand block with the left arm.

### 32) Zenkutsu-dachi/Migi tate-ken gyaku-zuki
Thrusting off the right foot, shift into a front stance while delivering a vertical-fist reverse punch with the right arm against the palm of the left hand.

### 33-A) Heisoku-dachi/Tsutsumi-ken
With the left hand wrapped around the right fist and the arms extended out in front of the chest, draw the left foot back to alongside the right foot into a closed parallel stance.

33) Jump back at an angle to the right, keeping both legs together while drawing the hands back a notch toward the chin.

34-A) Jump back again in the same direction while drawing the hands back a further notch closer to the chin.

### 34) Heisoku-dachi (Jiai no kamae)
Jump back once more to return to the original starting point, drawing the hands back further toward the chin with the elbows tucked in closely to the sides of the body.

### Yame
Draw the right foot out to the right side into an open V stance while lowering both fists to the front of the hips, the same natural-posture stance assumed prior to starting the kata.

## TECHNICAL ANALYSIS
### Movements 12–13

Upon blocking an opponent's lunge-punch attack using a knife-hand block (photo 1), immediately counter with a front snap kick (photo 2). As the attacker delivers a follow-up reverse punch, respond with a cross block (photo 3).

1

2

3

## TECHNICAL ANALYSIS
### Movements 13–14

Respond to a reverse-punch attack using a cross block (photo 1). As the opponent delivers a front snap kick, block with a scooping block (photo 2), following through with the motion of the blocking arm to throw the attacker (photos 3 and 4) and finishing with a hammer-fist strike (photo 5).

1

2

3

4

5

## TECHNICAL ANALYSIS
### Movements 16–18

Swing both hands downward to the side of the body to execute a two-handed centrifugal ridge-hand sweep in response to an attacker's front snap kick (photos 1 and 2), followed by an inside-to-outside block as he follows through with a reverse punch (photo 3). As the attacker delivers a subsequent front snap kick, assume a crane-leg stance while deflecting the attack with a downward block (photo 4).

1

2

3

4

## TECHNICAL ANALYSIS
### Movements 27–28

As an attacker approaches from behind, deliver a scissors strike to the rear (photo 1), turn 180 degrees to face the opponent (photo 2), and execute a follow-up scissors strike targeting the opponent's midsection (photo 3).

1

2

3

# Sōchin

The *kata* Sōchin is found only in the Shitō-ryū and Shōtōkan styles of karate. Within Shitō-ryū, it is classified as an Arakaki-faction *kata*. Within the Shōtōkan style, around the time that Master Funakoshi changed the characters used to write "karate," the *kata* was briefly called Hakkō. Sōchin is made up of techniques characterized by a solid, robust nature.

It is unclear whether the different ways each karate style performs this *kata* is the result of variations that existed when the *kata* was initially conceived, or whether changes occurred as a result of the way in which instructors taught it.

The most characteristic feature of this *kata* is, as its name suggests, *Sōchin-dachi* (Sōchin stance). This stance, also called *fudō-dachi* (rooted stance), represents a cross between a front stance (*zenkutsu-dachi*) and straddle-leg stance (*kiba-dachi*). It is a stance that is strong both to the front and sides, conveying the feeling of being firmly rooted to the ground with the knees bent and exerting force outward. With the center of gravity positioned slightly toward the front leg, *Sōchin-dachi* provides a foundation from which an opponent's attack can be solidly blocked and a powerful counterattack delivered.

In the Sōchin of Shitō-ryū, however, *neko-ashi-dachi* (cat stance) is the stance predominantly used throughout the *kata*, which concludes with the raising of both arms from a black tiger posture to perform a mountain-formation block, followed by a simultaneous middle-level front snap kick and double palm-heel scissors block. The reason why two *kata* bearing the same name differ in this way can be attributed to the fact that the origins and the creator of this *kata* remain unknown, as does the means by which it was passed down.

## Sōchin

Yōi

1-A

1-B

1

### *Yōi* (Ready position)
*Soto hachiji-dachi* (open V stance) with both fists positioned in front of the hips.

1-A) Drawing the right foot along a course in toward the left foot and then forward, drop the hips while driving the left fist downward and raising the right fist to above the head.

1-B) Sliding the right foot forward and out to the right at an angle, lower the right elbow in front of the body while raising the left forearm. Continue drawing out

the right foot while simultaneously lowering the right arm as if delivering a downward block and raising the left arm is if performing a rising block.

### 1) *Sōchin-dachi / Musō-gamae*
Assume a rooted stance (called Sōchin-stance within the Sōchin *kata*) as the upper body settles into an "incomparable posture." The right arm extends downward in front of the body like a downward block but with the elbow bent slightly more than usual, while the left arm is positioned like a rising block but with the forearm positioned directly in front of the forehead.

163

2-A) Draw the left foot forward toward the right foot while pulling the right hand, opened into a knife hand, back toward the body. At the same time, begin lowering the left elbow in front of the chest.

2-B) Continue stepping forward with the left foot, drawing the right hand up below the left underarm while pulling the left elbow downward in front of the body.

**2) *Sōchin-dachi/Migi chūdan tate shutō-uke***
Planting the left foot into a rooted stance, extend the right hand out in front of the chest to deliver a middle-level vertical knife-hand block while pulling the left fist back to above the left hip.

**3-A) *Sōchin-dachi/Hidari chūdan-zuki***
Maintaining a strong rooted stance, deliver a left middle-level punch.

**3) *Sōchin-dachi/Migi chūdan gyaku-zuki***
Deliver a right middle-level reverse punch.

4-A) Drawing the left foot back toward the right foot, drive the left fist up to above the right shoulder while extending the right arm across the front of the body.

**4) *Kōkutsu-dachi/Manji-uke***
Shifting into a right back stance facing the left, draw the right arm back strongly while driving the left arm downward to execute a hi-low block. The right arm performs an upper-level inside-to-outside block to the rear while the left arm delivers a downward block to the front.

5-A) Step forward with the right foot while maintaining the same position of the upper body.

5-B) Just before the right leg completes its step forward, begin to draw the right arm down while raising the left arm.

**5) *Sōchin-dachi/Musō-gamae***
Planting the right foot into a rooted stance, drive the right arm downward while raising the left elbow to assume an incomparable posture.

6-A) Stepping forward with the left foot, draw the right arm back toward the body and beneath the left arm while lowering the left elbow in front of the chest.

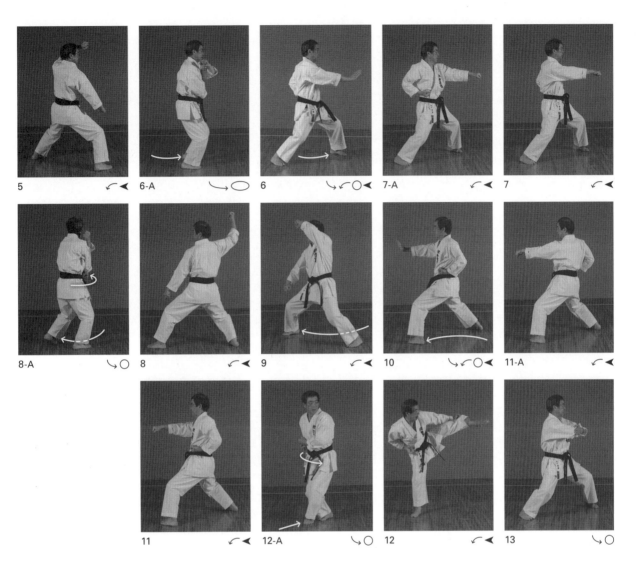

5    6-A    6    7-A    7

8-A    8    9    10    11-A

11    12-A    12    13

### 6) *Sōchin-dachi/Migi chūdan tate shutō-uke*

Complete the step forward with the left foot into a rooted stance while delivering a middle-level vertical knife-hand block with the right arm, pulling the left fist back to above the left hip.

### 7-A) *Sōchin-dachi/Hidari chūdan-zuki*

Deliver a left middle-level punch.

### 7) *Sōchin-dachi/Migi chūdan gyaku-zuki*

Deliver a right middle-level reverse punch.

8-A) Turning the head to the left to face the opposite direction, draw the left foot back and turn the body 180 degrees to the left. At the same time, drive the left fist up to above the right shoulder while extending the right arm across the front of the body toward the left.

### 8) *Kōkutsu-dachi/Manji-uke*

Assume a right back stance while pulling the right arm back strongly and driving the left arm downward to execute a hi-low block.

### 9) *Sōchin-dachi/Musō-gamae*

Step forward with the right foot into a rooted stance while assuming an incomparable posture.

### 10) *Sōchin-dachi/Migi chūdan tate shutō-uke*

Step forward with the left foot into a rooted stance while delivering a vertical knife-hand block with the right arm.

### 11-A) *Sōchin-dachi/Hidari chūdan-zuki*

Deliver a left middle-level punch.

### 11) *Sōchin-dachi/Migi chūdan gyaku-zuki*

Deliver a right middle-level reverse punch.

### 12-A) *Koshi-gamae*

Pivoting on the right foot, turn the head to the left to face the opposite side while drawing the left foot back toward the right foot and pulling both fists to above the right hip.

### 12) *Hidari yoko ke-age/Hidari yoko-mawashi uraken-uchi*

Deliver a left side snap kick while simultaneously executing a left side round back-fist strike.

### 13) *Sōchin-dachi/Migi empi-uchi*

Plant the left foot in the direction of the kick into a rooted stance while simultaneously delivering a right front elbow strike against the palm of the left hand.

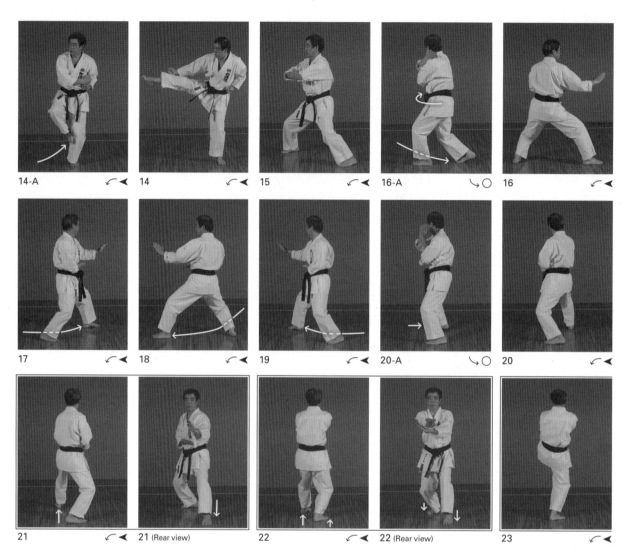

14-A) 14    15    16-A    16

17    18    19    20-A    20

21    21 (Rear view)    22    22 (Rear view)    23

### 14-A) *Koshi-gamae*

Turning the head to the right, draw the right foot up to the inside of the left knee in preparation to launch a side snap kick to the right-hand side while pulling both fists down to above the left hip.

### 14) *Migi yoko ke-age/Migi yoko-mawashi uraken-uchi*

Deliver a right side snap kick while executing a right side round back-fist strike.

### 15) *Sōchin-dachi/Hidari empi-uchi*

Plant the right foot in the direction of the kick into a rooted stance while delivering a left front elbow strike against the palm of the right hand.

16-A) Pivoting on the left foot, draw the right foot back along the right side of the body to turn 180 degrees to the right. At the same time, bring the right hand up to above the left shoulder while extending the left arm across the front of the body to the right.

### 16) *Kōkutsu-dachi/Migi chūdan shutō-uke*

Shift into a left back stance while executing a right middle-level knife-hand block.

### 17) *Kōkutsu-dachi/Hidari chūdan shutō-uke*

Stepping forward with the left foot at a 45-degree angle to the left, assume a right back stance while delivering a left middle-level knife-hand block.

### 18) *Kōkutsu-dachi/Hidari chūdan shutō-uke*

Drawing the left foot back, turn the hips 135 degrees to the left, assuming a left back stance while executing a left middle-level knife-hand block.

### 19) *Kōkutsu-dachi/Migi chūdan shutō-uke*

Step forward with the right foot at a 45-degree angle to the right, shifting into a left back stance while delivering a middle-level knife-hand block with the right arm.

20-A) Pivoting on the left foot, slide the right foot across to the right to turn 45 degrees to the right, bringing the right hand back to above the left shoulder while extending the left arm across the front of the body to the right-hand side.

### 20) *Kōkutsu-dachi/Migi chūdan shutō-uke*

Assume a left front stance while executing a middle-level knife-hand block with the right arm.

23 (Rear view)

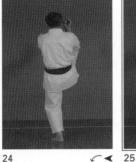

24    ↶ ◄

25    ☀ ↶ ◄

25 (Rear view)

26    ↶ ◄

27    ↶ ◄

28    ↶ ◄

29    ↶ ◄

30    ↶ ◄

31    ↶ ◄

### 21) *Kōkutsu-dachi/Hidari chūdan shutō-uke*

Step forward with the left foot into a right back stance while delivering a left middle-level knife-hand block.

### 22) *Kyo-dachi/Hidari osae-uke/Migi nukite*

Thrusting off the right foot, slide the left foot forward slightly and pull the right leg under the body into a transient stance (a foreshortened back stance with the rear foot turned inward at a 45-degree angle). At the same time, draw the left hand back toward the body to perform a pressing block while simultaneously thrusting the right hand forward with the palm of the hand facing upward to deliver spear-hand attack.

### 23) *Hidari mae-geri*

Maintaining the same upper-body position, deliver a front snap kick with the left leg.

### 24) *Migi mae-geri/Nagashi-uke/Uraken-uchi*

Immediately deliver a front snap kick with the right leg while executing a sweeping block past the right side of the head with the right arm and a back-fist strike to the front with the left arm.

### 25) *Sōchin-dachi/Nagashi-uke/Uraken-uchi*

Plant the right foot forward into a rooted stance, simultaneously executing a sweeping block past the left side of the head with the left arm while delivering a back-fist strike to the front with the right arm. This technique is performed with a *kiai*.

### 26) *Migi jōdan mikazuki-geri*

Pivoting on the left foot, lift the right foot up in a sweeping arc while turning 180 degrees to the left to face the opposite direction, delivering a right crescent kick against the open left hand while lifting the right fist to above the head.

### 27) *Sōchin-dachi/Musō-gamae*

Drop the right foot into a rooted stance while shifting into an incomparable posture.

### 28) *Sōchin-dachi/Hidari chūdan uchi-uke*

Step forward at a 45-degree angle to the left into a rooted stance while executing a middle-level inside-to-outside block with the left arm.

### 29) *Sōchin-dachi/Migi chūdan oi-zuki*

Step forward with the right foot into a rooted stance while delivering a right middle-level lunge punch.

### 30) *Sōchin-dachi/Migi chūdan uchi-uke*

Pivoting on the left foot, slide the right foot across to the right side to turn the body 90 degrees in the same direction, assuming a rooted stance while executing a right middle-level inside-to-outside block.

### 31) *Sōchin-dachi/Hidari chūdan oi-zuki*

Step forward with the left foot into a rooted stance while delivering a left middle-level lunge punch.

32    33-A    33    34    35-A

35    36-A    36    Yame-A    Yame

### 32) Sōchin-dachi/Hidari chūdan uchi-uke

Pivoting on the right foot, slide the left to the left side to turn the body 45 degrees to the left while executing a middle-level inside-to-outside block with the left arm.

33-A) Maintaining a strong rooted stance, draw the right fist across the front of the body and underneath the left arm.

### 33) Sōchin-dachi/Migi chūdan uchi-uke/Gyaku-hanmi

Draw the right arm out to deliver an inside-to-outside block, turning the hips to gyaku-hanmi (45-degree angle to the front, with the hip on the side opposite to the front leg pushed forward).

### 34) Migi mae-geri

Keeping the arms in place, deliver a front snap kick with the right leg.

35-A) Plant the right foot to the rear, resuming a rooted stance while drawing the right elbow directly to the rear and extending the left arm out in front of the body.

### 35) Sōchin-dachi/Hidari yumi-zuki

Complete the motion of the arms to deliver a left bow punch, with the left arm executing a middle-level straight punch and the right elbow pulled back to the rear. The right fist is positioned in front of the right side of the chest with the back of the fist facing upward. The position of the hands suggests the pulling back of a bow string in preparation to shoot an arrow.

### 36-A) Sōchin-dachi/Migi chūdan gyaku-zuki

Deliver a right middle-level reverse punch.

### 36) Sōchin-dachi/Hidari chūdan-zuki

Deliver a left middle-level punch with a kiai.

Yame-A) Draw the left foot back, positioning it in line with the right foot into an open V stance while pulling the left fist back toward the right-hand side of the body and extending the right arm across the front of the body in the opposite direction.

### Yame

Return to a natural-posture stance with the arms extended downward in front of the body, maintaining a state of physical and mental readiness (zanshin).

---

### TECHNICAL ANALYSIS
### Movements 21–25

Upon deflecting an opponent's lunge punch with a knife-hand block (photo 1), use the same blocking hand to suppress a subsequent reverse punch using a pressing block (photo 2). Drive the right hand forward to counter with a spear hand thrust (photo 3), followed by a short front kick (photo 4). As the attacker follows with a front punch,

1    2

respond with an inside-to-outside block while delivering a front snap kick with the opposite leg (photo 5). The same technique can also be used in response to an opponent's reverse punch attack, with the front snap kick delivered simultaneously with a combination sweeping block and back-fist strike to the face (photo 6). As the opponent then counters with an upper-level punch, respond by stepping forward with a subsequent sweeping block while delivering a back-fist strike (photo 7).

3

4

5

6

7

## TECHNICAL ANALYSIS
## Movements 33–35

After blocking an opponent's lunge punch attack with a reverse inside-to-outside block (photo 1), counter with a front snap kick (photo 2), followed by a bow punch to the midsection, performed while pulling the attacker forward to ensure a more powerful technique (photo 2).

1

2

3

# Meikyō (Rōhai)

Among the techniques employed in karate, *sankaku-tobi*, or triangle jump, is one that has reached something approaching legendary status, considered to be perhaps a secret or spiritual technique. According to some theories, the horizontal *sankaku-tobi* that appears near the end of this *kata* is believed to be something similar to this legendary technique. The name Meikyō, however, is what this *kata* is called within the Shōtōkan style, a name that was assigned by Master Gichin Funakoshi around the time that he changed the characters used to write "karate."

This *kata*, named Rōhai in other karate styles in the past, was made up of three versions, numbered one to three (*shodan, nidan* and *sandan*), and was characterized by techniques performed in a heron-leg stance. By comparision, Meikyō is not divided into multiple versions. Additionally, while Meikyō includes a response to an attack by an opponent wielding a staff, there is no such technique in Rōhai.

One major feature, however, found in the three Rōhai *kata* (*shodan* to *sandan*)—an openhanded reverse wedge block performed from *shiko-dachi* (square stance)—is also found in Meikyō. This common attribute provides evidence that both Meikyō and Rōhai are related *kata*.

The Rōhai comprising Rōhai Shodan, Nidan and Sandan belongs to the Itosu-school of karate and are known as Itosu Rōhai. The Tomari-based Rōhai, derived from the Matsumora school, is called Matsumora Rōhai and features a variety of resourceful techniques based on close-range exchanges. These include the ensnaring of an opponent's arm upon blocking from a heron-leg stance, followed by a middle-level front snap kick, after which a knife-hand block is performed, the opponent's wrist is seized, and a leg sweep is delivered and followed with a downward punch.

If we assume that Meikyō began as Rōhai, further research is needed to determine at what point it branched off to become the *kata* it is today.

## Meikyō

Yōi

1-A

1-B

1-C

### *Yōi* (Ready position)

*Soto hachiji-dachi* (open V stance) with both fists positioned in front of the hips.

1-A) Draw the right foot out to the right while extending both arms out to the sides, opening the hands as they move away from the body.

1-B) Draw the hands upward around the body as if describing a large circle while lowering the hips.

1-C) Assume a straddle-leg stance while drawing the arms, still extended, down in front of the chest, crossing them at the wrists in front of the chest with the right arm above the left arm.

1-D) Draw the elbows back along the sides of the body while closing the hands into fists.

### 1) *Kiba-dachi/Ryō goshi-gamae*
Pull the elbows to the rear, drawing the fists back to above the hips.

2-A) Draw both hands, opened into knife hands, out and upward towards each other in front of the chest.

2-B) Raise the hands together in front of the face with the small fingers aligned and the backs of the hands facing forward.

### 2) *Kiba-dachi/Jōshin-gamae*
Draw the elbows apart and lower them slightly while turning the hands outward. This posture, with the forearms suggesting the sides of an imaginary triangle, is known as *jōshin-gamae* ("mind-cleansing" posture).

3-A) Pull the left foot in slightly toward the right foot, drawing the left hand back to above the right shoulder while extending the right arm out in front of the body at an angle to the left.

### 3) *Zenkutsu-dachi/Hidari gedan-barai*
Step forward with the left foot at a 45-degree angle to the left into a left front stance while executing a downward block with the left arm.

### 4) *Zenkutsu-dachi/Migi chūdan oi-zuki*
Step forward with the right foot into a right front stance while delivering a right middle-level lunge punch.

5-A) Pivoting on the left foot, slide the right foot across to the right-hand side, turning the body 90 degrees in the same direction while pulling the right fist back to above the left shoulder and extending the left arm out across the front of the body.

### 5) *Zenkutsu-dachi/Migi gedan-barai*
Shift into a right front stance while delivering a downward block with the right arm.

### 6) *Zenkutsu-dachi/Hidari chūdan oi-zuki*
Step forward with the left foot into a left front stance while performing a left middle-level lunge punch.

7-A) Sliding the right foot forward toward the left foot, turn the head 45 degrees to the left and draw both arms back, opening the hands with the palms facing downward.

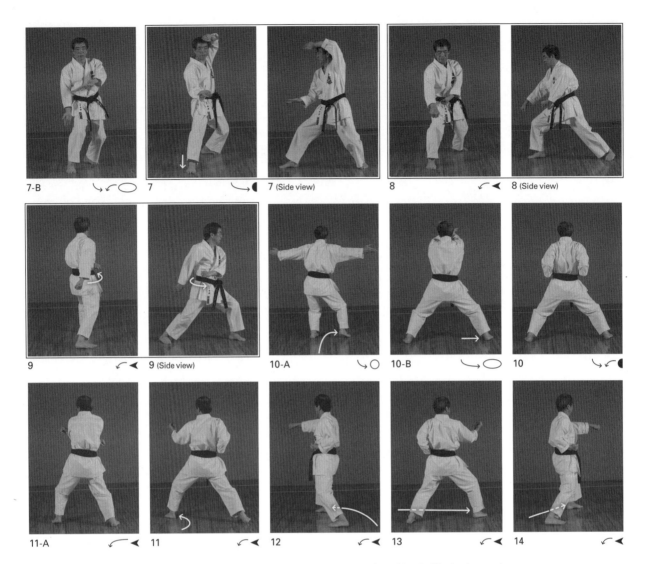

7-B) Slide the right foot forward alongside and past the left foot, drawing the right hand downward and out to the front in a scooping motion while simultaneously raising the left elbow.

### 7) *Kōkutsu-dachi/Morote jō-uke*

Assuming a left back stance, raise the right hand to approximately waist level and the left hand to above the forehead to perform a two-handed block against a *jō* (stick, or staff) attack. The right elbow is positioned against the right hip while the left forearm is above the head with the left elbow pulled back to the rear.

### 8) *Jō-zukami*

Thrusting off the left foot, drive the hips forward, transferring the center of gravity toward the right leg while thrusting both hands, closed into fists, downward at an angle in front of the body to execute a *jō* grab. The right fist is directed forward with the back of the fist facing upward while the inside of the left wrist rests against the lower abdomen with the back of the fist facing the floor.

9) Thrusting off the right foot, drive the hips back toward the rear, turning the hips to the left to face the opposite direction without changing the position of the feet. At the same time, keep the hands in the same location while rotating the fists inward.

10-A) Draw the right foot forward and out toward the right in line with the left foot while drawing the arms straight out to the sides of the body with the hands open.

10-B) Lowering the hips as the right foot slides out to the right side, draw the hands upward around the body and down in front of the chest, crossing the arms at the wrists with the right arm above the left arm.

### 10) *Kiba-dachi/Ryō goshi-gamae*

Assuming a straddle-leg stance, pull the elbows to the rear, drawing the fists back to above the hips.

11-A) Pull the left foot in slightly toward the right foot, drawing the left fist back to below the right underarm while extending the right arm out in front of the body at an angle to the left.

15-A

15-B

15

16

17

18-A

18-B

18

19-A

19

20

### 11) *Zenkutsu-dachi/Hidari chūdan uchi-uke*
Step forward with the left foot at a 45-degree angle to the left into a left front stance while delivering a middle-level inside-to-outside block with the left arm.

### 12) *Zenkutsu-dachi/Migi chūdan oi-zuki*
Step forward with the right foot into a right front stance while delivering a right middle-level lunge punch.

### 13) *Zenkutsu-dachi/Migi chūdan uchi-uke*
Pivoting on the left foot, slide the right foot across to the right, turning the body 90 degrees to the right into a right front stance while delivering a middle-level inside-to-outside block with the right arm.

### 14) *Zenkutsu-dachi/Hidari chūdan oi-zuki*
Step forward with the left foot into a left front stance while performing a left middle-level lunge punch.

15-A) Slide the right foot forward toward the left foot while opening the hands and drawing the arms back.

15-B) Sliding the right foot past the left foot, draw the right hand out to the front in a low scooping motion while raising the left elbow.

### 15) *Kōkutsu-dachi/Morote jō-uke*
Assume a right back stance while raising the arms into a two-handed *jō* block.

### 16) *Jō-zukami*
Thrust off the left foot and drive both hands, closed into fists, downward at an angle in front of the body to execute a *jō* grab.

17) Thrust off the right foot and drive the hips toward the rear, turning to face the opposite direction while keeping the hands in the same location and rotating the fists inward.

18-A) Draw the right foot forward and out toward the right while extending the arms out to the sides of the body with the hands open.

18-B) Lowering the hips into a straddle-leg stance as the right foot slides out to the right side, draw the hands upward around the body and down in front of the chest, crossing the arms at the wrists with the right arm above the left arm.

### 18) *Kiba-dachi/Ryō goshi-gamae*
Draw the elbows to the rear, pulling the fists back to above the hips.

19-A) Draw the left foot back slightly toward the right foot, turning the hips to the left while extending the right arm upward in front of the body at an angle to the left.

### 19) *Zenkutsu-dachi/Hidari jōdan age-uke*
Step forward with the left foot at a 45-degree angle to the left into a left front stance while delivering an upper-level rising block with the left arm.

### 20) *Zenkutsu-dachi/Migi chūdan oi-zuki*
Step forward with the right foot into a right front stance while delivering a right middle-level lunge punch.

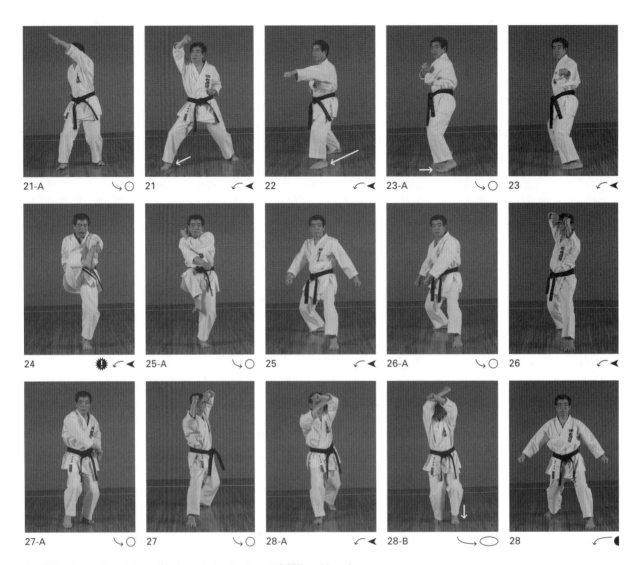

21-A) Pivoting on the left foot, slide the right foot back toward the left foot and turn the hips 90 degrees to the right. At the same time, pull the right fist back to above the right hip while extending the left arm upward at an angle to the right.

### 21) *Zenkutsu-dachi/Migi jōdan age-uke*
Step forward with the right foot into a right front stance while delivering an upper-level rising block with the right arm.

### 22) *Zenkutsu-dachi/Hidari chūdan oi-zuki*
Step forward with the left foot into a left front stance while performing a left middle-level lunge punch.

23-A) Shift the left foot 45 degrees to the left, positioning it in line with the right foot while pulling the left fist back toward the right side of the body and extending the right arm across the chest in the opposite direction.

### 23) *Kiba-dachi/Hidari chūdan tettsui-uchi*
Assume a straddle-leg stance while driving the left fist out to the left side to deliver a middle-level hammer-fist strike.

### 24) *Mikazuki-geri*
Keeping the right fist positioned above the right hip, drive the right foot up and around the front of the body to deliver a crescent kick against the palm of the left hand with a *kiai*.

25-A) Retracting the right foot, draw the left fist back to above the right shoulder while extending the right arm out in front of the body at an angle toward the left.

### 25) *Kōkutsu-dachi/Ryōwan gedan kakiwake-uke*
Plant the right foot to the rear into a right back stance while driving the fists out to the sides of the body to deliver a double downward separating block. The arms remain straight as they travel downward and to the sides.

26-A) Draw both arms back in a sweeping motion, generating momentum to deliver a powerful block to the front.

### 26) *Kōkutsu-dachi/Morote haiwan-uke*
Pull both arms up in a sharp, whipping motion to perform a left upper-level inside-to-outside back-arm block, accompanied by the right arm to provide additional momentum.

29-A   29   30-A   30   31-A

31   32   33   34   Yame-A

Yame

27-A) Stepping forward with the right foot, draw the arms down past the left side of the body and back in a sweeping motion to the rear.

### 27) Kōkutsu-dachi/Morote haiwan-uke
Completing the step forward into a left back stance, pull both arms up to deliver an upper-level inside-to-outside back-arm block with the right arm, accompanied by the left arm to provide added momentum.

28-A) Stepping forward with the left foot, draw the right elbow back while drawing the left elbow forward.

28-B) As the left foot moves forward, cross the arms at the wrists in front of the forehead with the right arm positioned between the left arm and the head.

### 28) Zenkutsu-dachi/Ryōwan gedan kakiwake-uke
Complete the step forward into a left front stance while driving the arms downward and out to the sides to deliver a double downward separating block.

29-A) Stepping forward with the right foot, cross the arms in front of the chest with the left arm positioned above the right.

### 29) Kōkutsu-dachi/Ryōwan uchi-uke
Complete the step forward with the right foot into a left back stance while delivering a double inside-to-outside block.

### 30-A) Kōkutsu-dachi/Morote kizami ura-zuki
Thrust off the left foot, sliding the right foot forward slightly while delivering a two-handed close punch upward.

30) Draw the elbows downward immediately following the two-handed close punch.

31-A) Turning the head to the left to face the rear, rotate the hips in the same direction while extending the right arm upward in the direction of the left leg.

### 31) Kōkutsu-dachi/Hidari jōdan age-uke
Shift the center of gravity toward the right leg, assuming a right back stance while executing a left upper-level rising block.

### 32) Sankaku-tobi/Empi-uchi
Launch the right knee forward in front of the body and leap upward off the left leg, turning the body to the left to perform a triangle jump while delivering a right elbow strike against the palm of the left hand with a *kiai*. When executing the triangle jump, the feeling should be of the body circling around the right elbow.

### 33) Kōkutsu-dachi/Migi chūdan shutō-uke
Completing a 180-degree turn to the left, plant the right foot immediately followed by the left into a left back stance while executing a right middle-level knife-hand block.

### 34) Kōkutsu-dachi/Hidari chūdan shutō-uke
Step back with the right foot into a right back stance while executing a left middle-level knife-hand block.

Yame-A) Draw the left foot back and out to the left-hand side, positioning it in line with the right foot in an open V stance. At the same time, extend the left arm across the chest to the right side of the body and above the right arm, which extends to the left side of the body.

### Yame
Return to a natural-posture stance with the arms extended downward in front of the body, maintaining a state of physical and mental readiness (*zanshin*).

## TECHNICAL ANALYSIS
### Movements 7–9

Upon grasping the staff following an opponent's *jō* attack (photo 1), counter-attack by thrusting the staff forward toward the attacker (photo 2). Then, turning the hips sharply to the left, disarm the attacker while turning to face an opponent approaching from the opposite direction (photo 3).

1

2

3

## TECHNICAL ANALYSIS
### Movements 31–33

After blocking an upper-level lunge punch attack (photo 1), leap around the opponent using a triangle jump while simultaneously countering with an elbow strike (photos 2 and 3), landing on the opposite side of the attacker in a back stance prepared to respond to any subsequent attacks (photo 4).

1

2

3

4

# Nijūshiho

Although this *kata*, which also goes by the name Nīsēshi, has been passed down to the Shōtōkan, Shitō-ryū and Wadō-ryū styles of karate, little is known about its creator or its origins. With many similarities to Unsū, it is quite likely that Nijūshiho belongs to the Nīgaki family of *kata* along with Sōchin.

Nijūshiho opens with a slowly executed pressing block in response to a middle-level punching attack from the front, followed by a strong reverse punch, and then a relatively slow elbow strike. The initial block is performed from a back stance, with the right foot sliding to the rear in a gliding step. The reverse punch is also delivered from a back stance upon thrusting forward off the rear foot to generate power in the direction of the punch. And finally, the elbow strike that completes the opening sequence is executed from a natural posture. This slow-quick-slow rhythm in which the opening sequence is performed is unique to Nijūshiho.

Other characteristics of this *kata* include five elbow strikes, executed both to the front and the side, a variety of punches delivered at various-level targets, and two-handed thrusting techniques, including U-punches and two-handed palm-heel thrusts. Among the diverse techniques Nijūshiho contains is an overhead back-hand slap intended to momentarily distract an opponent prior executing a combination scooping block/knee takedown. The *kata* ends with a two-handed palm-heel thrust delivered from an hourglass stance, performed while regulating the breathing to coincide with the execution of the technique.

## Nijūshiho

Yōi

1-A    ↘ ○

1-A (Side view)

1    ↘ ↶

### *Yōi* (Ready position)
*Soto hachiji-dachi* (open V stance) with both fists positioned in front of the hips.

1-A) Turning the hips to the right, step back with the right foot while opening both hands and extending the arms out at a 45-degree angle to the left relative to the hips.

### 1) *Kōkutsu-dachi/Ryūsui no kamae*
Assuming a right back stance, pull the right hand, closed into a fist, back to the right hip while drawing the left forearm toward the body at chest level to perform a middle-level pressing block. This posture is known as *ryūsui no kamae* (flowing-water posture).

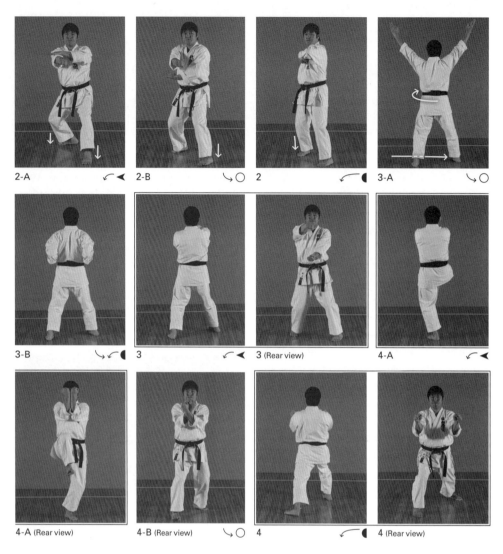

2-A    ↙◀    2-B    ↘○    2    ↙●    3-A    ↘○

3-B    ↘↙●    3    ↙◀    3 (Rear view)    4-A    ↙◀

4-A (Rear view)    4-B (Rear view)    ↘○    4    ↙●    4 (Rear view)

### 2-A) *Kōkutsu-dachi/Ryūsui-zuki*

Thrusting forward off the right foot, drive the right fist out in front of the body just beneath the left hand to deliver a flowing-water punch while maintaining a strong back stance.

2-B) Sliding the left foot forward, open the left hand and pull it back to beneath the right underarm, rotating the wrist so that the palm of the left hand faces upward.

### 2) *Shizentai/Hidari zempō empi-uchi*

Draw the right foot forward and raise the hips to assume a natural posture while drawing the left elbow out in front of the body and upward to deliver a forward elbow strike.

3-A) Pivoting on the left foot, slide the right foot across the back while turning the hips to the right to face the opposite direction. At the same time, extend both arms directly out to the sides while opening the hands with the palms facing upward, and immediately swing them upward at an angle toward the front.

### 3-B) *Sanchin-dachi/Ryōgoshi-gamae*

Assuming an hourglass stance, bring the arms down in front of the body, crossing them as they pass in front of

the chest, and then pull the elbows straight back to draw the hands, closed into fists, to above the hips.

### 3) *Sanchin-dachi/Awase-zuki*

Deliver a U-punch with the right arm performing an upper-level punch as the left arm performs a middle-level punch.

### 4-A) *Musō-uke (Hasami-uke/Hiza-gamae)*

Draw the forearms together with the elbows at chest level to execute a scissors block while raising the right knee in front of the body. This combination upper-level/ lower-level block is known as *musō-uke* (incomparable block).

4-B) Stepping forward with the right foot, draw the fists away from the body, crossing the arms at the wrists with the left fist positioned on the far side of the right fist.

### 4) *Zenkutsu-dachi/Chūdan kakiwake-uke*

Plant the right foot forward into a right front stance while drawing the fists apart to deliver a middle-level separating block.

5-A     5     5 (Rear view)     6-A     6-A (Rear view)

6     7-A     7     8-A     8

9-A     9     9 (Rear view)     10-A

### 5-A) *Zenkutsu-dachi/Hidari jōdan age-uke*

Pivoting on the right foot, step out to the left with the left foot, assuming a left front stance while executing a left upper-level rising block.

### 5) *Zenkutsu-dachi/Migi tate empi-uchi*

Drive the right elbow up to deliver an upward elbow strike, pulling the right fist back to the right side of the head with the back of the fist facing outward.

6-A) Turning the head to the right, open the right hand into a knife hand and pull it across to the opposite side of the head while sliding the right foot across the rear, bringing it in line with the left foot.

### 6) *Kiba-dachi/Migi sokumen tate shutō-uke*

Assuming a straddle-leg stance, draw the right arm around the body to the right-hand side to execute a vertical knife-hand block.

### 7-A) *Yoko-geri kekomi/Hiki-yose*

Deliver a right thrust kick to the right while simultaneously pulling the right hand, which closes into a fist, back to the right hip. The motion of the hand should be synchronized with the delivery of the kick.

### 7) *Kiba-dachi/Hidari sokumen-zuki*

Plant the right foot in the direction of the kick, again assuming a straddle-leg stance while delivering a side punch with the left arm.

8-A) Turning the head to the left, open the left hand into a knife hand and draw the left arm around the body to the left-hand side.

### 8) *Kiba-dachi/Hidari sokumen tate shutō-uke*

Complete the motion of the left arm to perform a vertical knife-hand block to the left.

### 9-A) *Yoko-geri kekomi/Hiki-yose*

Deliver a left thrust kick to the left while simultaneously pulling the left hand, closed into a fist, back to the left hip.

### 9) *Kiba-dachi/Migi sokumen-zuki*

Plant the left foot on the floor into a straddle-leg stance while executing a side punch with the right arm.

10-A) Draw the left foot back one half-step toward the right foot, turning the hips to the left while opening and "flipping" the right hand over as if to hook it over an opponent's wrist.

10-B     10-B (Rear view)     10-C     10-C (Rear view)     10

10 (Rear view)     11     12     13-A     13-B

13-C     13     14-A     14     15

### 10-B) *Han zenkutsu-dachi/Migi chūdan tekubi kake-uke*

Settling into a left half-front stance, lower the right hand to complete a wrist-hook block.

10-C) Step forward at a 45-degree angle to the left with the right foot, drawing the right hip forward to the right hand, which remains in place as if pressed against an immovable object. At the same time, open the left hand into a palm heel and "roll" it upward along the side of the torso, keeping the left wrist pressed against the body as the hand moves.

### 10) *Zenkutsu-dachi/Teishō awase-zuki*

Complete the step forward with the right foot into a right front stance while extending both arms out in front of the body to deliver a two-handed palm-heel thrust. Wait until the right hip meets the right hand before moving the arms, thrusting the left palm heel upward at an angle while simultaneously driving the right palm heel downward in front of the midsection.

### 11) *Zenkutsu-dachi/Tenchi haitō-uchi*

Shift the left leg across the rear and turn the body 180 degrees to the left, driving the hips forward into a left front stance facing the opposite direction while swinging both arms around the body to deliver a hi-low ridge-hand strike. The right arm travels upward to execute an upper-level ridge-hand strike to the front while the left arm moves downward to deliver a lower-level ridge-hand strike to the rear.

### 12) *Heisoku-dachi/Hidari haishu age-uchi*

Draw the right foot forward, positioning it alongside the left foot into a closed parallel stance while swinging the left hand upward in an arcing motion to execute a rising back-hand strike with a *kiai*. Bring the back of the left hand up sharply against the palm of the right hand.

13-A) Stepping back with the left foot, drop the left hand in preparation to execute a scooping block while drawing the right hand toward the right underarm.

### 13-B) *Zenkutsu-dachi/Kokō hiza-kuzushi*

Assuming a right front stance, complete the scooping block with the left hand while driving the right hand down to execute a knee takedown.

13-C) Drawing both elbows to the rear, pull the hands, closed into fists, back to the hips.

16-A

16

17-A

17

18-A

18

19-A

19

20

### 13) *Fudō-dachi/Gedan awase-zuki*

Shift into a rooted stance while simultaneously driving both fists down to deliver a downward U-punch with the left fist positioned above the right fist.

14-A) Turn the head to the left and shift the left foot slightly to the left while assuming a right back stance. At the same time, open the left hand into a knife hand and draw the left arm back across the front of the chest and below the right arm while extending the right arm in the opposite direction.

### 14) *Kōkutsu-dachi/Hidari chūdan haishu-uke*

Draw the left arm out to the left side of the body to execute a middle-level back-hand block.

### 15) *Kiba-dachi/Migi sokumen tate empi-uchi*

Stepping forward with the right foot in the same direction as the preceding back-hand block, assume a straddle-leg stance while delivering an upward elbow strike with the right arm to the right-hand side.

### 16-A) *Kiba-dachi/Migi ude-uke/Hidari gedan-zuki*

Thrust off the left foot to drive the right foot out to the right side with a gliding step (*suri-ashi*), immediately followed by the left foot into a strong straddle-leg stance. At the same time, deliver a downward punch across the front of the body with the left arm while simultaneously pulling the right elbow down toward the chest to execute a forearm block.

### 16) *Kiba-dachi/Migi sokumen gedan-barai*

Thrusting off the right foot to shift the body in the opposite direction, drive the right arm down to the right side of the body to deliver a downward block.

17-A) Turning the head to the left to face the opposite direction, open the left hand into a knife hand and draw the left arm across the front of the chest and below the right arm while extending the right arm in the opposite direction.

### 17) *Kōkutsu-dachi/Hidari chūdan haishu-uke*

Turn the left foot 90 degrees counter-clockwise while shifting the center of gravity back toward the right leg to assume a right back stance while drawing the left arm out to the left to execute a middle-level back-hand block.

### 18-A) *Kiba-dachi/Migi mae empi-uchi*

Keeping the left hand in place, step forward with the right foot in the direction of the outstretched left arm, turning the hips 180 degrees to the left into a straddle-leg stance while delivering a right front elbow strike against the palm of the left hand

### 18) *Kiba-dachi/Migi gedan-barai/Hidari soete*

Drive the right fist down to deliver a downward block. The left hand closes into a fist and rests just above the right elbow during the technique.

19-A) Draw the left foot in toward the right foot and then directly in front of the right foot while pulling the left hand, opened into a knife hand, back below the right arm and extending the right arm across the front of the chest to the left-hand side.

### 19) *Kōkutsu-dachi/Hidari chūdan haishu-uke*

Completing the step forward with the left foot into a right back stance, draw the left arm out to the left to execute a middle-level back-hand block.

### 20) *Kiba-dachi/Migi sokumen tate empi-uchi*

Step forward with the right foot in a straight line into a straddle-leg stance while delivering an upward elbow strike with the right arm to the right-hand side.

21-A    21    22-A    22-B    22

23    24-A    24-B    24-C    24

**21-A) *Kiba-dachi/Migi ude-uke/Hidari gedan-zuki***
Thrusting off the left foot in the direction of the preceding elbow strike, deliver a downward punch across the front of the body with the left arm while pulling the right arm back to execute a right forearm block.

**21) *Kiba-dachi/Migi sokumen gedan-barai***
Thrusting off the right foot in the opposite direction, drive the right arm down to the right side of the body to deliver a downward block.

22-A) Pivoting on the left foot, slide the right foot toward the left foot, turning the hips 135 degrees to the left. At the same time, extend both arms directly out to the sides, opening the hands with the palms facing upward, and then swing them upward around the body.

**22-B) *Ōfuri kōsa-barai***
Continuing with the motion of the right leg initiated in the previous step, draw the right foot out to the right side of the body while swinging the arms up above the head and then downward in front of the body to perform a swinging cross-arm sweep. The arms cross in front of the chest as they travel downward with the right arm positioned above the left arm.

**22) *Sanchin-dachi/Ryōgoshi-gamae***
Draw the left foot in toward the right foot, assuming an hourglass stance while pulling the elbows straight back to draw the hands, closed into fists, to above the hips.

**23) *Sanchin-dachi/Awase-zuki***
Deliver a U-punch with a *kiai*. The right arm performs an upper-level punch while the left arm performs a middle-level punch.

24-A) Open the hands with the palms facing each other

and bend the wrists so as to draw the hands back toward the body.

24-B) Drawing the right foot in toward the left foot and forward, rotate the hands in a circular motion in front of the body, with the right hand moving to the right and downward while the left hand moves to the left and upward.

**24-C) *Sanchin-dachi/Mawashi kake-uke***
Assuming an hourglass stance, follow through with the rotation of the arms to complete a circular hooking block. Pull the elbows back upon completing a 180-degree rotation of the hands, drawing the hands back toward the torso.

**24) *Sanchin-dachi/Teishō awase-zuki***
Extend both arms out in front of the body to deliver a two-handed palm-heel thrust, paying special attention to keep the elbows tucked inward close to the body.

*Yame*-A) Draw the right foot back, positioning it alongside the left foot while lowering the left arm so that the arms cross in front of the body.

**Yame**
Return to a natural-posture stance with the arms extended downward in front of the body, maintaining a state of physical and mental readiness (*zanshin*).

Yame-A

Yame

### TECHNICAL ANALYSIS
**Movements 8–9**

Upon blocking a lunge-punch attack from the left side with a vertical knife-hand block (photo 1), grab the opponent's wrist and pull him in while delivering a side thrust kick (photo 2), and then follow with a side punch (photo 3).

1

2

3

### TECHNICAL ANALYSIS
**Movements 10-A–10**

Block an opponent's lunge punch using a wrist-hook block (photo 1) and counter by stepping forward with a two-handed palm-heel thrust (photo 2).

1

2

### TECHNICAL ANALYSIS
**Movements 22-A–24**

After deflecting a double-fist punch attack with a downward cross-arm sweep (photo 1), draw the fists back to the hips (photo 2) and counter with a U-punch (photo 3). Then "hook" the hands around the opponent's wrists (photo 4) and rotate the arms to topple the opponent (photos 5 and 6).

1

2

3

4

5

6

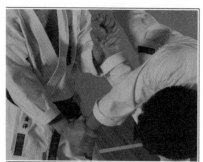
6 (Detail)

# Unsū

Although not believed to be very old, the origins of this *kata*, which has been passed down to the Shōtōkan and Shitō-ryū styles of karate, are not clearly known. Due to its many similarities to Nīsēshi (Nijūshiho), it is thought to belong to the Arakaki family of *kata*.

Around the time that he changed the characters used to write "karate," Master Gichin Funakoshi altered the names of multiple *kata* in his book *Karate-dō: My Way of Life*. Among the *kata* introduced in the book, there was no mention of Unsū.

In 1922, however, Funakoshi published *Ryūkyū Kempō Karate*, in which Unsū appeared for the first time along with a diverse variety of other *kata*, including the five Heian *kata*, the three Naihanchi *kata*, the Dai and Shō versions of Bassai, and the Dai and Shō versions of Kūshankū.

The movement with which Unsū opens—first raising the palms in front of the chest in a scooping motion with the outer edges of the hands touching each other, then pushing the hands out to the sides—which appears two times within the *kata*, is referred to in terms of parting the clouds with the hands. This separating movement of the hands can be interpreted defensively as the sweeping away of an attacker's fist following a scissors block, or offensively as simultaneous vertical knife-hand strikes to the sides.

Unsū is written using the Chinese characters 雲手, meaning "cloud" and "hand(s)," respectively. In addition to hand, 手 can also mean "technique" or "usage." As such, it is believed that the name Unsū refers not to any single technique, but rather to the collective movements of the entire *kata*. In the same way that clouds invite winds, thundershowers and violent storms, the movements that make up Unsū call to mind the elusive, ever-changing nature of clouds during a tempest.

Containing such diverse techniques as chicken-head-wrist blocks, one-finger spear hand strikes, roundhouse kicks delivered while lying on the floor, and a 360-degree turning jump that begins with a crescent kick and ends with a back kick, Unsū is an advanced *kata* intended for high-ranking black belt practitioners.

## Unsū

Shizentai          Yōi-A

### Shizentai (Natural posture)
*Soto hachiji-dachi* (open V stance) with both fists positioned in front of the hips.

### Yōi-A
Slide the right foot in toward the left foot to assume a closed parallel stance (*heisoku-dachi*) while bringing the arms together in front of the body, crossing them at the forearms.

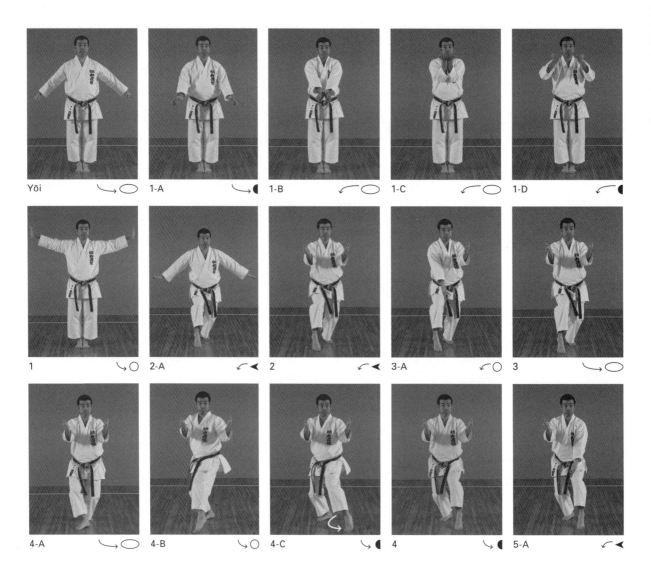

Yōi    1-A    1-B    1-C    1-D

1    2-A    2    3-A    3

4-A    4-B    4-C    4    5-A

### *Yōi* (Ready position)

Draw the arms out to the sides of the body.

1-A) Keeping the arms extended downward, draw the inner wrists together in front of the body in a fluid motion, bending the hands back upon initiating the motion and gradually opening the hands along the way.

1-B) Rotate the wrists outward as the hands approach each other so that the little-finger sides of the hands make contact.

1-C) Continuing with the fluid motion from the preceding step, draw the hands upward in front of the chest while pulling the forearms together so that the elbows touch once the hands reach the level of the chin.

1-D) As soon as the elbows make contact, draw the arms out to the sides, leading with the elbows while forming the hands into vertical knife hands.

### 1) *Heisoku-dachi/Kaiun no te*

Completing the fluid motion initiated in step 1-A, fully extend the arms out to the sides level with the shoulders. This posture is known as *kaiun no te* (cloud-parting hands).

2-A) Draw the right foot forward into a cat stance while swinging both arms down sharply to the sides of the body.

### 2) *Neko-ashi-dachi/Morote keitō-uke*

Continuing with the motion initiated in the previous step, sweep the hands past the sides of the body and upward in front of the chest while forming them into chicken-head wrists to deliver a double chicken-head-wrist block. Pay special attention to keep the elbows tucked in near the body.

### 3-A) *Neko-ashi-dachi/Migi ippon-nukite*

Employing a snapping motion of the elbow, drive the right hand down to deliver a one-finger spear-hand attack.

5

6-A

6-B

6

7-A

7

8-A

8

9-A

9-B

9

### 3) *Neko-ashi-dachi/Ni-keitō-gamae*

Snap the right hand back to its previous position following the strike to assume a double chicken-head-wrist posture.

4-A) Pivoting on the toes, turn the right foot outward so the toes point at a 45-degree angle to the right and lower the heel to the floor.

### 4-B) (*Ura ashi-gake*)

Transferring the weight of the body to the right leg, raise the heel of the left foot and slide the toes forward along the surface of the floor past the right foot and to the right.

### 4-C) (*Ura ashi-gake*)

Continuing the motion of the left foot, draw the toes out to the left along a circular path.

### 4) *Neko-ashi-dachi/Ura ashi-gake*

Draw the toes back toward the body along the same circular course, completing a back leg hook while settling into a cat stance.

### 5-A) *Neko-ashi-dachi/Hidari ippon-nukite*

Drive the left hand down in a quick snapping motion to deliver a one-finger spear-hand attack.

### 5) *Neko-ashi-dachi/Ni-keitō-gamae*

Snap the left hand back to its previous position.

6-A) Pivoting on the toes, turn the left foot outward and lower the heel to the floor.

### 6-B) (*Ura ashi-gake*)

Sliding on the toes, draw the right foot forward and in front of the left foot.

### 6) *Neko-ashi-dachi/Ura ashi-gake*

Draw the toes around to the right and then back toward the body along a circular path to execute a back leg hook while settling again into a cat stance.

### 7-A) *Neko-ashi-dachi/Migi ippon-nukite*

Snap the right hand down to deliver a one-finger spear-hand attack.

### 7) *Neko-ashi-dachi/Ni-keitō-gamae*

Snap the right hand back to its previous position.

### 8-A) *Zenkutsu-dachi/Hidari shutō-uke*

Turning the head to the left, step out with the left foot to the left-hand side, assuming a left front stance while thrusting the left arm in front of the body to execute a vertical knife-hand block.

### 8) *Zenkutsu-dachi/Migi chūdan gyaku-zuki*

Immediately deliver a right middle-level reverse punch.

9-A) Turning the head to the right to face the opposite direction, slide the right foot along the back to the opposite side, pivoting on the left foot to turn the hips to the right while drawing the right hand, opened into a knife hand, around the body in the same direction.

### 9-B) *Zenkutsu-dachi/Migi shutō-uke*

Completing a 180-degree turn to the right, assume a right front stance while executing a vertical knife-hand block with the right arm.

### 9) *Zenkutsu-dachi/Hidari chūdan gyaku-zuki*

Immediately deliver a left middle-level reverse punch.

10-A) Turning the head to the left, step out with the left foot to the left side, swinging the left arm in the same direction while opening the left hand into a knife hand.

**10-B) *Zenkutsu-dachi/Hidari shutō-uke***
Assume a left front stance while executing a left vertical knife-hand block.

**10) *Zenkutsu-dachi/Migi chūdan gyaku-zuki***
Immediately deliver a right middle-level reverse punch.

11-A) Turning the head to the right to face the opposite direction, slide the right foot along the back, pivoting on the left foot to turn the hips to the right while drawing the right hand around the body in the same direction.

**11-B) *Zenkutsu-dachi/Migi shutō-uke***
Assume a right front stance facing the opposite direction while executing a right vertical knife-hand block.

**11) *Zenkutsu-dachi/Hidari chūdan gyaku-zuki***
Immediately deliver a left middle-level reverse punch.

12-A) Pulling the right foot back, drop the upper body to the floor at an angle to the right.

**12-B) *Migi tai-otoshi***
Keeping the head raised, land with the palms of the hands facing downward and the right forearm resting against the floor. Raise the left knee immediately upon landing.

**12-C) *Hidari kasei mawashi-geri***
Deliver an upward roundhouse kick with the left leg.

12) Snap the left leg back following the delivery of the kick.

13-A) "Roll" the torso to the left while drawing the knees under the body so as to remain in the same location on the floor.

**13-B) *Hidari tai-otoshi***
Drop the left side of the body to the floor and immediately raise the right knee, assuming a mirror-image of the position assumed in step 12-B.

**13-C) *Migi kasei mawashi-geri***
Deliver an upward roundhouse kick with the right leg.

13) Retract the right leg following the delivery of the kick.

13-A (Rear view)　　13-B　　↘○ 13-B (Rear view)　　13-C　　↙◀ 13-C (Rear view)

13　　↙○ 13 (Rear view)　　14-A　　↘○◗ 14-A (Side view)

14-B　　↘○◗ 14-B (Side view)　　14　　↙◗◀ 14 (Side view)

15-A　　↘○ 15-A (Side view)　　15-B　　↘○ 15-B (Side view)

14-A) Pushing off the left arm to upright the body, place the right foot alongside the left foot and bring the hands together in front of the chest with the palms facing upward.

14-B) Turning the head to the right, slide the right foot out to the right while extending the arms out to the sides, leading with the elbows.

**14)** *Kiba-dachi/Kaiun no te*

Assuming a straddle-leg stance, fully extend the arms out to the sides with the hands formed into vertical knife hands positioned level with the shoulders.

15-A) Keeping the arms in place, draw the right foot back to alongside the left foot while turning the hips to the right so they face in the direction of the outstretched right arm.

15-B) Stepping forward with the left foot, draw the left hand around the body and below the right underarm.

15    15 (Side view)    16-A    16-A (Side view)    16-B

16-B (Side view)    16    16 (Side view)    17-A    17

17 (Side view)    18-A    18-A (Side view)    18-B    18-B (Side view)

### 15) *Zenkutsu-dachi/Hidari keitō-uke/Migi ushiro teishō-barai*

Complete the step forward with the left foot into a left front stance while simultaneously delivering a chicken-head-wrist block to the front with the left arm and a palm-heel sweep to the rear with the right arm.

16-A) Keeping the arms in place, draw the left foot back, positioning it alongside the right foot while turning the hips to the left so they face squarely to the front.

16-B) Stepping forward with the right foot, draw the right hand around the body and below the left underarm.

### 16) *Zenkutsu-dachi/Migi keitō-uke/Hidari ushiro teishō-barai*

Complete the step forward with the right foot into a right front stance while executing a chicken-head-wrist block to the front with the right arm and a palm-heel sweep to the rear with the left arm.

17-A) Swing the left arm around the body to the front while pulling the right hand, formed into a fist, back to above the right hip.

### 17) *Zenkutsu-dachi/Hidari jōdan haitō-uchi*

Complete the motion of the left arm to deliver an upper-level ridge-hand strike to the front.

### 18-A) *Hidari jōdan mae-geri*

Keeping the left hand in place, deliver an upper-level front snap kick with the left leg.

18-B) Pivoting on the supporting leg, rotate the hips sharply to the right while retracting the kicking leg. At the same time, pull the left elbow back and draw the right elbow out to the side of the body.

### 18-C) *Ippon-dachi/Migi chūdan soto-uke*

Completing a 180-degree turn to the right to face the opposite direction, drive the right forearm inward to complete a middle-level outside-to-inside block. At the same time, draw the left knee, still raised following the kick, inward from the opposite side. Employing a sharp twisting of the hips, the block and the left knee converge simultaneously in front of the body from opposite directions.

18-C

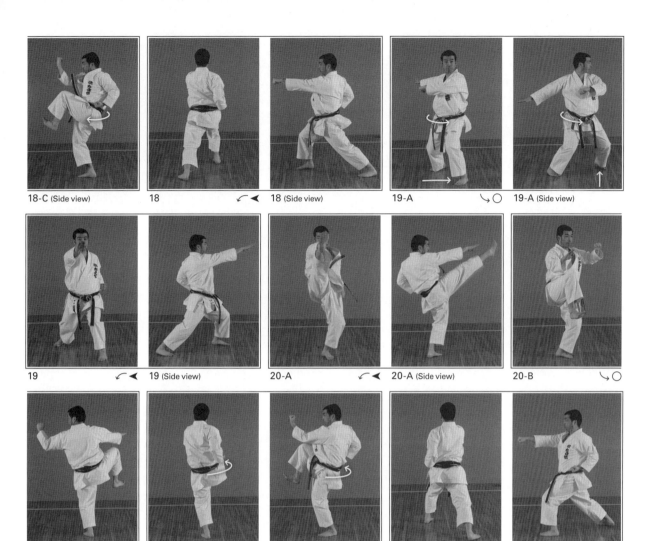

18-C (Side view)   18   18 (Side view)   19-A   19-A (Side view)

19   19 (Side view)   20-A   20-A (Side view)   20-B

20-B (Side view)   20-C   20-C (Side view)   20   20 (Side view)

**18) *Zenkutsu-dachi/Hidari chūdan gyaku-zuki***
Drive the left foot back into a right front stance while simultaneously delivering a left middle-level reverse punch.

19-A) Turning the head to the left to face the opposite direction, draw the left foot across the back to the right-hand side, turning the hips to the left while swinging the right arm around the body to the front.

**19) *Zenkutsu-dachi/Migi jōdan haitō-uchi***
Assuming a left front stance facing the opposite direction, deliver a right upper-level ridge-hand strike.

**20-A) *Migi jōdan mae-geri***
Deliver an upper-level front snap kick with the right leg.

20-B) Retracting the kicking leg, pivot on the left leg and rotate the hips sharply to the left while pulling the right elbow back and drawing the left elbow out to the side of the body.

**20-C) *Ippon-dachi/Hidari chūdan soto-uke***
Completing a 180-degree turn to the left to face the opposite direction, execute a middle-level outside-to-inside block with the left arm as the right knee reaches the front of the body from the right-hand side.

**20) *Zenkutsu-dachi/Migi chūdan gyaku-zuki***
Drive the right foot back into a left front stance while simultaneously delivering a right middle-level reverse punch.

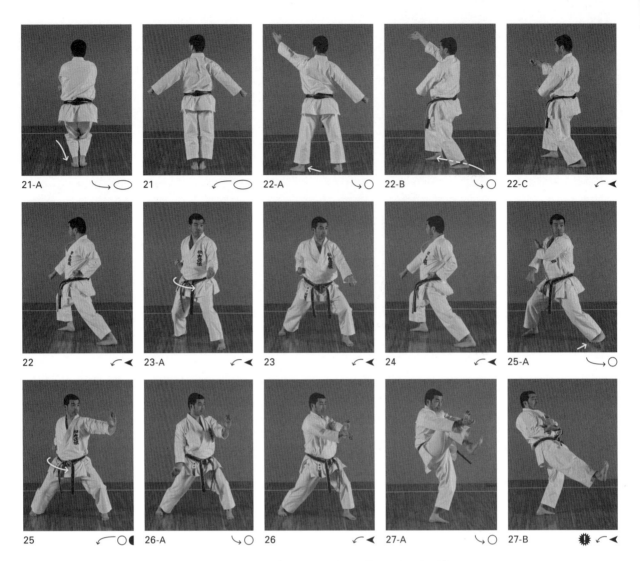

21-A) 〰️⭕  21 ⭕  22-A 〰️◯  22-B 〰️◯  22-C ◄

22 ◄  23-A ◄  23 ◄  24 ◄  25-A 〰️◯

25 ◯◖  26-A 〰️◯  26 ◄  27-A 〰️◯  27-B ✺ ◄

21-A) Turning the head 45 degrees to the left, draw the left foot back toward the right foot. At the same time, extend the left arm downward at an angle to the right while drawing the right fist to the left-hand side so that the arms cross in front of the body.

### 21) *Heisoku-dachi/Ryōwan-gamae*
Assuming a closed parallel stance, draw the arms back to the sides of the body.

22-A) Drawing the left foot out at a 45-degree angle to the left, raise the outstretched left arm in the same direction with the left hand opened into a knife hand. The motion serves as a feint to divert the attention of an imagined opponent.

### 22-B) *Tenchi kenseitai*
Initiating a step forward, rapidly drop the left arm in front of the body while simultaneously raising the right arm to execute a hi-low feint.

22-C) Stepping forward with the right foot, drive the right hand downward in front of the body while closing the hand into a fist.

### 22) *Zenkutsu-dachi/Migi gedan oi-zuki*
Complete the step forward with the right foot into a right front stance while delivering a right downward lunge punch.

23-A) Without changing the position of the feet, turn the hips sharply to the left, shifting the center of gravity forward toward the left leg while initiating a downward punch with the left arm.

### 23) *Zenkutsu-dachi/Hidari gedan-zuki*
Assume a left front stance facing the opposite direction while delivering a left downward punch.

### 24) *Zenkutsu-dachi/Migi gedan-zuki*
Rotating the hips sharply to the right, shift the center of gravity back toward the right leg, assuming a right front stance facing the previous direction while delivering a right downward punch.

25-A) Turning the head to the left, draw the left foot across the back to the right-hand side, turning the hips to the left while pulling the left hand, opened into a vertical knife hand, up toward the right shoulder.

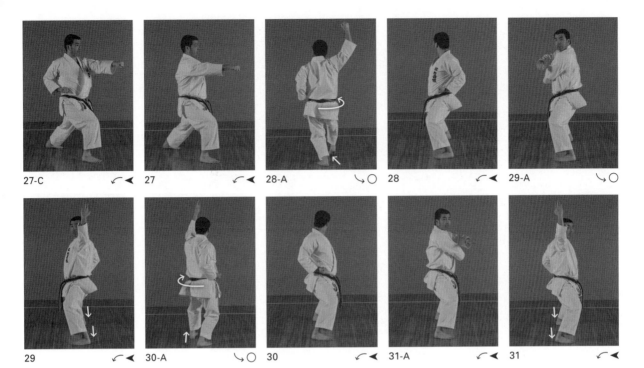

27-C    27    28-A    28    29-A

29    30-A    30    31-A    31

### 25) *Fudō-dachi/Hidari chūdan tate shutō-uke*
Completing a 180-degree turn to the left to face the opposite direction, assume a rooted stance while performing a middle-level vertical knife hand block with the left arm.

26-A) Drive the right hand downward in front of the body while opening it into a palm heel, and then upward in a scooping motion toward the left hand.

### 26) *Zenkutsu-dachi/Teishō tate hasami-uchi*
Shifting the hips forward to assume a front stance, bring the heel of the right hand up to meet the heel of the left hand to complete a vertical palm-heel scissors strike.

27-A) Keeping the arms in place, draw the right knee up sharply between the arms toward the chest.

### 27-B) *Mae ke-sage*
Thrust the heel of the right foot out in front of the body to deliver a front thrust kick with a *kiai* while pulling the hands back toward the chest.

### 27-C) *Zenkutsu-dachi/Hidari chūdan gyaku-zuki*
Plant the kicking foot forward in the direction of the kick, assuming a right front stance while executing a middle-level reverse punch with the left arm.

### 27) *Zenkutsu-dachi/Migi chūdan jun-zuki*
Deliver a middle-level front punch with the right arm.

28-A) Turning the head to the left, draw the right foot across the front of the left foot to the far side, pivoting on the left foot to turn the hips to the left. At the same time, lift the right fist upward and over the head.

### 28) *Kiba-dachi/Migi sokumen gedan-barai*
Slide the right foot out at a 135-degree angle relative to its previous position, assuming a straddle-leg stance while dropping the right arm to deliver a side downward block.

29-A) Turning the head to the left to face the opposite side, draw the left hand, opened into a ridge hand, across the front of the abdomen to the right-hand side of the body while extending the right arm across the chest in the opposite direction.

### 29) *Kiba-dachi/Hidari sokumen jōdan haitō-uke*
Thrust off the right foot to drive the left foot out to the left side with a gliding step (*suri-ashi*), immediately followed by the right foot, into a strong straddle-leg stance while delivering a side upper-level ridge-hand block with the left arm.

30-A) Turning the head to the right, draw the left foot across the front of the right foot and out to the opposite side, turning the hips 180 degrees to the right.

### 30) *Kiba-dachi/Hidari sokumen shutō gedan-barai*
Assuming a straddle-leg stance, drive the left arm down to the left-hand side of the body to deliver a side knife-hand downward block.

31-A) Turning the head to the right, draw the left arm across the front of the chest to the right-hand side of the body while extending the right arm below the left arm in the opposite direction.

### 31) *Kiba-dachi/Migi sokumen jōdan haitō-uke*
Thrusting off the left foot to slide the feet to the right while maintaining a strong straddle-leg stance, execute a side upper-level ridge-hand block with the right arm.

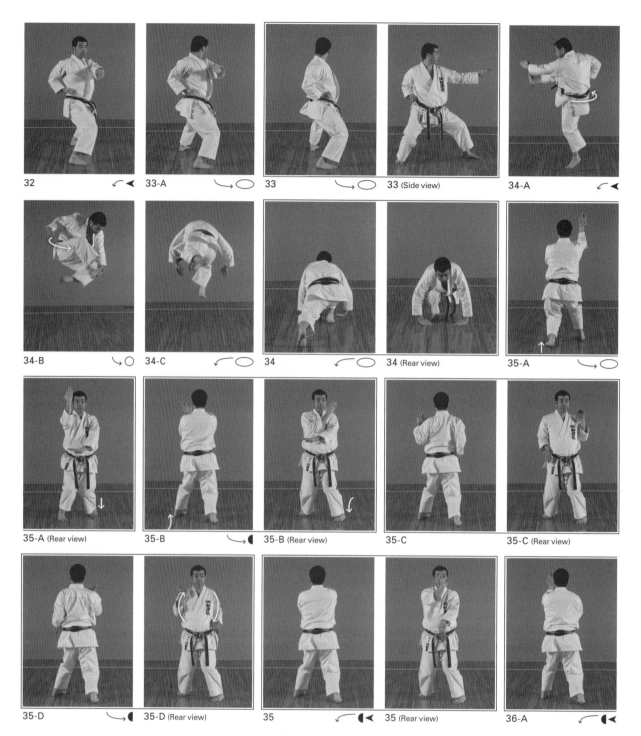

32    33-A    33    33 (Side view)    34-A

34-B    34-C    34    34 (Rear view)    35-A

35-A (Rear view)    35-B    35-B (Rear view)    35-C    35-C (Rear view)

35-D    35-D (Rear view)    35    35 (Rear view)    36-A

**32) *Kiba-dachi/Hidari sokumen-zuki***
Deliver a side punch with the left arm.

33-A) Turning the head to the left to face the opposite direction, rotate the left foot 90 degrees to the left while shifting the hips back toward the right leg. At the same time, draw the left hand, open and formed into a knife hand, out around the body to the left-hand side.

**33) *Kōkutsu-dachi/Hidari chūdan haishu-uke***
Assuming a right back stance, complete the motion of the left arm to deliver a back-hand block.

34-A) Turning the hips to the left, swing the right leg sharply across the front of the body, striking the palm of the left hand with the sole of the right foot while leaping into the air off the left leg.

**34-B) *Sempū tobi-geri***
Follow through with the rotation of the body in midair to perform a whirlwind jumping kick.

36-A (Rear view)

36-B

36-B (Rear view)

36-C

36-C (Rear view)

36-D

36-D (Rear view)

36

36 (Rear view)

37-A

37-B

37

### 34-C) *Ushiro-geri*

Completing a 360-degree turn, thrust the left leg back to deliver a back kick while lowering the hands in preparation for landing.

### 34) *Ryōte-fuse*

Land face down supported by the hands, which are positioned approximately shoulder-width apart and turned inward at an angle, with the right foot positioned roughly beneath the right shoulder and the left leg extending straight back with the heel of the left foot pointing upward.

35-A) Standing upright, step forward with the left foot while simultaneously raising the right forearm along the right side of the body with the back of the hand facing forward and dropping the left hand in front of the right hip with the palm facing downward.

35-B) Completing the step forward with the left foot into an hourglass stance, draw the right hand across toward the left shoulder while bringing the left hand up in front of the right-hand side of the body.

35-C) Draw the right hand down to the right hip while pulling the left hand up to the left shoulder. The right hand passes between the chest and the left arm as it approaches the right hip.

### 35-D) *Sanchin-dachi/Mawashi kake-uke*

"Roll" the hands around the sides of the torso to complete a circular hooking block.

### 35) *Sanchin-dachi/Teishō awase-zuki*

Drive both arms out in front of the body to deliver a two-handed palm-heel thrust with the right hand targeting the head and the left hand targeting the midsection.

36-A) Stepping forward with the right foot, raise the left forearm along the left side of the body while drawing the right hand in front of the left hip beneath the left elbow.

36-B) Completing the step forward with the right foot into an hourglass stance, draw the left hand across toward the right shoulder while bringing the right hand up in front of the left-hand side of the body.

36-C) Draw the left hand down to the left hip while pulling the right hand up to the right shoulder. The left hand travels between the chest and the right arm as it moves to the left hip.

### 36-D) *Sanchin-dachi/Mawashi kake-uke*

"Roll" the hands around the sides of the torso to complete a circular hooking block.

### 36) *Sanchin-dachi/Teishō awase-zuki*

Drive the arms forward to deliver a two-handed palm-heel thrust with the left hand above the right hand.

37-A) Pivoting on the right foot, slide the left foot along the rear to the opposite side, turning 180 degrees to the left to face the opposite direction while extending right arm up at an angle and pulling the left hand back towards the left hip.

### 37-B) *Zenkutsu-dachi/Hidari jōdan age-uke*

Step forward with the left foot into a left front stance while executing a left upper-level rising block.

### 37) *Zenkutsu-dachi/Migi chūdan gyaku-zuki*

Immediately deliver a right middle-level reverse punch with a *kiai*.

Yame-A

Yame

Shizentai

*Yame*-A) Pull the left foot back, positioning it alongside the right foot into closed parallel stance while drawing the right fist back toward the left-hand side of the body and extending the left arm across the midsection in the opposite direction.

*Yame*-B) Draw the arms back so that they extend downward to the sides, the same ready position in which the *kata* began.

**Yame**

Draw the right foot out to the right side into an open V stance while bringing the fists in to the front of the hips, the same natural-posture stance assumed prior to starting the *kata*.

---

**TECHNICAL ANALYSIS**
## Movements 1-C–1

Block an attacker's lunge-punch attack with an upward double-handed palm-heel block (photo 1) and, grabbing the wrist, pull him off-balance by drawing the blocking arm out to the side, away from the body (photo 2).

1

2

**TECHNICAL ANALYSIS**
## Movement 2

In response to a lunge-punch attack, hook the front leg behind the front leg of the attacker's while blocking with a chicken-head-wrist block (photos 1 and 2). Draw the front leg back to topple the attacker (photo 3) and counter with a one-finger spear-hand strike to the base of the neck (photo 4).

1

2

3

4

## TECHNICAL ANALYSIS
### Movements 12-A–13

As an opponent attacks with a reverse punch, lunge forward beneath the punch (photo 1) and counter with a roundhouse kick from below (photo 2). As the attacker responds with a downward punch, roll over to the opposite side (photo 3) and deliver a roundhouse kick from the reverse direction (photo 4).

1

2

3

4

## TECHNICAL ANALYSIS
### Movements 16–18

Block a lunge punch from the front with a chicken-head-wrist block while suppressing a front snap kick from the rear with a palm-heel block (photo 1). Deliver a ridge-hand strike to the attacker in front (photo 2) followed by a front snap kick (photo 3). As the attacker to the rear attacks with a reverse punch, block with a reverse outside-to-inside block (photo 4) followed by a reverse punch (photo 5).

1

2

3

4

5

# Wankan

Wankan, also known by the names Shōfū and Hitō, has been passed down as a *kata* from the Tomari region. Representative of the Tomari-te style, unique features of the *kata* include an augmented block delivered with one leg raised followed by a counterattack, and a takedown maneuver that reflects some of the mystique surrounding techniques unique to karate. The takedown, in response to an opponent's attack, comprises an instantaneous evasive shifting of the body and throwing technique performed so quickly that the attacker would find himself on the floor before he realized what had taken place.

Although recognized as a Matsumora-school *kata*, Wankan has been incorporated into the Shōtōkan and Shitō-ryū styles. Within these two styles, however, the same *kata* has taken on significant differences in appearance.

Reflecting its Tomari-te roots, the Wankan practiced within the Shōtōkan style is distinguished by techniques targeting the joints, including a scissors block performed with one leg raised, a hammer-fist strike, and a knee takedown.

With the fewest number of movements of any Shōtōkan *kata*, Wankan is a difficult *kata* to express well. The final wide-U punch is the high point of the *kata*, and must be performed with the hips very low.

## Wankan

Yōi     1-A     1-B     1-C     1

### *Yōi* (Ready position)
*Soto hachiji-dachi* (open V stance) with both fists positioned in front of the hips.

### 1-A) *Hidari shahō sashi-ashi*
Turning the head 45 degrees to the left, step forward with the right foot at a 45-degree angle to the left, placing it in front of the left foot with the toes pointing directly to the front. At the same time, raise the fists while drawing them together in front of the chest with the backs of the hands facing forward. The left fist is positioned on the far side of the right fist.

1-B) Step forward with the left foot at a 45-degree angle to the left with the heel raised while lifting the fists in front of the face with the elbows drawn together.

1-C) Settling into a cat stance, pull the elbows back toward the body and begin drawing the fists apart.

### 1) *Neko-ashi-dachi/Chūdan kakiwake-uke*
Complete the motion of the arms to perform a middle-level separating block.

### 2-A) *Migi shahō sashi-ashi*
Keeping the arms in place, turn the head to the right and draw the left foot across the front of the left foot to the right-hand side.

2-B) Stepping forward with the right foot at a 45-degree angle to the right with the heel raised, draw the fists together in front of the body, positioning the right fist on the far side of the left fist.

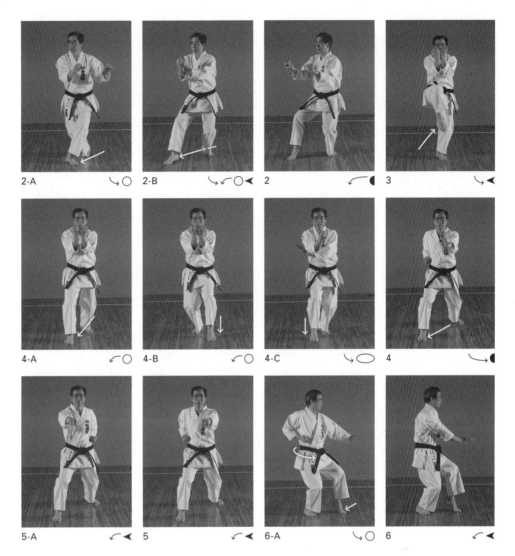

2-A    2-B    2    3

4-A    4-B    4-C    4

5-A    5    6-A    6

### 2) *Neko-ashi-dachi/Chūdan kakiwake-uke*

Assuming a cat stance, draw the fists apart to perform a middle-level separating block.

### 3) *Musō-uke* (*Hasami-uke/Hiza-gamae*)

Turning the head to the left to face the front, draw the forearms together with the elbows at chest level to execute a scissors block while raising the right knee in front of the body with the toes pointing downward. This combination upper-level/lower-level block is known as *musō-uke* (incomparable block).

### 4-A) *Migi sashi-ashi/Hasami-uke*

Keeping the forearms drawn together in front of the chest, step forward with the right foot, placing it on the floor approximately one foot's length ahead of the left foot.

### 4-B) *Hidari sashi-ashi/Hasami-uke*

Step forward with the left foot, placing it on the floor in front of the right foot.

4-C) Stepping forward with the right foot, pull the left hand, opened into a knife hand, back toward the right-hand side of the body.

### 4) *Zenkutsu-dachi/Hidari chūdan gyaku tate shutō-uke*

Complete the step forward with the right foot into a right front stance while extending the left arm out in front of the body to deliver a middle-level reverse vertical knife-hand block.

### 5-A) *Zenkutsu-dachi/Migi chūdan jun-zuki*

Drive the right fist forward to deliver a middle-level front punch.

### 5) *Zenkutsu-dachi/Hidari chūdan gyaku-zuki*

Deliver a middle-level reverse punch with the left arm.

6-A) Turning the head to the left, draw the left foot forward while turning the hips to the left. At the same time, extend the left arm out to the left-hand side of the body while opening the left hand.

### 6) *Neko-ashi-dachi/Kokō hiza-kuzushi*

Assuming a cat stance, draw the left hand back toward the abdomen to perform a scooping block while driving the right hand downward in front of the body to execute a knee takedown.

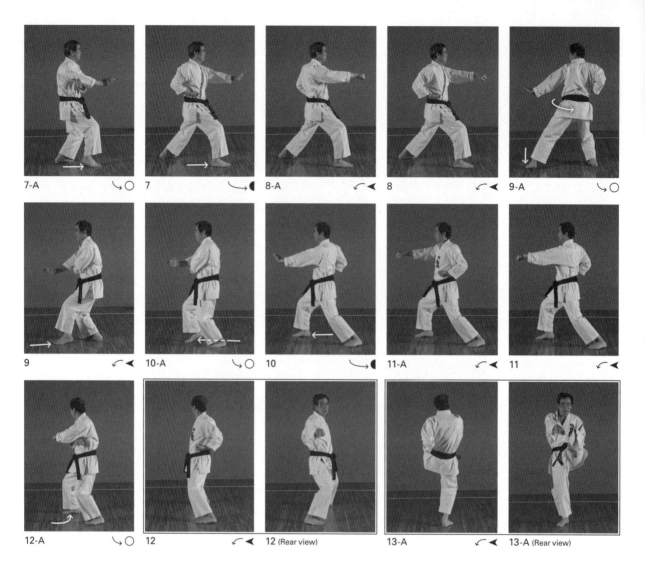

7-A) Stepping forward with the right foot, extend the right arm forward while keeping the left hand in front of the right-hand side of the body.

**7)** *Zenkutsu-dachi/Hidari chūdan gyaku tate shutō-uke*
Complete the step forward with the right foot into a right front stance while performing a middle-level reverse vertical knife-hand block with the left arm.

**8-A)** *Zenkutsu-dachi/Migi chūdan jun-zuki*
Deliver a middle-level front punch with the right arm.

**8)** *Zenkutsu-dachi/Hidari chūdan gyaku-zuki*
Deliver a middle-level reverse punch with the left arm.

9-A) Pivoting on the right foot, slide the left foot along the back to the opposite side, turning the hips to the left while drawing the left hand, opened into a knife hand, around the body in the same direction.

**9)** *Neko-ashi-dachi/Kokō hiza-kuzushi*
Drawing the left foot back to assume a cat stance facing the opposite direction, execute a scooping block with the left hand while delivering a knee takedown with the right hand.

10-A) Step forward with the right foot while extending the right arm out in front of the body.

**10)** *Zenkutsu-dachi/Hidari chūdan gyaku tate shutō-uke*
Complete the step forward with the right foot into a right front stance while executing a left middle-level reverse vertical knife-hand block.

**11-A)** *Zenkutsu-dachi/Migi chūdan jun-zuki*
Deliver a middle-level front punch with the right arm.

**11)** *Zenkutsu-dachi/Hidari chūdan gyaku-zuki*
Deliver a middle-level reverse punch with the left arm.

12-A) Turning the head to the right, draw the right foot back in line with the left foot and then out to the right-hand side. At the same time, draw the right fist across the midsection to below the left underarm while extending the left arm across the front of the chest in the opposite direction.

**12)** *Kiba-dachi/Migi tettsui-uchi*
Assuming a straddle-leg stance, drive the right fist out to the right side of the body to deliver a hammer-fist strike.

13

14-A

14

15-A

15

16-A

16

Yame-A

Yame

**13-A)** *Hidari mae-geri*
Turning the hips to the right, deliver a front snap kick with the left leg in the same direction as the hammer-fist strike.

**13)** *Zenkutsu-dachi/Hidari jun-zuki*
Plant the left foot forward into a left front stance while executing a left front punch.

**14-A)** *Migi mae-geri*
Deliver a right front snap kick.

**14)** *Zenkutsu-dachi/Migi jun-zuki*
Plant the right foot forward into a right front stance while executing a right front punch.

**15-A)** *Hidari mae-geri*
Deliver a left front snap kick.

**15)** *Zenkutsu-dachi/Hidari jun-zuki*
Plant the left foot forward into a left front stance while executing a left front punch.

16-A) Turning the head to the right to face the opposite direction, slide the right foot across the rear to the opposite side while drawing both fists to the left hip.

**16)** *Fudō-dachi/Yama-zuki*
Assuming a rooted stance, deliver a wide-U punch to the front with a *kiai*, with the left fist targeting an imagined opponent's face, and the right fist delivering a close punch to the midsection. In the completed position, the fists should be aligned vertically.

*Yame*-A) Pulling the right foot back in alignment with the left foot, extend the right arm across the front of the midsection while drawing the left fist across toward the right-hand side of the body.

**Yame**
Return to a natural-posture stance with the arms extended downward in front of the body, maintaining a state of physical and mental readiness (*zanshin*).

---

**TECHNICAL ANALYSIS**
## Movement 3

Block an opponent's simultaneous two-level attack with a combination scissors block and shin block (photo 1). This can then be immediately followed with an upper-level punch (photo 2).

1

2

## TECHNICAL ANALYSIS
### Movements 5–8

As an opponent launches a kick from the side (photo 1), turn to the left and deflect the attack with a scooping block combined with a knee takedown (photo 2). Stepping forward, draw the attacker's kicking leg forward while suppressing his upper body to topple him (photos 3 and 4), and counter with a downward punch (photo 5) followed by a downward reverse punch (photo 6).

1

2

3

4

5

6

五十四歩

# Gojūshiho Dai

This *kata*, also known as Ūsēshī, is most likely the most advanced representative *kata* of the Itosu school of Shuri-te. Master Gichin Funakoshi named it Hōtaku around the time that he changed the characters used to write "karate." This name (written using the characters 鳳啄, meaning "phoenix" and "peck") was likely assigned to the *kata* after having viewed a woodpecker alighting on a tree and opening a hole in the bark with its sharp beak to hunt for insects.

Gojūshiho Dai's sibling *kata*, Gojūshiho Shō, incorporates several advanced open-handed techniques and is characterized by such sequences as a chicken-head-wrist block followed by consecutive one-finger spear-hand strikes, and a two-handed chicken-head-wrist block followed by an ox jaw strike to an opponent's collarbone.

I have assigned the "Dai" designation to the Gojūshiho *kata* that contains the flowing cloud block followed by three consecutive four-finger spear-hand strikes, while the other version, which includes a chicken-head-wrist block followed by one-finger spear-hand strikes, I have labeled "Shō."

Master Kenwa Mabuni, the founder of the Shitō-ryū style of karate, introduced improvements to the *kata* and named it Ūsēshī while within the Shōtōkan style it became known as Gojūshiho (Dai and Shō) as the name Hōtaku falls into disuse. Through Master Kanken Tōyama, the *kata* Koryū Gojūshiho, which was his specialty, was introduced into the Shōtōkan style as what is called Gojūshiho Shō within the SKIF organization. The author believes that the Shō and Dai designations for the two versions of the Gojūshiho *kata* became reversed at the time of their introduction. Accordingly, SKIF recognizes the version that follows, which begins with a back-fist strike in a right front stance followed by a separating block, as Gojūshiho Dai.

## Gojūshiho Dai

Yōi     1-A     1    

2-A    

2

### *Yōi* (Ready position)
*Soto hachiji-dachi* (open V stance) with both fists positioned in front of the hips.

1-A) Drawing the right foot in toward the left foot and then forward, lower the hips while driving the left fist downward and raising the right fist to above the head.

### 1) *Zenkutsu-dachi/Migi uraken-uchi*
Stepping forward with the right foot into a right front stance, lower the right arm to deliver a back-fist strike

while raising the left forearm to meet the right elbow in front of the chest.

2-A) Turning the head to the left, step forward and out at a 45-degree angle to the left with the left foot while raising the left forearm so the wrists cross in front of the chest.

### 2) *Kōkutsu-dachi/Chūdan kakiwake-uke*
Assuming a right back stance, draw the fists apart to execute a middle-level separating block.

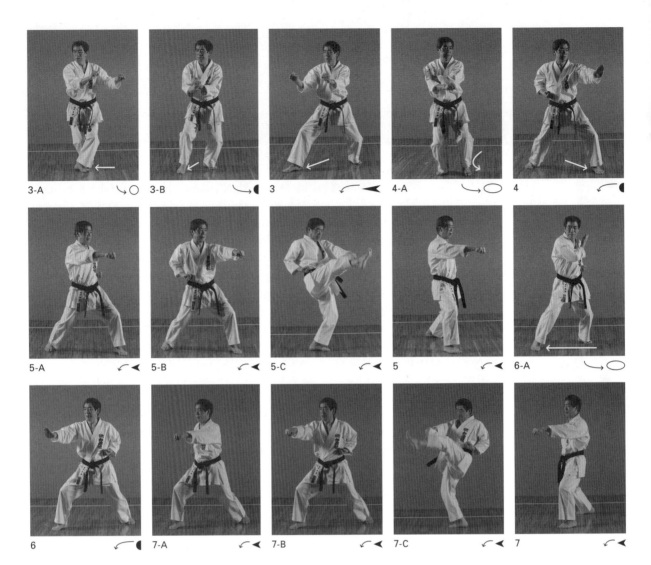

3-A) Without changing the position of the arms or the orientation of the upper body, turn the head to the right and cross the left foot in front of the right, placing it on the far side of the right foot.

3-B) Draw the right foot out at a 45-degree angle to the right while crossing the arms in front of the chest with the back of the left wrist resting against the inside of the right wrist.

### 3) *Kōkutsu-dachi/Chūdan kakiwake-uke*
Assume a left back stance while drawing the fists apart to perform a middle-level separating block.

4-A) Drawing the left foot in toward the right foot and then forward at a 45-degree to the left, extend the right arm across the front of the body toward the left-hand side while pulling the left arm back and above the right arm with the left hand opened into a knife hand.

### 4) *Zenkutsu-dachi/Hidari chūdan tate shutō-uke*
Complete the step forward with the left foot into a left front stance while performing a left middle-level vertical knife-hand block.

### 5-A) *Zenkutsu-dachi/Migi chūdan gyaku-zuki*
Deliver a middle-level reverse punch with the right arm.

### 5-B) *Zenkutsu-dachi/Hidari chūdan zuki*
Deliver a middle-level punch with the left arm.

### 5-C) *Migi mae-geri*
Maintaining the same upper body position, deliver a right front snap kick.

### 5) *Zenkutsu-dachi/Migi chūdan oi-zuki*
Plant the right foot forward into a right front stance while delivering a right middle-level lunge punch.

6-A) Draw the right hand, opened into a knife hand, back to above the left shoulder while shifting the right foot 90 degrees to the right.

### 6) *Zenkutsu-dachi/Migi chūdan tate shutō-uke*
Assume a right front stance at a 45-degree angle to the right while executing a right middle-level knife-hand block.

### 7-A) *Zenkutsu-dachi/Hidari chūdan gyaku-zuki*
Deliver a left middle-level reverse punch.

### 7-B) *Zenkutsu-dachi/Migi chūdan zuki*
Deliver a right middle-level punch.

### 7-C) *Hidari mae-geri*
Keeping the arms in place, deliver a left front snap kick.

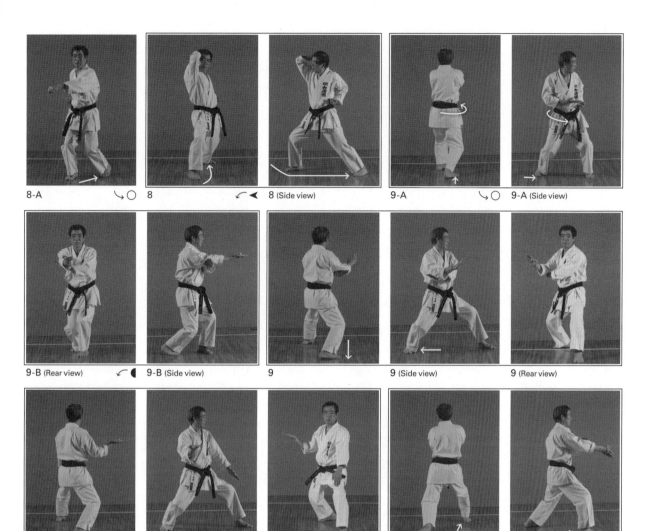

8-A    ↘○   8    ↙◄   8 (Side view)     9-A    ↘○   9-A (Side view)

9-B (Rear view)   ↙◑   9-B (Side view)    9     9 (Side view)     9 (Rear view)

10    ↙◄   10 (Side view)     10 (Rear view)     11    ↙◄   11 (Side view)

### 7) Zenkutsu-dachi/Hidari chūdan oi-zuki

Plant the left foot forward into a left front stance while delivering a left middle-level lunge punch.

8-A) Draw the left foot back sharply, directing it along a course past the right foot and directly back while pulling the left elbow back toward the body.

### 8) Zenkutsu-dachi/Migi tate empi-uchi

Plant the left foot to the rear in line with the right foot, assuming a narrow right front stance while driving the right elbow up to deliver an upward elbow strike.

9-A) Turn the head to the left to face the rear and, without raising the hips, draw the right foot one half-step toward the left foot while turning the hips to the left. At the same time, drop the right elbow to the right hip and open the right hand into a knife hand with the palm of the hand facing upward.

9-B) Extend the right arm out in front of the body while drawing the left arm across the chest, pressing the back of the left hand, also opened into a knife hand with the palm facing downward, against the right arm just above the elbow.

### 9) Kōkutsu-dachi/Ryū-un no uke

Draw the right foot back into a right back stance while performing a "flowing cloud block." The right arm executes a middle level knife-hand block at a 45-degree angle to the right with the left hand "hooked" behind the right arm above the elbow.

### 10) Kōkutsu-dachi/Kaishu kōsa-gamae

Drive the left arm downward in front of the body to deliver a downward knife-hand block while thrusting the right hand back at a 90-degree angle to the right, rotating the right wrist outward so the palm of the hand faces upward. Upon completion of the technique, the right hand should be parallel to the floor.

### 11) Zenkutsu-dachi/Migi shihon-nukite

Step forward with the right foot into a right front stance while delivering a right four-finger spear-hand attack with the left hand positioned against the inside of the right elbow.

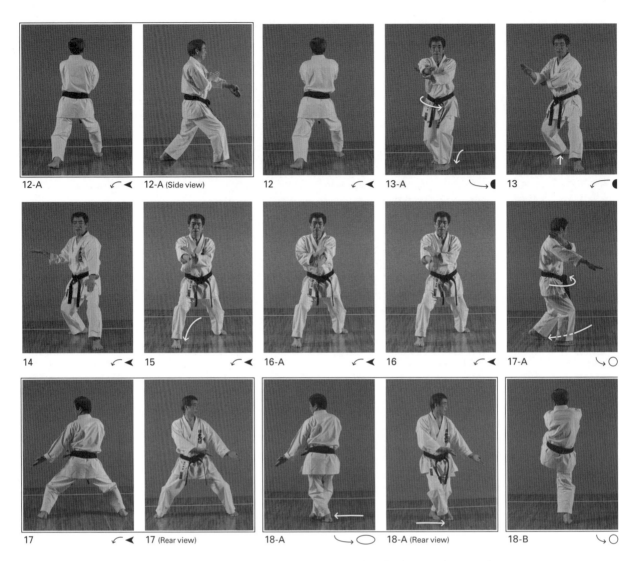

12-A (Side view)

12

13-A

13

14

15

16-A

16

17-A

17

17 (Rear view)

18-A

18-A (Rear view)

18-B

**12-A) *Zenkutsu-dachi/Hidari shihon-nukite***
Launching the left hand out in front of the body along a path traveling directly above the right wrist, deliver a four-finger spear-hand attack with the left hand while pulling the right hand back to the inside of the left elbow.

**12) *Zenkutsu-dachi/Migi shihon-nukite***
Deliver another right four-finger spear-hand attack, pulling the left hand back to the inside of the right elbow.

13-A) Turn the head to the left and draw the right foot one half-step toward the left foot while turning the hips to the left and extending the right arm out in front of the body with the back of the left hand pressing against the right arm just above the elbow.

**13) *Kōkutsu-dachi/Ryū-un no uke***
Drawing the right foot back into a right back stance, perform a "flowing cloud block" with the right arm executing a middle level knife-hand block at a 45-degree angle to the right and the left hand positioned behind the right arm above the elbow.

**14) *Kōkutsu-dachi/Kaishu kōsa-gamae***
Deliver a downward knife-hand block with the left arm

while driving the right hand back to a 90-degree angle to the right.

**15) *Zenkutsu-dachi/Migi shihon-nukite***
Step forward with the right foot into a right front stance while delivering a four-finger spear-hand attack with the right arm, pulling the left hand back to the inside of the right elbow.

**16-A) *Zenkutsu-dachi/Hidari shihon-nukite***
Deliver a four-finger spear-hand attack with the left hand, pulling the right hand back to the inside of the left elbow.

**16) *Zenkutsu-dachi/Migi shihon-nukite***
Deliver another right four-finger spear-hand attack, pulling the left hand back to the inside of the right elbow.

17-A) Draw the left foot across the rear to the right side, pivoting on the right foot to turn the hips 180 degrees to the left so they face the opposite direction. At the same time, pull the left hand up to above the right shoulder and thrust the right arm out to the right-hand side of the body.

18-B (Rear view)

18

↶◀ 18 (Rear view)

19 ↶◀ 19 (Rear view)

20-A

↘⬭ 20-A (Rear view)

20-B

↘○ 20-B (Rear view)

20

↶◀ 21-A ↘○

21 ↶◗

22 ↶◀

## 17) *Kiba-dachi/Morote kaishu gedan-uke*

Draw the left foot out to the left side into a straddle-leg stance while driving both arms downward to the left to deliver a two-handed open-hand downward block.

## 18-A) *Kōsa-dachi*

Without moving the upper body or raising the hips, cross the right foot in front of the left leg, placing it on the far side of the left foot to assume a cross-legged stance.

18-B) Turning the head to face the front, draw the left leg up sharply in front of the body while swinging both arms straight out in front of the chest. The right hand is positioned approximately 10 centimeters (4 inches) above the left hand with the palms of the hands facing each another.

## 18) *Kiba-dachi/Fumikomi/Hidari koshi-gamae*

Plant the left foot out to the left to deliver a stamping kick, assuming a straddle-leg stance while sharply pulling both fists back to above the left hip.

## 19) *Kiba-dachi/Morote kaishu gedan-uke*

Turning the head to the right, thrust both arms downward at an angle to the right to execute a two-handed open-hand downward block.

## 20-A) *Kōsa-dachi*

Cross the left foot in front of the right leg, placing it on the far side of the right foot to assume a cross-legged stance.

20-B) Turning the head to face the front, draw the right leg up sharply in front of the body while swinging both arms straight out in front of the chest with the left hand positioned above the right hand and the palms facing each other.

## 20) *Kiba-dachi/Fumikomi/Migi koshi-gamae*

Deliver a stamping kick to the right side of the body, assuming a straddle-leg stance while sharply pulling both fists back to above the right hip.

## 21) *Kōkutsu-dachi/Ryū-un no uke*

Draw the right foot in toward the left foot and then back to the rear, assuming a right back stance while performing a flowing cloud block.

## 22) *Kōkutsu-dachi/Kaishu kōsa-gamae*

Execute a downward knife-hand block with the left arm while thrusting the right hand back to a 90-degree angle to the right.

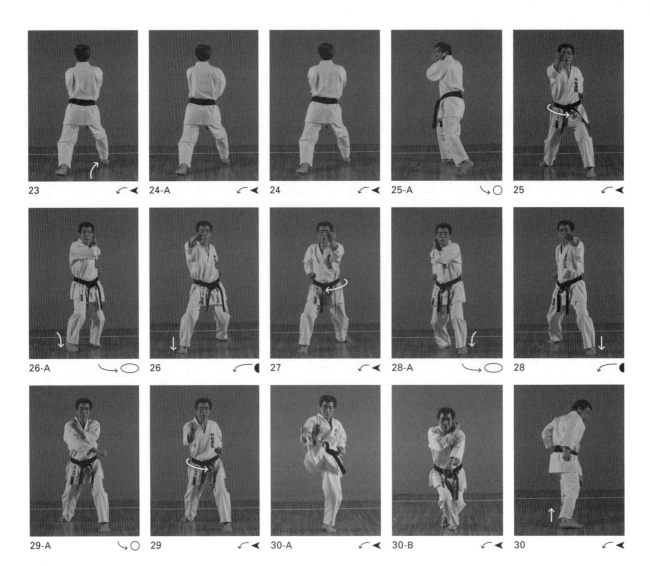

23    24-A    24    25-A    25

26-A    26    27    28-A    28

29-A    29    30-A    30-B    30

### 23) Zenkutsu-dachi/Migi shihon-nukite

Step forward with the right foot into a right front stance while delivering a four-finger spear-hand attack with the right hand, pulling the left hand to the inside of the right elbow.

### 24-A) Zenkutsu-dachi/Hidari shihon-nukite

Deliver a four-finger spear-hand attack with the left hand while pulling the right hand back to the inside of the left elbow.

### 24) Zenkutsu-dachi/Migi shihon-nukite

Deliver another right four-finger spear-hand attack, pulling the left hand back to the inside of the right elbow.

25-A) Turning the head to the left to face the rear, slide the left foot across the back to the opposite side while drawing the left hand around to the left and pulling the right elbow out sharply to the right side of the body.

### 25) Zenkutsu-dachi/Migi jōdan shutō-uchi/Gyaku-hanmi

Assuming a left front stance, turn the hips sharply to the left to *gyaku-hanmi* (45-degree angle to the front, with

the hip on the side opposite to the front leg pushed forward) while delivering a right upper-level knife-hand strike.

26-A) Step forward with the right foot while drawing the right knife hand back to above the left shoulder with the back of the hand facing outward.

### 26) Zenkutsu-dachi/Migi jōdan shutō-uke

Complete the step with the right foot into a right front stance while executing a right upper-level knife-hand strike.

### 27) Zenkutsu-dachi/Hidari jōdan shutō-uchi/Gyaku-hanmi

Draw the left elbow back and then deliver a left upper-level knife-hand strike, turning the hips sharply to the right to *gyaku-hanmi*.

28-A) Step forward with the left foot while drawing the right knife-hand back to above the left shoulder with the back of the hand facing outward.

31-A    31    32    33

34-A    34    35-A    35

### 28) *Zenkutsu-dachi/Hidari jōdan shutō-uke*
Complete the step forward with the left foot into a left front stance while executing an upper-level knife-hand strike with the left arm.

29-A) Pull the left hand, closed into a fist, back to above the right shoulder while drawing the right fist across the front of the body to the left-hand side.

### 29) *Zenkutsu-dachi/Migi chūdan gyaku uchi-uke/Gyaku-hanmi*
Deliver a middle-level inside-to-outside block with the right arm, turning the hips sharply to the left to *gyaku-hanmi*.

### 30-A) *Migi mae-geri*
Maintaining the same upper body position, deliver a right front snap kick.

### 30-B) *Kōsa-dachi/Migi nagashi-uke/Hidari otoshi-zuki*
Plant the right foot forward, immediately followed by the left foot into a cross-legged stance while dropping the hips. At the same time, deliver a downward punch with the left arm while simultaneously pulling the right fist back to above the left shoulder to perform a sweeping block.

### 30) *Zenkutsu-dachi/Migi ushiro gedan-barai*
Thrusting off the right foot, step straight back with the left foot into a narrow elongated left front stance, leaning the upper body over the left leg while executing a downward block to the rear. Throughout the movement, the head faces the same direction, with the eyes trained toward the downward block.

31-A) Turning the head to the left to face the opposite direction, draw the right foot one half-step toward the left foot while extending the right arm out in front of the body with the back of the left hand hooked beneath the right arm just above the elbow.

### 31) *Kōkutsu-dachi/Ryū-un no uke*
Draw the right foot back into a right back stance while performing a flowing cloud block.

### 32) *Kōkutsu-dachi/Kaishu kōsa-gamae*
Execute a downward knife-hand block with the left arm while driving the right hand back to a 90-degree angle to the right.

### 33) *Zenkutsu-dachi/Migi shihon-nukite*
Step forward with the right foot into a right front stance while delivering a four-finger spear-hand attack with the right hand, pulling the left hand to the inside of the right elbow.

### 34-A) *Zenkutsu-dachi/Hidari shihon-nukite*
Execute a four-finger spear-hand attack with the left hand, drawing the right hand back to the inside of the left elbow.

### 34) *Zenkutsu-dachi/Migi shihon-nukite*
Deliver another right four-finger spear-hand attack, pulling the left hand back to the inside of the right elbow.

35-A) Draw the left foot across the rear to the right side, pivoting on the right foot to turn the hips 180 degrees to the left so they face the opposite direction. At the same time, pull the left hand up to above the right shoulder and thrust the right arm out to the right-hand side of the body.

### 35) *Kiba-dachi/Morote kaishu gedan-uke*
Draw the left foot out to the left side of the body into a straddle-leg stance while driving both arms downward at an angle to the left to deliver a two-handed open-hand downward block.

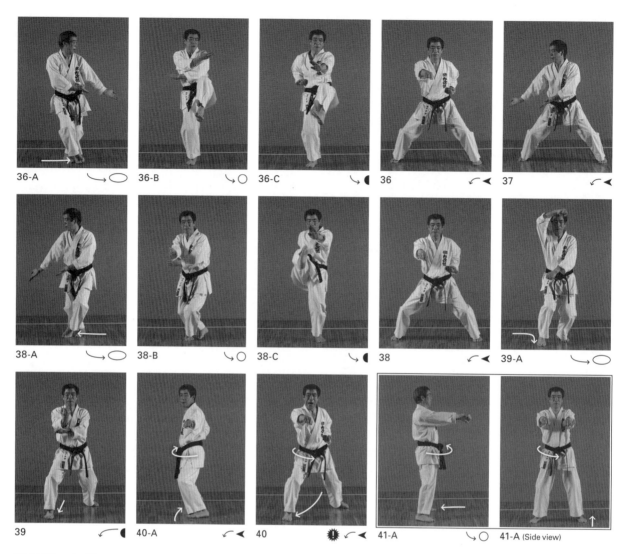

36-A    36-B    36-C    36    37

38-A    38-B    38-C    38    39-A

39    40-A    40    41-A    41-A (Side view)

### 36-A) *Kōsa-dachi*

Without moving the upper body or raising the hips, cross the right foot in front of the left leg, placing it on the far side of the left foot to assume a cross-legged stance.

36-B) Turning the head to face the front, draw the left leg up sharply in front of the body while driving the left hand across to the right-hand side of the body and beneath the right arm.

36-C) As the left leg reaches the peak of its upward path, thrust the left arm out in front of the body to deliver a middle-level vertical knife-hand block while pulling the right fist back to above the right hip.

### 36) *Kiba-dachi/Fumikomi/Migi chūdan zuki*

Plant the left foot out to the left to deliver a stamping kick, assuming a straddle-leg stance while executing a right middle-level punch.

### 37) *Kiba-dachi/Morote kaishu gedan-uke*

Turning the head to the right, thrust both arms downward at an angle to the right to execute a two-handed open-hand downward block.

### 38-A) *Kōsa-dachi*

Cross the left foot in front of the right leg, placing it on the far side of the right foot to assume a cross-legged stance.

38-B) Turning the head to the left to face the front, extend the right arm out in front of the body.

38-C) Drawing the right leg up sharply in front of the body, thrust the left hand out to the front to deliver a middle-level vertical knife-hand block while pulling the right fist back to above the right hip.

### 38) *Kiba-dachi/Fumikomi/Migi chūdan zuki*

Deliver a stamping kick to the right, assuming a straddle-leg stance while executing a middle-level punch with the right arm.

39-A) Draw the right foot in toward the left foot while driving the left fist downward and raising the right fist to above the head.

### 39) *Zenkutsu-dachi/Migi uraken-uchi*

Stepping forward with the right foot into a right front stance, lower the right arm to deliver a back-fist strike while raising the left forearm to meet the right elbow in front of the chest.

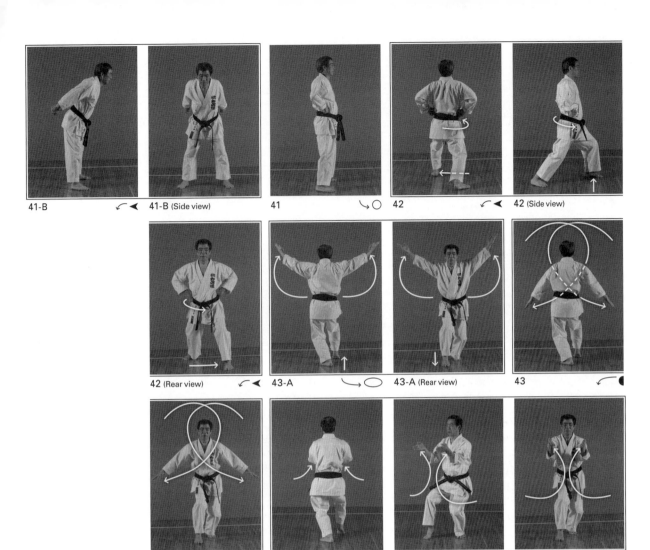

41-B     41-B (Side view)     41     42     42 (Side view)

42 (Rear view)     43-A     43-A (Rear view)     43

43 (Rear view)     44     44 (Angle view)     44 (Rear view)

### 40-A) *Kiba-dachi/Hidari chūdan tettsui-uchi*
Draw the right foot back sharply, aligning it with the left foot into a straddle-leg stance while delivering a left middle-level hammer-fist strike to the left-hand side of the body.

### 40) *Zenkutsu-dachi/Migi chūdan oi-zuki*
Step forward with the right foot into a right front stance while delivering a right middle-level lunge punch with a *kiai*.

### 41-A) *Shizentai/Ryōwan zenpō-nobashi*
Drawing the left foot in line with the right foot, turn the head and hips 90 degrees to the left while raising the hips to assume a natural-posture open V stance. At the same time, swing the right arm horizontally 90 degrees to the left and extend the left arm out in front of the chest so that both arms extend toward the front.

### 41-B) *Ushiro tettsui hasami-uchi*
Thrusting the hips to the rear, drive both fists around the body and downward to deliver a back hammer-fist scissors strike.

### 41) *Shizentai/Ryōken koshi-gamae*
Straighten the upper body while bringing the fists forward to the hips, pressing the first knuckles of the index and middle fingers into the sides of the body with the elbows extending out to the sides.

### 42) *Zenkutsu-dachi/Ryōken koshi-gamae*
Stepping out to the left and back with the left foot, turn the hips 90 degrees to the left to assume a left front stance.

43-A) Stepping forward with the right foot, extend the arms out to the sides and upwards to describe a large circle around the body. Open the hands with the palms facing upward upon initiating the motion.

### 43) *Neko-ashi-dachi/Ryō kaishu-gamae*
Complete the step forward with the right foot into a cat stance while drawing the arms downward in front of the body and out to the sides. The arms cross in front of the chest as they travel downward in front of the body.

### 44) *Neko-ashi-dachi/Morote keitō-uke*
Draw both hands inward and upward, forming them into chicken-head wrists to deliver a two-handed chicken-head-wrist block.

45

45 (Rear view)

46-A

46

Yame-A

Yame

**45) *Neko-ashi-dachi/Morote seiryūtō-uchi***
Thrust forward off the left foot into cat stance while executing a two-handed ox-jaw strike targeting an opponent's hips with a *kiai*.

**46-A)** Turning the head to the left while rotating the feet in place, turn the hips 180 degrees to the left and extend the right arm out in front of the body with the back of the left hand hooked beneath the right arm just above the elbow.

**46) *Kōkutsu-dachi/Ryū-un no uke***
Draw the right foot back into a right back stance while performing a flowing cloud block.

*Yame*-A) Draw the left foot back and out to the left-hand side, positioning it in line with the right foot in an open V stance. At the same time, draw the right arm back and out to the left-hand side of the body and above the left arm, which extends to the right side of the body.

**Yame**
Return to a natural-posture stance with the arms extended downward in front of the body, maintaining a state of physical and mental readiness (*zanshin*).

**TECHNICAL ANALYSIS**
**Movements 9–12-A**

Block an opponent's lunge punch using a "flowing cloud block" (photo 1), followed by a cross block in response to a subsequent reverse punch (photo 2). As the attacker grabs the wrist (photo 3), break the hold by using the opposite arm to deliver a spear-hand thrust (photos 4 to 6), repeating the process for the other side when the opponent again grabs the wrist (photos 7 and 8).

1

2

3
4
5
6
7
8

**Movements 25–30-A**

After launching a knife-hand strike to the neck (photo 1), step forward while delivering a subsequent knife-hand strike targeting the opposite side of the neck using the same hand (photo 2), immediately followed by another knife-hand strike to the neck using the opposite hand (photo 3). As the opponent retreats and responds with a reverse punch, block with an inside-to-outside block while turning the hips sharply in the opposite direction (photo 4) and counter with a front snap kick (photo 5).

1

2

3

4

5

## TECHNICAL ANALYSIS
**Movements 44–45**

In response to an opponent grasping the lapels with both hands (photo 1), break the hold with a two-handed chicken-head-wrist block (photo 2) and counter with a two-handed ox-jaw strike targeting the attacker's hips (photo 3).

1

2

3

# Gojūshiho Shō

Also known by the name Ūsēshī, this *kata*, as mentioned in the previous chapter, is the most advanced *kata* of the Itosu school of Shuri-te.

Around the time that Master Gichin Funakoshi changed the characters used to write "karate," he renamed this *kata* Hōtaku (written using the characters 鳳啄, meaning "phoenix" and "peck," respectively). The image of a woodpecker perched on a tree limb pecking away at the bark with its sharp beak while looking for insects applies to the "Shō" version of this *kata*.

Relatively early in the *kata*, Gojūshiho Shō introduces a variety of advanced techniques, including consecutive sequences delivered from a cat stance that begin with a chicken-head-wrist block, followed by a simultaneous chicken-head-wrist block-sweep and downward knife-hand press, and then successive one-finger spear-hand strikes to the sternum. After these come a sequence beginning with a two-handed downward block followed by an upper-level two-handed block against a stick attack, which is then repeated on the opposite side. This sequence is then followed with the chicken-head-wrist block and successive one-finger spear-hand strikes, after which consecutive downward knife-hand strikes are delivered.

Other unique characteristics that distinguish Gojūshiho Shō include a variety of highly advanced techniques, such as an eagle hand dropping strike, immediately followed by an eagle hand rising strike. These techniques, in turn, are soon followed by a simultaneous upper-level elbow strike and back downward block. It goes without saying, however, that the most striking feature of Gojūshiho Shō is the sequence that begins with the chicken-head-wrist block and finishes with three successive one-finger spear-hand strikes, which appears repeatedly throughout the *kata*. Accordingly, it is obvious why Master Funakoshi chose to assign it the name Hōtaku.

As a *kata* for advanced practitioners, Gojūshiho Shō is highly deserving of diligent study.

## Gojūshiho Shō

Yōi     1-A     1-B     1     2-A

### *Yōi* (Ready position)
*Soto hachiji-dachi* (open V stance) with both fists positioned in front of the hips.

1-A) Drawing the right foot in toward the left foot, lower the hips while driving the left fist downward and raising the right fist in front of the body.

1-B) Step forward with the right foot while raising the right fist up and over the head.

### 1) *Zenkutsu-dachi/Migi uraken-uchi*
Completing the step forward with the right foot into a right front stance, lower the right arm to deliver a backfist strike while raising the left forearm to meet the right elbow in front of the chest.

2-A) Turning the head to the left, step forward and out at a 45-degree angle to the left with the left foot while drawing both fists back to above the right hip, resting the left fist on top of the right fist.

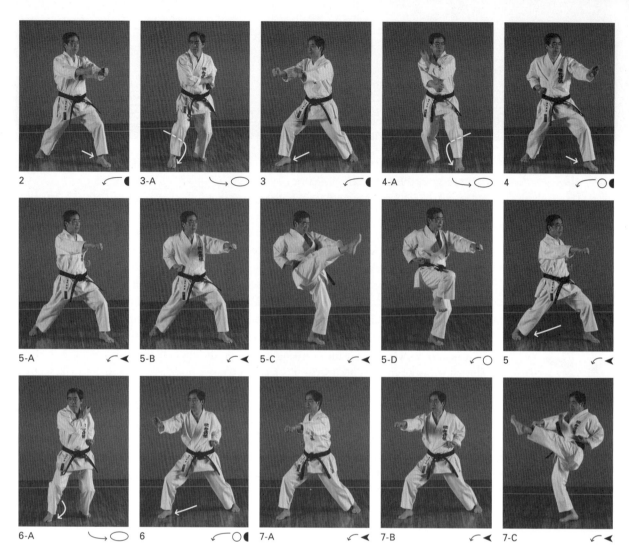

2    3-A    3    4-A    4

5-A    5-B    5-C    5-D    5

6-A    6    7-A    7-B    7-C

### 2) *Zenkutsu-dachi/Heikō tate-zuki*

Complete the step forward with the left foot into a left front stance while extending both arms straight out in front of the chest to deliver a parallel vertical-fist punch.

3-A) Turning the head to the right, draw the right foot forward and out at a 45-degree angle to the right while drawing both fists back to above the left hip, placing the right fist on top of the left fist.

### 3) *Zenkutsu-dachi/Heikō tate-zuki*

Complete the step forward with the right foot into a right front stance while extending both arms in front of the chest to deliver another parallel vertical-fist punch.

4-A) Drawing the left foot in toward the right foot and then forward at a 45-degree angle to the left, extend the right arm across the front of the body to the left-hand side while pulling the left hand, opened into a knife hand, back to above the right shoulder.

### 4) *Zenkutsu-dachi/Hidari chūdan tate shutō-uke*

Complete the step forward with the left foot into a left front stance while performing a left middle-level vertical knife-hand block.

### 5-A) *Zenkutsu-dachi/Migi chūdan gyaku-zuki*

Deliver a middle-level reverse punch with the right arm.

### 5-B) *Zenkutsu-dachi/Hidari chūdan jun-zuki*

Deliver a middle-level punch with the left arm.

### 5-C) *Migi mae-geri*

Maintaining the same upper body position, deliver a right front snap kick.

5-D) Keeping the punching arm extended, retract the kicking leg.

### 5) *Zenkutsu-dachi/Migi chūdan gyaku-zuki*

Plant the right foot to the rear, again assuming a left front stance while simultaneously executing a right middle-level reverse punch.

6-A) Turning the head to the right, draw the right foot in toward the left foot and then forward at a 45-degree angle to the right while pulling the right hand, opened into a knife hand, back to above the left shoulder.

### 6) *Zenkutsu-dachi/Migi chūdan tate shutō-uke*

Complete the step forward with the right foot into a right front stance while executing a right middle-level vertical knife-hand block.

7

8-A

8

9-A (Rear view)

9

9 (Rear view)

10-A (Rear view)

10

10 (Rear view)

11

11 (Rear view)

12

12 (Rear view)

### 7-A) *Zenkutsu-dachi/Hidari chūdan gyaku-zuki*
Deliver a left middle-level reverse punch.

### 7-B) *Zenkutsu-dachi/Migi chūdan jun-zuki*
Deliver a right middle-level punch.

### 7-C) *Hidari mae-geri*
Keeping the arms in place, deliver a left front snap kick.

### 7) *Zenkutsu-dachi/Hidari chūdan gyaku-zuki*
Plant the left foot to the rear, returning to a right front stance while delivering a left middle-level reverse punch.

### 8-A)
Turning the head to the left to face the front, draw the right foot forward while pulling the left elbow back toward the body.

### 8) *Zenkutsu-dachi/Tate-empi*
Complete the step forward with the right foot, assuming a narrow right front stance while driving the right elbow up to deliver an upward elbow strike.

### 9-A)
Turning the head to the left to face the rear, slide the left foot across the back to the opposite side while turning the hips to the left. At the same time, extend the left arm downward to the rear with the left hand open in preparation for a scooping block while opening the right hand and lowering the right elbow.

### 9) *Zenkutsu-dachi/Kokō hiza-kuzushi*
Assuming a left front stance, execute a scooping block with the left hand while driving the right hand down to deliver a knee takedown.

### 10-A)
Stepping forward with the right foot, draw the right hand up along a circular path in front of the left-hand side of the body while forming it into a chicken-head wrist. At the same time, begin rotating the left hand inward so the back of the hand faces the front.

### 10) *Neko-ashi-dachi/Migi keitō-uke* (*Kitsutsuki no kamae*)
Complete the step forward with the right foot into a cat stance while bringing the right hand up in front of the right shoulder to execute a chicken-head-wrist block. At the same time, complete the rotation of the left hand while forming it into a chicken-head wrist, "hooking" it underneath the right arm above the elbow. This position is also known as *kitsutsuki no kamae* (woodpecker posture).

### 11) *Neko-ashi-dachi/Migi keitō uke-nagashi/Hidari gedan shutō-osae*
Draw the right elbow back, level with the shoulder to execute a chicken-head-wrist block-sweep while extending the left hand, still formed into a chicken-head wrist, downward in front of the body to deliver a downward knife-hand press.

### 12) *Neko-ashi-dachi/Migi ippon-nukite*
Thrusting off the left foot, drive the right leg forward with a gliding step (*suri-ashi*), immediately followed by the left leg, again assuming a cat stance while delivering a right one-finger spear hand strike with the left hand positioned against the inside of the right elbow. When delivering the one-finger spear-hand strike, snap the wrist downward at an angle at the moment of impact.

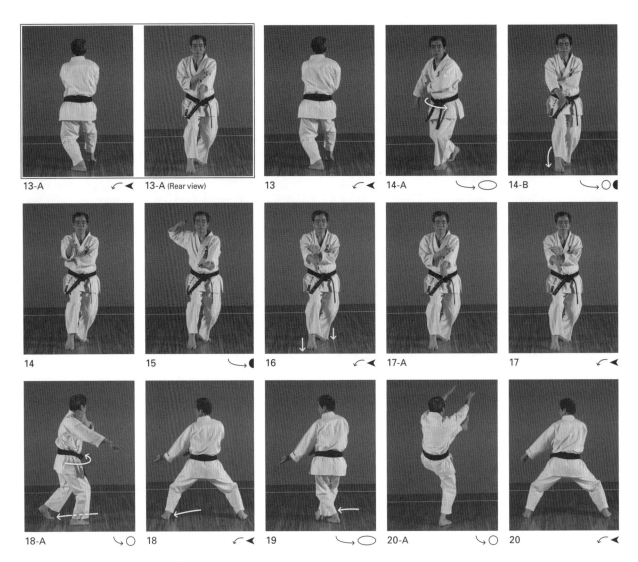

13-A    13-A (Rear view)    13    14-A    14-B

14    15    16    17-A    17

18-A    18    19    20-A    20

**13-A) *Neko-ashi-dachi/Hidari ippon-nukite***
Launch the left hand directly out in front of the body to deliver another one-finger spear-hand strike while retracting the right hand to the inside of the left elbow.

**13) *Neko-ashi-dachi/Migi ippon-nukite***
Deliver another right one-finger spear-hand attack while retracting the left hand to the inside of the right elbow.

**14-A)** Rotating the feet in place, turn the hips 180 degrees to the left to face the opposite direction, dropping the right arm to the right-hand side of the body while bringing the left hand back below the right underarm.

**14-B)** Drawing the right foot forward, bring the right hand toward the front of the body in a sweeping motion to the left.

**14) *Neko-ashi-dachi/Migi keitō-uke***
Complete the step forward with the right foot into a cat stance, executing a chicken-head-wrist block with the right hand, hooking the left hand behind the right elbow.

**15) *Neko-ashi-dachi/Migi keitō uke-nagashi/Hidari gedan shutō-osae***
Draw the right elbow back to perform a chicken-head-wrist block-sweep while extending the left hand forward to deliver a downward knife-hand press.

**16) *Neko-ashi-dachi/Migi ippon-nukite***
Thrust forward off the left foot with a gliding step into cat stance while delivering a right one-finger spear hand strike with the left hand positioned against the inside of the right elbow.

**17-A) *Neko-ashi-dachi/Hidari ippon-nukite***
Thrust the left hand in front of the body to deliver another one-finger spear-hand strike, retracting the right hand to the inside of the left elbow.

**17) *Neko-ashi-dachi/Migi ippon-nukite***
Deliver another right one-finger spear-hand attack while retracting the left hand to the inside of the right elbow.

21 ↰◄

22 ↘◯

23-A ↘◯

23 ↰◄

24 ↘◖

25 ↘◖

26 ↰◄

27-A ↰◄

27 ↰◄

18-A) Draw the left foot across the rear to the far side of the right foot, pivoting on the right foot to turn the hips 180 degrees to the left so they face the opposite direction. At the same time, pull the left hand up to above the right shoulder and thrust the right arm out to the right-hand side of the body.

### 18) *Kiba-dachi/Morote kaishu gedan-uke*
Draw the left foot out to the left into a straddle-leg stance while driving both arms downward to the left to deliver a two-handed open-hand downward block.

### 19) *Kōsa-dachi*
Without moving the upper body or raising the hips, cross the right foot in front of the left leg to assume a cross-legged stance.

### 20-A) *Jōdan kokō morote-uke*
Swinging the left leg up across the front of the body, drive the arms upward to the right with the palms facing each other to execute an upper-level two-handed block.

### 20) *Kiba-dachi/Fumikomi/Sokumen gedan morote-otoshi*
Deliver a stamping kick with the left leg, assuming a straddle-leg stance while drawing the hands, closed into fists, downward at an angle to the left to perform a side downward two-handed drop.

### 21) *Kiba-dachi/Morote kaishu gedan-uke*
Turn the head to the right and, opening both hands into knife hands, first draw the right hand up to the left shoulder and raise the left arm, then drive both arms downward to the right to deliver a two-handed open-hand downward block.

### 22) *Kōsa-dachi*
Without moving the upper body, cross the left foot in front of the right leg to assume a cross-legged stance.

### 23-A) *Jōdan kokō morote-uke*
Swinging the right leg up across the front of the body, thrust both arms upward to the left to perform an upper-level two-handed block.

### 23) *Kiba-dachi/Fumikomi/Sokumen gedan morote-otoshi*
Deliver a stamping kick with the right leg, assuming a straddle-leg stance while drawing the hands, closed into fists, downward at an angle to the right to perform a side downward two-handed drop.

### 24) *Neko-ashi-dachi/Migi keitō-uke*
Turning the head to the left, draw the right foot toward the left foot and then forward into a cat stance while delivering a chicken-head-wrist block with the right hand, hooking the left hand behind the right elbow.

### 25) *Neko-ashi-dachi/Migi keitō uke-nagashi/Hidari gedan shutō-osae*
Draw the right elbow back to perform a chicken-head-wrist block-sweep while extending the left hand forward to deliver a downward knife-hand press.

### 26) *Neko-ashi-dachi/Migi ippon-nukite*
Thrust forward off the left foot into a cat stance while delivering a right one-finger spear hand strike with the left hand against the inside of the right elbow.

### 27-A) *Neko-ashi-dachi/Hidari ippon-nukite*
Deliver another one-finger spear-hand attack with the left hand while pulling the right hand back to the inside of the left elbow.

### 27) *Neko-ashi-dachi/Migi ippon-nukite*
Deliver another one-finger spear-hand attack with the right hand, retracting the left hand to the inside of the right elbow.

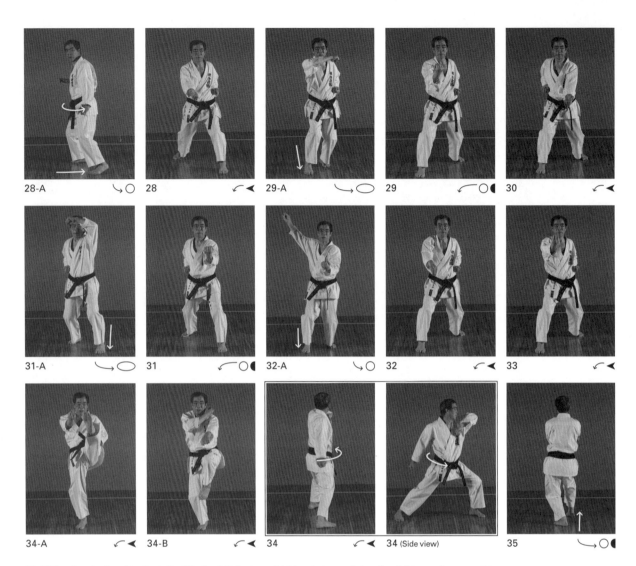

28-A    28    29-A    29    30

31-A    31    32-A    32    33

34-A    34-B    34    34 (Side view)    35

28-A) Turning the head to the left, slide the left foot across the back and out at an angle in preparation to assume a left front stance facing the opposite direction. At the same time, draw the left hand downward and across the front of the body to the left while pulling the right elbow out sharply to the right.

### 28) *Zenkutsu-dachi/Migi gedan shutō-uchi (Hira-nukite)*

Turning the hips sharply to the left, assume a left front stance while thrusting the right hand, formed into a knife hand, downward at an angle in front of the body with the palm facing upward to deliver a downward knife-hand strike. (Depending on the application, this technique could also be a downward horizontal spear-hand attack.)

29-A) Stepping forward with the right foot, close the right hand into a fist while drawing it back in a fluid motion toward the left-hand side of the body, past the left ear and above the head. The left fist remains in place against the right hip.

### 29) *Zenkutsu-dachi/Migi uraken-uchi*

Completing the step forward with the right foot into a right front stance, bring the right arm downward to deliver a back-fist strike.

### 30) *Zenkutsu-dachi/Hidari gedan shutō-uchi (Hira-nukite)*

Thrust the left hand, formed into a knife hand, downward at an angle in front of the body with the palm facing upward to deliver a downward knife-hand strike. (This technique could also be a downward horizontal spear-hand attack.)

31-A) Stepping forward with the left foot, draw the left hand, closed into a fist, back toward the right-hand side of the body, past the right ear and above the head.

### 31) *Zenkutsu-dachi/Hidari uraken-uchi*

Completing the step forward with the left foot into a left front stance, lower the left arm to deliver a back-fist strike.

32-A) Stepping forward with the right foot, swing the right arm upward and over in a large sweeping motion from the rear while forming the right hand into an eagle hand. At the same time, pull the left fist back to above the left hip.

36     37     38-A     38

39-A     39     40     41-A

### 32) *Zenkutsu-dachi/Migi washide otoshi-uchi*
Completing the step forward with the right foot into a right front stance, follow through with the motion of the right arm to deliver an eagle hand dropping strike.

### 33) *Zenkutsu-dachi/Migi washide age-uchi*
Immediately drive the right hand upward while rotating the wrist clockwise to perform an eagle hand rising strike.

### 34-A) *Hidari mae-geri*
Keeping the arms in place, deliver a front snap kick with the left leg.

### 34-B) *Ippon-dachi/Gedan kōsa-zuki*
As the kicking leg returns, pull the right hand, closed into a fist, back toward the left shoulder while thrusting the left arm downward in front of the body to deliver a downward cross punch.

### 34) *Zenkutsu-dachi/Hidari jōdan empi-uchi/Migi ushiro gedan-uke*
Turning the head to the left, plant the left foot straight back, pivoting on the right foot while turning the hips sharply to the left to assume a narrow left front stance facing the opposite direction. At the same time, drive the left elbow forward to execute an upper-level elbow strike while driving the right arm back to deliver a back downward block.

### 35) *Neko-ashi-dachi/Migi keitō-uke*
Step forward with the right foot into a cat stance while performing a chicken-head-wrist block with the right hand, hooking the left hand behind the right elbow.

### 36) *Neko-ashi-dachi/Migi keitō uke-nagashi/Hidari gedan shutō-osae*
Draw the right elbow back to perform a chicken-head-wrist block-sweep while extending the left hand

downward in front of the body to deliver a downward knife-hand press.

### 37) *Neko-ashi-dachi/Migi ippon-nukite*
Thrust forward off the left foot, again assuming a cat stance while delivering a right one-finger spear hand strike, pulling the left hand back to the inside of the right elbow.

### 38-A) *Neko-ashi-dachi/Hidari ippon-nukite*
Deliver another one-finger spear-hand attack with the left hand, pulling the right hand back to the inside of the left elbow.

### 38) *Neko-ashi-dachi/Migi ippon-nukite*
Deliver another one-finger spear-hand attack with the right hand, pulling the left hand back to the inside of the right elbow.

39-A) Draw the left foot across the rear to the far side of the right foot, pivoting on the right foot to turn the hips 180 degrees to face the opposite direction. At the same time, pull the left hand up to above the right shoulder and thrust the right arm out to the right-hand side of the body.

### 39) *Kiba-dachi/Morote kaishu gedan-uke*
Drawing the left foot out to the left-hand side of the body, assume a straddle-leg stance while driving both arms downward at an angle to the left to deliver a two-handed open-hand downward block.

### 40) *Kōsa-dachi*
Keeping the arms in place, cross the right foot in front of the left leg, placing it on the far side of the left foot to assume a cross-legged stance.

41-A) Turning the head to the right, transfer the body's weight to the right leg, raising the left knee while drawing the left arm back toward the body beneath the right arm.

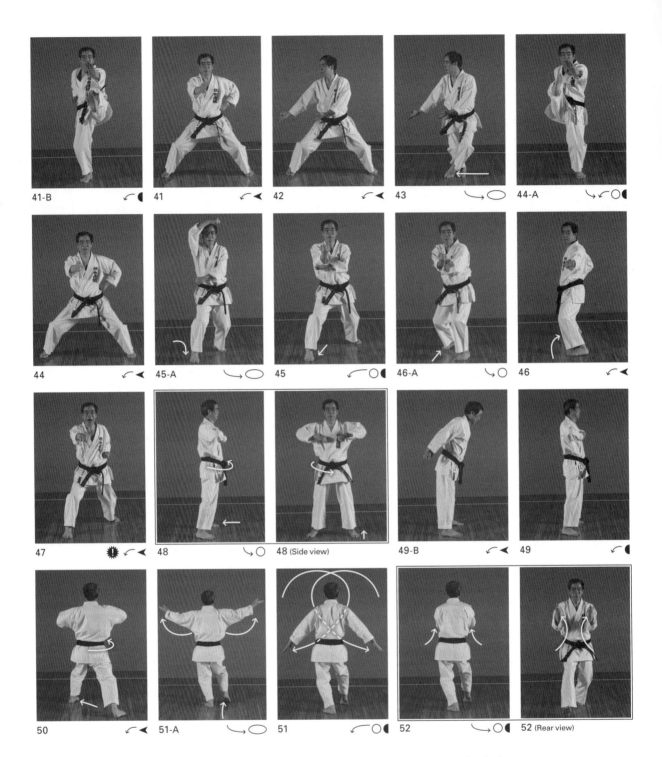

41-B     41     42     43     44-A

44     45-A     45     46-A     46

47     48     48 (Side view)     49-B     49

50     51-A     51     52     52 (Rear view)

### 41-B) *Hidari chūdan tate shutō-uke*

Drawing the left leg up sharply in front of the body, thrust the left arm forward to deliver a middle-level vertical knife-hand block while pulling the right hand, closed into a fist, back to above the right hip.

### 41) *Kiba-dachi / Fumikomi / Migi tate nukite / Hidari yoko hari-empi*

Plant the left foot out to the left-hand side to deliver a stamping kick, assuming a straddle-leg stance while driving the right hand, opened into a spear hand, for-ward to execute a vertical spear-hand strike. At the same time, pull the left hand, closed into a fist, back to the left hip with the elbow extending out to the side of the body.

### 42) *Kiba-dachi/Morote kaishu gedan-uke*

Turning the head to the right, first draw the right hand back to above the left shoulder while extending the left arm out to the left-hand side of the body, then drive both arms downward to the right to deliver a two-handed open-hand downward block.

53-A

53-A (Rear view)

53-A (Side view)

53

53 (Rear view)

53 (Side view)

54-A

54

### 43) *Kōsa-dachi*

Cross the left foot in front of the right leg to assume a cross-legged stance.

### 44-A) *Hidari chūdan tate shutō-uke*

Turning the head to the left, draw the right leg up sharply in front of the body while delivering a middle-level vertical knife-hand block with the left arm and pulling the right fist back to above the right hip

### 44) *Kiba-dachi / Fumikomi / Migi tate nukite / Hidari yoko hari-empi*

Plant the right foot out to the right-hand side to execute a stamping kick, assuming a straddle-leg stance while driving the right hand forward to deliver a vertical spear-hand strike and pulling the left fist back to the left hip with the elbow extending out to the side.

45-A) Draw the right foot in toward the left foot while driving the left fist downward and raising the right fist to above the head.

### 45) *Zenkutsu-dachi/Migi uraken-uchi*

Stepping forward with the right foot into a right front stance, lower the right arm to deliver a back-fist strike while raising the left forearm to meet the right elbow in front of the chest.

46-A) Draw the right foot back sharply past the left foot, rotating the hips to the right while pulling the left fist back toward the right-hand side of the body.

### 46) *Kiba-dachi/Hidari chūdan tettsui-uchi*

Assuming a straddle-leg stance with the right foot in alignment with the left foot, draw the left arm out sharply to the left-hand side of the body to deliver a middle-level hammer-fist strike.

### 47) *Zenkutsu-dachi/Migi chūdan oi-zuki*

Stepping forward with the right foot into a right front stance, deliver a right middle-level lunge punch with a *kiai*.

### 48) *Shizentai/Suihei hiji-gamae*

Drawing the left foot in line with the right foot, turn the head and hips 90 degrees to the left while raising the hips to assume a natural-posture open V stance. At the same time, pull both fists up to the chest with the elbows extending out to the sides.

### 49-A) *Shizentai/Ushiro tettsui hasami-uchi*

Thrusting the hips to the rear, drive the fists around the body and downward to deliver a back hammer-fist scissors strike.

### 49) *Shizentai/Suihei hiji-gamae*

Bring the fists back up to the chest with the elbows extending out to the sides.

### 50) *Zenkutsu-dachi/Suihei hiji-gamae*

Turning the head to the left, step out at an angle to the left with the left foot, turning the hips 90 degrees to the left to assume a left front stance.

51-A) Stepping forward with the right foot, extend the arms out to the sides, opening the hands with the palms facing upward.

### 51) *Neko-ashi-dachi/Ryō kaishu-gamae*

Complete the step forward with the right foot into a cat stance while drawing the arms upward to describe a large circle around the body, and then down in front of the body and out to the sides. The arms cross in front of the chest as they travel downward in front of the body.

### 52) *Neko-ashi-dachi/Morote keitō-uke*

Draw both hands inward and upward, forming them into chicken-head wrists to deliver a two-handed chicken-head-wrist block.

### 53-A) *Neko-ashi-dachi/Morote gedan ippon-nukite*

Thrust forward off the left foot with a gliding step into cat stance while delivering a two-handed downward one-finger spear hand strike with a *kiai*.

### 53) *Neko-ashi-dachi/Morote keitō-uke*

Snap both hands upwards into a two-handed chicken-head-wrist block.

54-A) Rotating the feet in place, turn the hips 180 degrees to the left to face the opposite direction, drawing the right arm out to the right-hand side of the body while bringing the left hand back below the right underarm.

### 54) *Neko-ashi-dachi/Migi keitō-uke*

Draw the right foot forward into a cat stance while executing a chicken-head-wrist block with the right hand, hooking the left hand behind the right elbow.

Yame-A          Yame

*Yame*-A) Draw the right foot back and out to the right-hand side, positioning it alongside the left foot while extending the right arm out to the left-hand side of the body.

### Yame

Return to a natural-posture stance with the arms extended downward in front of the body, maintaining a state of physical and mental readiness (*zanshin*).

---

### TECHNICAL ANALYSIS
### Movements 32–34-A

In response to an opponent's lunge-punch attack, deliver an eagle hand dropping strike targeting the wrist (photo 1). As the attacker counters with a reverse punch, use the same hand to execute an eagle hand rising strike (photo 2) followed by a front snap kick (photo 3).

1

2

3

### TECHNICAL ANALYSIS
### Movements 48–50

In response to an opponent grabbing from behind (photo 1), raise both elbows out to the sides of the body to break the hold (photo 2) and then drive the fists around the sides of the body to the rear to deliver a back hammer-fist scissors strike (photo 3). This can then be followed with a back round elbow strike (photo 4).

1

2

3

4

# Koryū Gankaku (Gankaku Shō)

The *kata* Gankaku, introduced in an earlier chapter, was originally known as Chintō. In Okinawa, it was previously called Mukandi and had been among the oldest of the old-style *kata*.

The *kata* Koryū Gankaku (called Gankaku Shō in the SKIF organization), which contains these original, older movements, is introduced for the first time in this book. One of the unique characteristics of Koryū Gankaku is its *embusen*, or performance line. While the *embusen* of all three Tekki *kata* describe a straight horizontal line, and that of Gankaku a straight vertical line, Koryū Gankaku's *embusen* is a straight diagonal line that extends forward at an angle to the left and back at an angle to the right. One of the theories behind this diagonal performance line states that it was to make it difficult for an outside observer to secretly steal the techniques used in the *kata*. According to another theory, the diagonal performance line is to ensure that the person practicing the *kata* never directly turns his back to the Shinto gods.

Other characteristics of Koryū Gankaku include numerous offensive and defensive techniques performed upon pivoting on one foot to complete a 180-degree turn, as well as the frequent appearance of hidden-knee cross-legged stances.

Long ago in Okinawa the names that had been attributed to various karate *kata* frequently made use of regional dialect and were written using Chinese characters based on phonetic equivalents rather than actual meaning. It was Master Gichin Funakoshi, recognized as the father of mainland Japan's karate world, who freed karate from its provincialism, bringing order to techniques from a Japanese perspective and changing the names of *kata*. Chintō was renamed Gankaku (written using the Chinese characters meaning "rock" and "crane") based on the image of a crane standing on a rock.

Chintō is an advanced *kata*, the essence of which can only be appreciated through diligent practice, which is why, within some circles, it is considered to be highly esoteric.

## Koryū Gankaku

Shizentai     Yōi     1     2

### *Yōi* (Ready position)
*Soto hachiji-dachi* (open V stance) with both fists positioned in front of the hips.

### Yōi *(Ready position)/Riken-gashō*
Slide the right foot in to assume a closed V stance (*musubi-dachi*) while drawing both hands up in front of the chin. The right hand is closed into a fist with the back resting against the palm of the open left hand.

1) Keeping the back of the right fist against the palm of the left hand, lower the hands along a vertical line so that both arms extend downward in front of the body.

2) Slowly turn the head 45 degrees to the left.

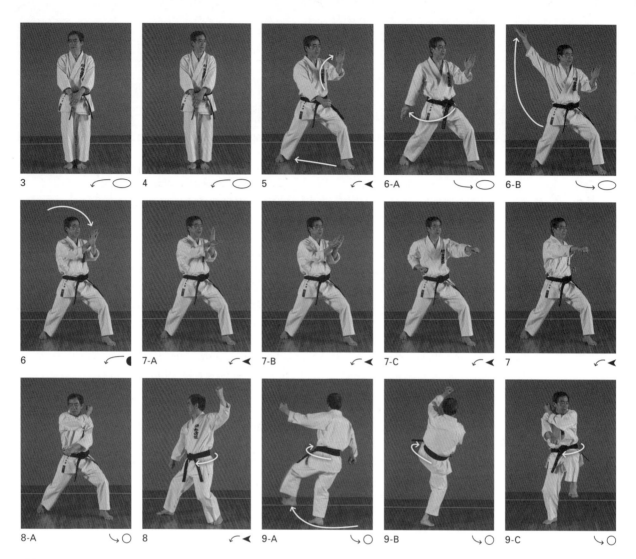

3      4      5      6-A      6-B

6      7-A      7-B      7-C      7

8-A      8      9-A      9-B      9-C

3) Slowly turn the head 90 degrees to the right, directing the face at a 45-degree angle to the right.

4) Slowly turn the head 90 degrees to the left, again directing the face at a 45-degree angle to the left.

### 5) *Zenkutsu-dachi/Hidari haishu-uke/Migi gedan tate-zuki*
Step back at a 45-degree angle to the right with the right foot into a left front stance, drawing the left hand up sharply in an arcing motion centered on the elbow to execute a back-hand block while driving the right fist down to deliver a downward vertical-fist punch.

6-A) Without moving the left arm, begin lowering the right arm while opening the right hand.

6-B) Draw the right arm back and around in a large circular motion while rotating the right wrist outward (clockwise) as the arm travels upward.

### 6) *Zenkutsu-dachi/Kaishu jūji-tori*
As the right arm approaches the left arm, begin bending the right elbow and position the right wrist above the left wrist to perform an open-hand X-grasp.

7-A) Keeping the wrists crossed, drop the right hand

down toward the left while rotating the left hand so that the palm faces upward.

### 7-B) *Gyaku te-dori*
Swing the left hand back toward the right hand using the wrist as a pivot while drawing the right hand back along the same path to perform a reverse hand grasp.

### 7-C) *Zenkutsu-dachi/Hidari chūdan jun-zuki*
As the hands drop level with the chest, immediately deliver a middle-level punch with the left arm while pulling the right hand, formed into a fist, back sharply to above the right hip.

### 7) *Zenkutsu-dachi/Migi chūdan gyaku-zuki*
Deliver a right middle-level reverse punch.

8-A) Turning the head to the right, pull the right fist back to above the left shoulder while driving the left fist downward across the front of the body to the right-hand side.

### 8) *Kōkutsu-dachi/Manji-uke*
Turning the hips sharply to the right, assume a left back stance facing the opposite direction while driving the left hand back and thrusting the right arm downward to perform a hi-low block.

9

10

11-A

11

12

13-A

13-B

13-C

13

14-A

14

9-A) Pivoting on the right foot, draw the left foot forward and around the front of the right leg while turning the hips in the same direction. Perform the turn with the feeling of maintaining a consistent center of gravity, keeping the hips in the general vicinity of where the left leg had been prior to initiating the turn.

9-B) Swing the left leg around the body while raising the left fist up above the head.

9-C) Prior to completing the turn, pull the left fist back to above the right shoulder.

### 9) *Kiba-dachi/Hidari sokumen gedan-barai*
Upon completing a 360-degree turn to the right, plant the left foot into a straddle-leg stance while simultaneously driving the left arm down to deliver a side downward block.

### 10) *Zenkutsu-dachi/Hidari haishu-uke/Migi gedan tate-zuki*
Slide the left foot back one half-step while turning the hips to the left and shifting them forward into a left front stance while executing a simultaneous left backhand block and right downward vertical-fist punch.

11-A) Without moving the left arm, lower the right arm while opening the right hand, drawing it back and around in a large circular motion while rotating the right wrist outward.

### 11) *Zenkutsu-dachi/Kaishu jūji-tori*
Bend the right elbow slightly and lower the right wrist onto the left wrist to perform an open-hand X-grasp.

### 12) *Tora-dachi/Hiki-yose-gamae*
Pulling the hips to the rear, draw the left foot back approximately one half-step, assuming a tiger stance while pulling the elbows down toward the chest and closing the hands into fists to assume a "pull-in" posture.

### 13-A) *Nidan-geri (Migi tobi mae-geri)*
Maintaining the same upper-body position, deliver a double jump kick, first thrusting off the left leg to deliver a jumping front kick with the right leg.

### 13-B) *Nidan-geri (Hidari tobi mae-geri)*
Immediately retract the right leg and deliver a jumping front kick with the left leg.

### 13-C) *Nidan-geri*
Upon completing the second kick, pull the fists back toward the right hip in preparation for the subsequent blocking technique.

### 13) *Zenkutsu-dachi/Gedan jūji uke-zuki*
Plant the left foot out in front of the right foot, assuming a left front stance while delivering a downward X-block/punch. The left arm performs a downward block while the right arm delivers a downward vertical-fist punch.

14-A) Turning the hips to the right, draw the left foot back alongside and past the right foot while pulling both fists back to above the right hip.

### 14) *Zenkutsu-dachi/Gedan jūji uke-zuki*
Completing a 180-degree turn to the right to face the opposite direction, complete the step forward with the left foot into a left front stance while delivering a downward X-block/punch, with the left arm performing a downward block and the right arm a downward vertical-fist punch.

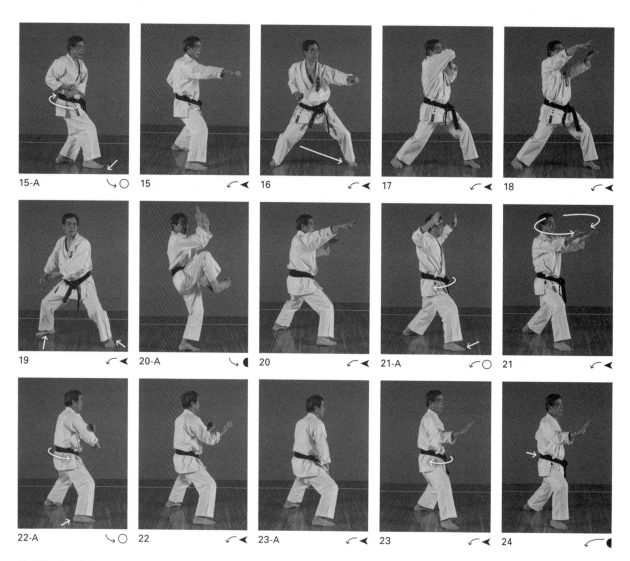

15-A) Turning the head to the right, shift the right foot across the rear and turn the hips sharply to the right to face the opposite direction while pulling both fists back to above the right hip.

### 15) *Fudō-dachi/Migi chūdan jun-zuki*
Assuming a rooted stance, launch the right fist forward to deliver a middle-level front punch while pulling the left fist back to above the left hip.

### 16) *Fudō-dachi/Hidari chūdan oi-zuki*
Step forward with the left foot into a rooted stance while delivering a left middle-level lunge punch.

### 17) *Zenkutsu-dachi/Migi jōdan mae-empi*
Thrusting off the right foot, drive the right hip forward, shifting into a left front stance while launching the right elbow forward to deliver an upper-level front elbow strike against the palm of the left hand.

18) Thrust both arms upward at an angle in front of the body with the palms facing each other.

### 19) *Shiko-dachi/Morote hiki-otoshi*
Driving the hips back toward the right leg to assume a square stance, draw the hands, closed into fists, down sharply at an angle to the right to perform a two-handed pull-down.

### 20-A) *Jō-chū awase-uke*
Draw the right knee up across the front of the body while swinging both arms around in the same direction to perform an upper-lower combined block. As the arms travel around the body, open the hands into knife hands and draw the elbows together above the right knee at approximately shoulder height.

### 20) *Shiko-dachi/Jōdan soto shutō-uchi*
Plant the right foot forward into a square stance while driving the arms out to the right-hand side of the body to deliver an upper-level outside knife-hand strike. The palm of the right hand faces the floor while the palm of the left hand faces upward.

21-A) Turn the hips to the right, shifting the right foot out to the right-hand side while drawing the elbows out to the sides of the body.

25-A

25-B

25

26-A

26

27

28-A

28-B

28

29-A

### 21) *Zenkutsu-dachi/Jōdan awase shutō-uchi*

Shifting the center of gravity toward the right leg to assume a right front stance, draw the hands along circular paths in front of the body to perform an upper-level two-handed knife-hand strike.

22-A) Turning the head to the left, turn the hips in the same direction and shift the right foot to the left-hand side. At the same time, extend the right arm downward at an angle to the left and draw the left hand across the top of the right elbow.

### 22) *Kiba-dachi/Ryōwan uchi-uke*

Assuming a straddle-leg stance, execute a double inside-to-outside block.

### 23-A) *Kiba-dachi/Kensei hirate komata-uchi*

Drop both hands and slap the inner thighs, a technique intended as a feint to momentarily distract an opponent.

### 23) *Kōkutsu-dachi/Migi chūdan shutō-uke*

Turning the head to the right, shift the hips toward the left leg to assume a left back stance while executing a right middle-level knife-hand block to the right.

### 24) *Zenkutsu-dachi/Migi chūdan shutō-gamae*

Keeping the arms in place, slowly shift the hips forward to assume a right front stance.

25-A) Draw the right foot back toward the left foot.

25-B) Continue to draw the right foot back, pulling it past the left foot to the opposite side while turning the hips to the right. At the same time, draw the right elbow back toward the body while bringing the open left hand out to meet the right elbow.

### 25) *Kiba-dachi/Hineri-kaeshi*

Turning the head to the right, assume a straddle-leg stance while drawing the right elbow out to the right-

hand side of the body with the forearm extending upward and the left hand providing support above the elbow to perform a twist return.

### 26-A) *Kiba-dachi/Migi hirate otoshi-uchi*

Turning the head to the left to face forward, drop the right hand along a circular course centered on the elbow to perform an open-hand drop strike.

### 26) *Shiko-dachi/Otoshi-zuki*

Grasping the right wrist with the left hand, deliver a downward punch with a *kiai*, dropping the hips while turning the feet outward to assume a square stance.

### 27) *Kiba-dachi/Ryōwan uchi-uke*

Turning the feet inward and raising the hips to again assume a straddle-leg stance, deliver a double inside-to-outside block.

### 28-A) *Kiba-dachi/Kensei hirate komata-uchi*

Drop the hands to slap the inner thighs as a feint to distract an opponent.

28-B) Keeping the feet in place, turn the hips to the right and draw the hands toward the right-hand side of the body while closing them into fists.

### 28) *Hiza-kakushi kōsa-dachi/Jōdan uchi-ude kaeshi-uke*

Completing a 135-degree turn of the hips to the right, assume a hidden-knee cross-legged stance while pulling both arms up in a sharp, whipping motion to perform an upper-level inside-to-outside reverse block. The right arm accompanies the technique to provide additional momentum.

### 29-A) *Hidari mae-geri*

Keeping the arms in place, deliver a front snap kick with the left leg.

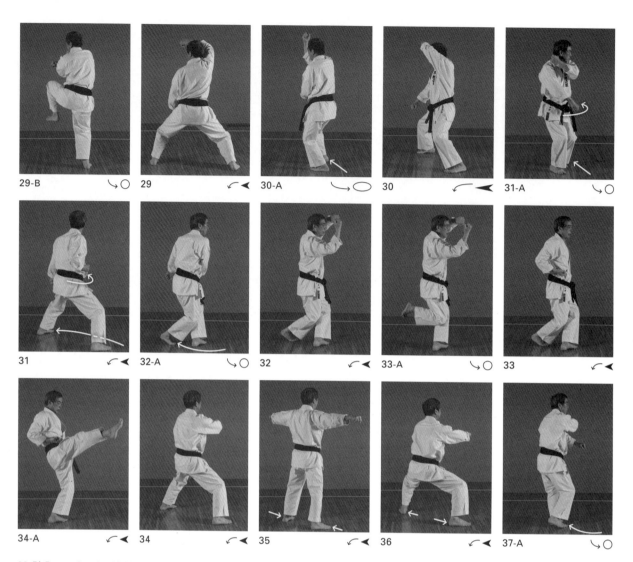

29-B) Retracting the kicking leg, draw the right fist across the front of the chest to the left while extending the left arm in the opposite direction below the right arm.

### 29) *Fudō-dachi/Musō-gamae*

Plant the left foot forward into a rooted stance while assuming an "incomparable posture." The left arm extends downward in front of the body as in a downward block but with the elbow bent slightly more than usual while the right arm is positioned like a rising block but with the forearm positioned directly in front of the forehead.

30-A) Stepping forward with the right foot, extend the left arm across the midsection to the opposite side while pulling the right elbow across the chest toward the left shoulder.

### 30) *Fudō-dachi/Musō-gamae*

Completing the step forward with the right foot into a rooted stance, drive the right arm downward while raising the left elbow to again assume an incomparable posture.

31-A) Turning the head to the left, draw the left foot back past the right foot while turning the hips to the left. At the same time, drop the left elbow, lowering the left fist toward the right shoulder while extending the right arm downward across the front of the body.

### 31) *Kiba-dachi/Hidari sokumen gedan-barai*

Step out with the left foot to complete a 360-degree turn to the left, assuming a straddle-leg stance while driving the left arm down to deliver a side downward block.

32-A) Turning the head to the right, draw the right foot back to the opposite side of the left foot while extending the right arm across the front of the midsection to the left-hand side of the body.

### 32) *Hiza-kakushi kōsa-dachi/Jōdan uchi-ude kaeshi-uke*

Assuming a hidden-knee cross-legged stance, pull both arms up sharply to perform an upper-level inside-to-outside reverse block. The left arm accompanies the technique to provide momentum for a more powerful block.

33-A) Keeping the arms in place, raise the right foot behind the body.

37-B    37    38-A    38-B    38-C

38    39-A    39-B    39    40

### 33) *Hiza-kakushi kōsa-dachi/Kensei yuka-geri/Ryō goshi-gamae*

Bring the ball of the right foot down sharply, kicking the floor to create a distraction while simultaneously pulling both elbows back, drawing the fists to above the hips.

### 34-A) *Migi mae-geri*

Keeping the fists positioned at the hips, deliver a front snap kick with the right leg.

### 34) *Kiba-dachi/Migi mae empi-uchi*

Turning the head to the left, plant the right foot forward in the direction of the kick, assuming a straddle-leg stance while delivering a right front elbow strike against the palm of the left hand.

### 35) *Shizentai/Sokumen dōji-tsuki*

Straighten the knees and draw the feet toward each other to assume a natural posture while driving the fists out to the sides at shoulder height to deliver a simultaneous double-punch to the sides.

### 36) *Shiko-dachi/Hasami-zuki*

Drop the hips, drawing the feet out to the sides to assume a square stance while driving the fists toward each other in front of the chest to execute a scissors punch.

37-A) Turning the head to the right, draw the right foot back behind the left foot while pulling the right fist up to above the left shoulder and extending the left arm across the front of the midsection to the right.

### 37-B) *Hiza-kakushi kōsa-dachi/Migi gedan-barai*

Draw the right foot back to the opposite side of the left foot to assume a hidden-knee cross-legged stance while driving the right arm down to perform a downward block.

### 37) *Hiza-kakushi kōsa-dachi/Ryō goshi-gamae*

Pull the right elbow back sharply, drawing the right fist to above the right hip.

### 38-A) *Migi mae-geri*

Keeping the fists in place, deliver a right front snap kick.

38-B) Plant the right foot forward and immediately rotate the hips to the left, turning to face the opposite direction while drawing the left foot back to again assume a hidden-knee stance. At the same time, pull the left fist back to above the right shoulder.

### 38-C) *Hiza-kakushi kōsa-dachi/Hidari gedan-barai*

Drive the left arm down in front of the body to deliver a downward block.

### 38) *Hiza-kakushi kōsa-dachi/Ryō goshi-gamae*

Immediately pull the left elbow back, bringing the left fist to above the left hip.

### 39-A) *Hidari mae-geri*

Keeping the fists in place at the hips, deliver a left front snap kick.

39-B) Retracting the kicking leg, pull the left hand, opened into a knife hand, back to above the right shoulder while extending the right arm out in front of the body.

### 39) *Kōkutsu-dachi/Hidari chūdan shutō-uke*

Plant the left foot forward, assuming a right back stance while executing a left middle-level knife-hand block.

### 40) *Zenkutsu-dachi/Hidari chūdan shutō-uke*

Keeping the arms in place, slowly shift the hips forward to assume a left front stance.

41-A    41    42-A    42    43-A

43-B    43    44    45    Yame-A

**41-A)** *Migi jōdan mae-geri/Migi jōdan jun-zuki*
Deliver a right upper-level front snap kick while simultaneously executing a right upper-level front punch.

**41)** *Tachi-hiza/Hidari otoshi-zuki*
Upon completing the kick, drop the left knee as the right foot makes contact with the floor, delivering a left downward punch with a *kiai* while pulling the right fist back to above the right hip.

**42-A)** Turning the head to the left, raise the left knee and begin drawing the left foot out to the left-hand side of the body.

**42)** *Zenkutsu-dachi/Hidari haishu-uke/Migi gedan tate-zuki*
Assuming a left front stance, draw the left hand up sharply to execute a back-hand block while delivering a downward vertical-fist punch with the right arm.

**43-A)** Draw the right arm back and around in a large circular motion while rotating the right wrist outward as the arm travels upward behind the body.

**43-B)** Follow through with the motion, keeping the right arm extended with the back of the hand facing the right-hand side.

**43)** *Zenkutsu-dachi/Kaishu jūji-tori*
Begin bending the right elbow as the right arm approaches the left arm, positioning the right wrist above the left wrist to perform an open-hand X-grasp.

**44)** Turning the head to the right to face the front, slide the right foot forward to the left foot to assume a closed V stance (*musubi-dachi*) while drawing both hands up in front of the chin with the back of the right hand, closed into a fist, resting against the palm of the open left hand.

**45)** Keeping the back of the right fist against the palm of the left hand, lower the hands so that both arms extend downward in front of the body.

*Yame*-A) Lower the arms to the sides of the body, opening the right hand as it moves downward.

**Yame**
Draw the right foot out to the right into an open V stance while closing the hands into fists and drawing them out to the front of the hips, the same natural-posture stance assumed prior to starting the *kata*.

Yame

## TECHNICAL ANALYSIS
### Movements 20-A–22-A

Upon blocking an opponent's simultaneous kick and punch attack with an upper-lower combined block (photo 1), counter with an outside knife-hand strike to the head (photo 2) followed by a two-handed knife-hand strike to the neck (photo 3). The attacker's punching arm can then be grabbed and an armlock applied (photo 4).

1

2

3

4

## TECHNICAL ANALYSIS
### Movements 28–30

Block an attacker's lunge punch attack with a back-arm block (photo 1) and counter with a front snap kick (photo 2) followed by a hammer-fist strike to the midsection (photo 3). Step forward and around the opponent while driving the right arm across the opponent's chest, using the leverage provided by the front leg to throw him to the floor (photo 4). This response can then be followed with a downward punch (photo 5).

1

1 (Reverse-angle view)

2

2 (Reverse-angle view)

3

3 (Reverse-angle view)

4 4 (Reverse-angle view)

5 5 (Reverse-angle view)

# GLOSSARY OF JAPANESE KARATE TERMS

## Note regarding pronunciation of basic karate terms for punch, kick and stance

Although many students of karate are familiar with the Japanese names of specific punching/kicking techniques and stances, there remains confusion over the correct pronunciation of the basic terms for punch (*tsuki*), kick (*keri*) and stance (*tachi*).

### TSUKI VS. ZUKI

In Japanese, the term *tsuki* is used to refer to the punching techniques used in karate. Due to a pronunciation characteristic of the Japanese language, when *tsuki* immediately follows a descriptive component, it is pronounced *zuki*, as in *gyaku-zuki* (reverse punch) and *oi-zuki* (lunge punch). However, when referring to punching techniques in general (as opposed to a specific type of punch), the proper pronunciation is *tsuki* (not *zuki*).

### KERI VS. GERI

*Keri* is the basic Japanese term used to refer to kicking techniques. In the same way that *tsuki* becomes *zuki* depending on its usage, *keri* also changes in a similar manner. When *keri* follows a descriptive component, it is pronounced *geri*, as in *yoko-geri* (side kick) and *mawashi-geri* (roundhouse kick). When referring to kicking techniques in general, however, the correct pronunciation is *keri*.

### TACHI VS. DACHI

*Tachi* is the Japanese word used to refer to stances used in karate. Like *tsuki* and *keri*, its pronunciation changes when affixed to a descriptive component. *Tachi* becomes *dachi* when describing specific types of stances, such as *zenkutsu-dachi* (front stance) and *kiba-dachi* (straddle-leg stance). But, when referring to stances in general, the correct pronunciation is *tachi*.

## Pronouncing Japanese

The Japanese terms appearing in this book have been written in accordance with the modified Hepburn romanization system. With only five vowel sounds, the pronunciation of Japanese is not overly difficult once the pronunciation of each vowel has been learned.

Each vowel is pronounced as follows:
a — *ah*, as the "a" in father
e — *eh*, as the "e" in get
i — *ee*, as the "ee" in feet
o — *oh*, as the "o" in go
u — *ooh*, as the "oo" in food

Vowels with a mark above them (as in the words *jōdan* and *chūdan*) indicate lengthened vowels. They are pronounced in the same fashion as their shorter counterparts but last a little longer when spoken.

---

**GENERAL**

*Ashi*: Foot, leg
*Awase*: Refers to a technique with combined elements, such as a two-handed block
*Chūdan*: Middle level of the body (chest area)

*Dōjō*: training hall
*Embusen*: Performance line (a pattern formed by the movements that make up a *kata*)
*Empi*: Elbow (also *hiji*)
*Gedan*: Lower level of the body, downward
*Gyaku*: Reverse or opposite

*Haimen*: Rear, back side

*Haishu*: Back hand

*Haitō*: Ridge hand

*Haiwan*: Back arm (the posterior surface of the forearm leading into the back of the hand)

*Heikō*: Parallel

*Hidari*: Left

*Hiji*: Elbow (also *empi*)

*Hirate*: Open hand

*Hiza*: Knee

*Jō*: stick, staff

*Jōdan*: Upper level of the body (face area)

*Kaishu*: Open hand(s)

*Kamae*: Posture or ready position (pronounced *gamae* when preceded by another word, as in *koshi-gamae*)

*Karate-dō*: Way or path of karate

*Kata*: Pre-arranged forms comprising a series of offensive and defensive techniques that are performed individually against imaginary opponents

*Keri*: Kick (pronounced *geri* when preceded by another word, as in *mae-geri*)

*Kiai*: A loud vocalization, such as "*yaah*," timed to coincide with a decisive technique

*Kōhō*: Rear direction

*Kōsa*: Refers to a technique or stance involving the crossing of either the arms or legs

*Mae*: Front, forward

*Migi*: Right

*Morote*: Refers to techniques performed with both hands or both arms

*Nai-wan*: Inner arm (the thumb side of the forearm)

*Ryō-hiji*: Refers to techniques performed with both elbows

*Ryō-ude*: Refers to techniques performed with both arms

*Ryōwan*: Refers to techniques performed with both arms

*Sashi-ashi*: Step-over

*Soete*: Accompanying hand (arm) used for augmented techniques

*Sokumen*: Side (used in connection with techniques delivered to either side of the body)

*Soto*: Outside, outside-to-inside

*Soto-ude*: Outer arm (the little-finger side of the forearm)

*Suri-ashi*: A "gliding" step, without raising the foot

*Tachi*: Stance (pronounced *dachi* when preceded by another word, as in *zenkutsu-dachi*)

*Tate*: Vertical or upward

*Te*: Hand

*Tekubi*: Wrist

*Tenchi*: Refers to techniques in which one arm performs an upper-level technique while the other arm performs a lower-level technique (literal translation: Heaven and Earth)

*Tenshin*: Body rotation

*Tsuki*: Punch or thrust (pronounced *zuki* when preceded by another word, as in *gyaku-zuki*)

*Uchi*: 1. Strike; 2. Inside, inside-to-outside

*Uchi-ude*: Inner arm (the thumb side of the forearm)

*Ude*: Arm

*Uke*: Block

*Ushiro*: Back, rear

*Yoko*: Side

*Yame*: Command to cease performing an activity or action

*Zanshin*: A state of physical and mental preparedness following the performance of a technique

*Zempō*: Indicating a direction to the front

## STANCES

*Fudō-dachi*: Rooted stance

*Gankaku-gamae*: A posture unique to the *kata* Gankaku in which the lower body assumes a crane-leg stance while the upper body is positioned as if having performed a hi-low block

*Gedan-gamae*: Downward-block posture

*Gyaku-hanmi*: Reverse half-front-facing position (hips at a 45-degree angle to the front, with the hip on the side opposite to the front leg pushed forward)

*Hachiji-dachi*: Open V stance (also *soto hachiji-dachi*)

*Haitō koshi-gamae*: A posture in which the hands are positioned beside one side of the hips, one closed into a fist with the other forming a ridge hand

*Hangetsu-dachi*: Half-moon stance

*Hanmi*: Half-front-facing position (hips at a 45-degree angle to the front)

*Han zenkutsu-dachi*: Half-front stance

*Heisoku-dachi*: Closed parallel stance

*Hiza-gamae*: A posture in which one knee is raised in front of the body

*Hiza-kakushi kōsa-dachi*: Hidden-knee cross-legged stance

*Jiai no kamae*: The ready position used at the start of such *kata* as Jion, Jitte and Jiin (literal translation: posture of benevolence)

*Jūji-gamae*: X-block posture

*Kagi-gamae*: A hook punch posture

*Kamae*: Posture or ready position (pronounced *gamae* when preceded by another word, as in *koshi-gamae*)

*Kasei kōkutsu-dachi*: Low back stance, a back stance in which the hips are positioned lower than in a conventional back stance

*Kata-ashi-dachi*: One-legged stance

*Kata-hiza-dachi*: Kneeling stance

*Kiba-dachi*: Straddle-leg stance

*Kitsutsuki no kamae*: Woodpecker posture

*Kokō-gamae*: A posture in which the hands are poised to grasp an opponent at the throat and groin (literal translation: "in the jaws of the tiger" posture)

*Kōkutsu-dachi*: Back stance

*Kōsa-dachi*: Cross-legged stance

*Koshi-gamae*: A posture in which both fists are

positioned beside one side of the hips

*Kyo-dachi*: Transient stance, a foreshortened back stance with the rear foot turned inward at a 45-degree angle

*Manji-gamae*: A posture in which the arms are positioned as if having just completed a hi-low block

*Mizu-nagare no kamae*: Water-flow posture

*Moto-dachi*: Slightly shortened front stance

*Musō-gamae*: A posture in which one arm extends downward similar to a downward block as the other arm is positioned similar to a rising block (literal translation: incomparable posture)

*Musubi-dachi*: Closed V stance

*Neko-ashi-dachi*: Cat stance

*Renoji-dachi*: L stance

*Ryōgoshi-gamae*: A posture in which each fist is positioned above its respective hip

*Ryōken koshi-gamae*: A posture in which each fist is positioned above its respective hip

*Ryōte-fuse*: Dropping face down with the hands pressing against the floor

*Ryōwan-gamae*: A posture in which the arms are extended downward to the sides of the body

*Ryūsui no kamae*: Flowing-water posture

*Sagi-ashi-dachi*: Heron-leg stance

*Sanchin-dachi*: Hourglass stance

*Sashi-ashi*: Step-over

*Shiko-dachi*: Square stance

*Shizentai*: Natural posture

*Sōchin-dachi*: Rooted stance (*Sōchin-dachi* is the name used instead of *fudō-dachi* to refer to rooted stances in the *kata* Sōchin)

*Soete koshi-gamae*: A posture in which both hands are positioned beside one side of the hips, with one hand formed into a fist pressing against the palm of the other hand

*Soto hachiji-dachi*: Open V stance (also *hachiji-dachi*)

*Suri-ashi*: A "gliding" step, without raising the foot

*Tachi*: Stance (pronounced *dachi* when preceded by another word, as in *zenkutsu-dachi*)

*Tachi-hiza*: A kneeling position in which one knee rests on the floor alongside the foot of the other leg

*Tate shutō-gamae*: Vertical knife-hand posture

*Tsuru-ashi-dachi*: Crane-leg stance

*Uraken-gamae*: A posture in which the arms are positioned as if having just completed a back-fist strike

*Yoko sashi-ashi*: Step-over to the side

*Zenkutsu-dachi*: Front stance

## HAND/ARM TECHNIQUES

*Age-uke*: Rising block

*Age-zuki*: Rising punch

*Awase shutō age-uke*: Two-handed knife-hand rising block

*Awase shutō-uchi*: Two-handed knife-hand strike

*Awase-zuki*: U-punch

*Chūdan oi-zuki*: Middle level lunge punch

*Chūdan shutō-uke*: Middle level knife-hand block

*Chūdan soto ude-uke*: Middle level outside-to-inside block (also *chūdan soto-uke*)

*Chūdan soto-uke*: Middle level outside-to-inside block (also *chūdan soto ude-uke*)

*Chūdan uchi ude-uke*: Middle level inside-to-outside block (also *chūdan uchi-uke*)

*Chūdan uchi-uke*: Middle level inside-to-outside block (also *chūdan uchi ude-uke*)

*Empi*: Elbow (also *hiji*)

*Empi-uchi*: Elbow strike

*Empi-uke*: Elbow block

*Enshin haitō-barai*: Centrifugal ridge-hand sweep

*Gedan awase-zuki*: Downward U-punch

*Gedan-barai*: Downward block (literal translation: downward sweep)

*Gedan-uke*: Downward block

*Gedan jūji-uke*: Downward X-block

*Gedan jūji uke-zuki*: Downward X-block/punch

*Gedan-kōsa-zuki*: Downward cross punch

*Gedan shutō-osae*: Downward knife-hand press

*Gedan shutō-uchi*: Downward knife-hand strike

*Gedan tettsui-uchi*: Downward hammer-fist strike

*Gyaku tate shutō-uke*: Reverse vertical knife-hand block

*Gyaku te-dori*: Reverse hand grasp

*Gyaku-zuki*: Reverse punch

*Haishu*: Back hand

*Haishu age-uchi*: Rising back-hand strike

*Haishu awase-uke*: Two-handed back-hand block

*Haishu-uke*: Back-hand block

*Haishu jūji-uke*: Back-hand X-block

*Haitō*: Ridge hand

*Haitō-barai*: Ridge-hand sweep

*Haitō sukui-nage*: Ridge-hand scooping throw

*Haitō-uchi*: Ridge-hand strike

*Haitō-uke*: Ridge-hand block

*Haiwan-uke*: Back-arm block

*Hasami-uchi*: Scissors strike

*Hasami-uke*: Scissors block

*Hasami-zuki*: Scissors punch

*Hazushi-te*: Hand release (a pull-away technique for releasing the hand from an opponent's grasp)

*Heikō ippon-ken*: Parallel one-knuckle fists

*Heikō tate-zuki*: Parallel vertical-fist punch

*Heishin*: The name of the final movement in the *kata* Kankūdai in which the arms travel upward around the body as if to describe a large circle (literal translation: closing of the mind or heart)

*Hiji-barai*: Sweeping elbow block

*Hiki-yose*: A pulling technique to draw an opponent closer (literal translation: pull in)

*Hiki-yose-gamae*: A posture in which the arms are formed as if having completed a pulling technique to draw an opponent closer

*Hineri-kaeshi*: Twist return

*Hira-nukite*: Horizontal spear hand

*Hirate*: Open hand

*Hirate otoshi-uchi*: Open-hand drop strike

*Ippon-ken*: One-knuckle fist

*Ippon-ken furi-otoshi*: Swinging one-knuckle fist drop

*Ippon-nukite*: One-finger spear hand

*Jō-chū awase-uke*: Upper-lower combined block

*Jōdan age-uke*: Upper-level rising block

*Jōdan awase shutō-uchi*: Upper-level two-handed knife-hand strike

*Jōdan empi-uchi*: Upper-level elbow strike

*Jōdan haishu jūji-uke*: Upper-level back-hand X-block

*Jōdan heikō ura-zuki*: Upper-level parallel close punch

*Jōdan kokō morote-uke*: Upper-level two-handed block (literal translation: upper-level "in the jaws of the tiger" two-handed block)

*Jōshin-gamae*: A posture similar to a reverse knife-hand wedge block with the forearms suggesting the sides of a triangle (literal translation: "mind-cleansing" posture)

*Jō tsuki-dashi*: *Jō* (stick, staff) thrust

*Jō-uke*: *Jō* (stick, staff) block

*Jō-zukami*: *Jō* (stick, staff) grab

*Jūji-gamae*: A posture in which the arms are formed into an X-block

*Jūji-uke*: X-block

*Jun-zuki*: Front punch

*Kaeshi-dori*: Reverse grasp

*Kaeshi-ude*: Arm return

*Kagi-gamae*: A posture in which the arms are positioned as if having just completed a hook punch

*Kagi-zuki*: Hook punch

*Kaishin*: The name of the opening movement in the *kata* Kankū Dai in which the arms open as if to describe a large circle around the body (literal translation: opening of the mind or heart)

*Kaishu*: Open hand(s)

*Kaishu haiwan-uke*: Open-hand back-arm block

*Kaishu jūji-tori*: Open-hand X-grasp

*Kaishu kōsa-gamae*: A posture in which one arm is positioned as if having completed a knife-hand downward block with the other hand open and directed to the side at a 90-degree angle

*Kaishu ryōwan-gamae*: A posture in which the arms are extended downward to the sides of the body with the hands open

*Kaishu yama-gamae*: Open-hand mountain posture

*Kake-dori*: Hooking grasp

*Kakiwake-uke*: Separating block

*Kamae*: Posture or ready position (pronounced *gamae* when preceded by another word, as in *koshi-gamae*)

*Kami-zukami*: Hair grab

*Kasui-ken*: Simultaneous downward block to the front and middle-level inside-to-outside block to the side (literal translation: fire and water fists)

*Kizami-zuki*: Jab

*Keitō*: Chicken-head wrist

*Keitō-uke*: Chicken-head-wrist block

*Keitō uke-nagashi*: Chicken-head-wrist block-sweep

*Kensei hirate komata-uchi*: A diversionary technique performed by slapping the inner thighs

*Kōhō tsuki-age*: Uppercut punch to the rear

*Kokō-dori*: A grasping technique in which the hands are positioned out in front of the body with one hand level with the face and other hand level with the midsection (literal translation: "in the jaws of the tiger" grasp)

*Kokō-gamae*: A posture in which the hands are poised to grasp an opponent at the throat and groin (literal translation: "in the jaws of the tiger" posture)

*Kokō hiza-kuzushi*: A takedown technique in response to a kick in which one hand performs a scooping block while the other hand presses against the knee to perform the takedown (literal translation: "in the jaws of the tiger" knee takedown)

*Kōsa-uke*: Cross block

*Koshi-gamae*: A posture in which both fists are positioned above one side of the hips

*Mae empi-uchi*: Front elbow strike

*Manji-gamae*: A posture in which the arms are positioned as if having just completed a hi-low block

*Manji-uke*: Hi-low block, a block in which one arm performs an upper-level inside-to-outside block to the rear while the other arm performs a downward block to the front

*Mawashi kake-uke*: Circular hooking block

*Mawashi-uke*: Circular block

*Mizu-nagare no kamae*: Water-flow posture

*Morote*: Refers to techniques performed with both hands or both arms

*Morote age-uke*: Two-handed rising block

*Morote enshin haitō-barai*: Two-handed centrifugal ridge-hand sweep

*Morote gedan-uke*: Two-handed downward block

*Morote gedan shutō-uke*: Two-handed downward knife-hand block

*Morote haiwan-uke*: Augmented back-arm block

*Morote hiki-otoshi*: Two-handed pull-down

*Morote jō-uke*: Two-handed *jō* (stick, staff) block

*Morote kaishu gedan-uke*: Two-handed open-hand downward block

*Morote keitō-uke*: Double chicken-head-wrist block

*Morote kizami ura-zuki*: Two-handed close punch

*Morote kubi-osae*: Two-handed head (or neck) hold

*Morote seiryūtō-uchi*: Two-handed ox-jaw strike

*Morote-uke*: Augmented block, two-handed block

*Morote yokoken-ate*: A technique that appears in the *kata* Hangetsu in which both fists are pulled in toward the chest with the elbows extending out to the sides

*Morote-zuki*: Double-fist punch

*Musō-gamae*: A posture in which one arm extends downward similar to a downward block as the other arm is positioned similar to a rising block (literal translation: incomparable posture)

*Nagashi-uke*: Sweeping block

*Nai-wan sukui-nage*: Inner-arm scooping throw

*Nakadaka ippon-ken*: Middle-finger one-knuckle fist

*Nihon-nukite*: Two-finger spear hand

*Ni-keitō-gamae*: Double chicken-head-wrist posture

*Nukite*: Spear hand

*Ōfuri kōsa-barai*: Swinging cross-arm sweep

*Oi-zuki*: Lunge punch

*Osae-uke*: Pressing block

*Otoshi-uke*: Dropping block

*Otoshi-zuki*: Dropping or downward punch

*Riken-gashō*: A positioning of the arms appearing at the start of the *kata* Gankaku Shō in which the back of the right fist rests against the palm of the open left hand

*Ryōgoshi-gamae*: A posture in which each fist is positioned above its respective hip

*Ryō-hiji harai-age*: Double rising elbow sweep

*Ryōken koshi-gamae*: A posture in which each fist is positioned above its respective hip

*Ryō-ude mawashi-uke*: Two-armed circular block

*Ryōwan*: Refers to techniques performed with both arms

*Ryōwan-gamae*: A posture in which the arms are extended downward to the sides of the body

*Ryōwan gedan kakiwake-uke*: Double downward separating block

*Ryōwan uchi-uke*: Double inside-to-outside block

*Ryōwan zempō-nobashi*: Both arms extended outward to the front

*Ryūsui no kamae*: Flowing-water posture

*Ryū-un no uke*: A blocking technique in which one arm delivers a knife-hand block at a 45-degree angle to the side supported by the opposite hand, which is positioned just above the elbow of the blocking arm (literal translation: flowing cloud block)

*Seiryūtō*: Ox-jaw hand

*Seiryūtō-uchi*: Ox-jaw strike

*Shihon-nukite*: Four-finger spear hand

*Shutō*: Knife hand

*Shutō gedan-barai*: Knife-hand downward block

*Shutō kakiwake-uke*: Knife-hand separating block

*Shutō-osae*: Knife-hand press

*Shutō-uchi*: Knife-hand strike

*Shutō-uke*: Knife-hand block

*Soeshō*: Refers to an arm technique assisted by the palm of the other hand

*Soete kake-dori*: Augmented hooking grasp

*Soete koshi-gamae*: A posture in which both hands are positioned beside one side of the hips, with one hand formed into a fist pressing against the palm of the other hand

*Sokumen dōji-tsuki*: Simultaneous double-punch to the sides

*Sokumen empi-uchi*: Side elbow strike

*Sokumen gedan-barai*: Side downward block

*Sokumen jōdan haitō-uke*: Side upper-level ridge-hand block

*Sokumen morote-zuki*: Side double-fist punch

*Sokumen shutō gedan-barai*: Side knife-hand downward block

*Sokumen tate empi-uchi*: Side upward elbow strike

*Sokumen tate shutō-uke*: Side vertical knife-hand block

*Sokumen-uke*: Side block

*Sokumen-zuki*: Side punch

*Soto ude-uke*: Outside-to-inside block

*Suihei hiji-gamae*: Horizontal elbow posture

*Suihei jō-dori*: Horizontal *jō* (stick, staff) grasp

*Sukui-nage*: Scooping throw

*Sukui-uke*: Scooping block

*Tate empi-uchi*: Upward elbow strike

*Tate-ken*: Vertical fist

*Tate-mawashi tettsui-uchi*: Vertical round hammer-fist strike

*Tate-mawashi uraken-uchi*: Vertical round back-fist strike

*Tate nukite*: Vertical spear hand

*Tate shutō-gamae*: Vertical knife-hand posture

*Tate shutō-uke*: Vertical knife-hand block

*Tate uraken-uchi*: Vertical back-fist strike

*Tate-zuki*: Vertical-fist punch

*Tekubi kake-uke*: Wrist-hook block

*Teishō*: Palm heel

*Teishō awase gedan-uke*: Two-handed downward palm-heel block

*Teishō awase-zuki*: Two-handed palm-heel thrust

*Teishō-barai*: Palm-heel sweep

*Teishō furi-uchi*: Swinging palm-heel strike

*Teishō morote-uke*: Double palm-heel block

*Teishō tate hasami-uchi*: Vertical palm-heel scissors strike

*Teishō-uchi*: Palm heel strike

*Tenchi haitō-uchi*: Hi-low ridge-hand strike, a striking technique in which one arm performs an upper-level ridge-hand strike to the front while the other arm performs a downward ridge-hand strike to the rear (literal translation: "Heaven and Earth" ridge-hand strike)

*Tenchi kenseitai*: Hi-low feint, a diversionary technique in which the arms move in opposite directions to momentarily confuse an opponent

*Tettsui*: Hammer fist

*Tettsui hasami-uchi*: Hammer-fist scissors strike

*Tettsui otoshi-uchi*: Downward hammer-fist strike

*Tettsui-uchi*: Hammer-fist strike

*Tsukami-dori*: Grasping clutch

*Tsukami-uke*: Grabbing block

*Tsuki*: Punch or thrust (pronounced *zuki* when

preceded by another word, as in *gyaku-zuki*)

*Tsuki-age*: Uppercut punch

*Tsutsumi-ken*: A hand position in which the fist is enveloped by the fingers of the other hand

*Uchi*: 1. Strike; 2. Inside, inside-to-outside

*Uchi haiwan-uke*: Inside-to-outside back-arm block

*Uchi-ude kaeshi-uke*: Inside-to-outside reverse block

*Uchi ude-uke*: Inside-to-outside block (also *uchi-uke*)

*Uchi-uke*: Inside-to-outside block (also *uchi ude-uke*)

*Ude*: Arm

*Ude-hasami*: Forearm scissors block

*Ude-uke*: Forearm block

*Uke*: Block

*Uke-nagashi*: Block-sweep

*Uke-zuki*: Blocking punch

*Uraken*: Back fist

*Uraken-gamae*: A posture in which the arms are positioned as if having just completed a back-fist strike

*Uraken-uchi*: Back-fist strike

*Ura-zuki*: Close punch

*Ushiro empi-uchi*: Back elbow strike

*Ushiro gedan-barai*: Back downward block

*Ushiro gedan-uke*: Back downward block

*Ushiro tettsui hasami-uchi*: Back hammer-fist scissors strike

*Washide*: Eagle hand

*Washide age-uchi*: Eagle-hand rising strike

*Washide otoshi-uchi*: Eagle-hand dropping strike

*Yama-gamae*: Mountain posture

*Yama kakiwake-uke*: Mountain separating block

*Yama-zuki*: Wide-U punch (literal translation: mountain punch)

*Yoko empi-uchi*: Side elbow strike

*Yoko hari-empi*: A positioning of the arm appearing in the *kata* Gojūshiho Shō in which the front of the fist rests against the hip with the elbow extending out to the side of the body

*Yokoken*: Side fist

*Yoko-mawashi uraken-uchi*: Side round back-fist strike

*Yoko ude-hasami*: Side forearm scissors block

*Yumi-zuki*: Bow punch, a punch in which the pulling hand is positioned as if pulling back the string of a bow prior to shooting an arrow

*Zempō empi-uchi*: Elbow strike to the front

## LEG/FOOT TECHNIQUES

*Ashi*: Foot, leg

*Ashi-barai*: Leg sweep

*Ashi-gake*: Leg hook

*Engetsu-kaeshi*: Circular return

*Fumikomi*: Stamping kick

*Gedan ke-sage*: Downward thrust kick

*Harai-fumikomi*: Sweeping stamping kick

*Hiza*: Knee

*Hiza-gamae*: A posture in which one knee is raised so as to protect the body

*Hiza-uchi*: Knee strike

*Jōhō kaiten-tobi*: Upwards turning jump

*Kasei mawashi-geri*: Underneath roundhouse kick (delivered from below while lying on the floor)

*Kekomi*: Thrust kick

*Kensei yuka-geri*: diversionary technique performed by kicking the floor with the ball of the foot

*Keri*: Kick (pronounced *geri* when preceded by another word, as in *mae-geri*)

*Mae-geri*: Front snap kick

*Mae ke-sage*: Front thrust kick

*Mikazuki-geri*: Crescent kick

*Mawashi-geri*: Roundhouse kick

*Nami-gaeshi*: Return-wave kick

*Nidan-geri*: Double jump kick

*Sashi-ashi*: Step-over

*Sempū tobi-geri*: Whirlwind jumping kick

*Suri-ashi*: A "gliding" step, without raising the foot

*Tobi ashi-barai*: Jumping leg sweep

*Tobi-geri*: Jumping kick

*Tobi mae-geri*: Jumping front kick

*Tobi ushiro-geri*: Jumping back kick

*Ura ashi-gake*: Back leg hook

*Ushiro-geri*: Back kick

*Yoko-geri*: Side kick

*Yoko-geri kekomi*: Side thrust kick (also *yoko-kekomi*)

*Yoko-geri ke-age*: Side snap kick (also *yoko ke-age*)

*Yoko ke-age*: Side snap kick (also *yoko-geri ke-age*)

*Yoko-kekomi*: Side thrust kick (also *yoko-geri kekomi*)

*Yoko sashi-ashi*: Step-over to the side